Wellington Against Junot

Wellington Against Junot

The First Invasion of Portugal
1807–1808

David Buttery

Pen & Sword
MILITARY

First published in Great Britain in 2011 by
Pen & Sword Military
an imprint of
Pen & Sword Books Ltd
47 Church Street
Barnsley
South Yorkshire
S70 2AS

ISBN 978-1-84884-142-0

A CIP catalogue record for this book is
available from the British Library.

Typeset in 11/13 Ehrhardt by Concept, Huddersfield, West Yorkshire
Printed and bound in England by CPI UK

Pen & Sword Books Ltd incorporates the imprints of Pen & Sword Aviation,
Pen & Sword Maritime, Pen & Sword Military, Wharncliffe Local History,
Pen & Sword Select, Pen & Sword Military Classics, Leo Cooper,
Remember When, Seaforth Publishing and Frontline Publishing.

For a complete list of Pen & Sword titles please contact
PEN & SWORD BOOKS LIMITED
47 Church Street, Barnsley, South Yorkshire, S70 2AS, England
E-mail: enquiries@pen-and-sword.co.uk
Website: www.pen-and-sword.co.uk

Contents

Now the Tyrant stubbornly insists,
With rights violated at his behest,
What will Britain do against this beast,
Who would fly at Heaven itself if he could?

The Canto Patriotico
Elman Solitaire[1]

Chronology

1750	3 December	Birth of Hew Dalrymple
1769	1 May	Birth of Arthur Wesley
	15 August	Birth of Napoleon Buonaparte
1771	24 September	Birth of Jean-Andoche Junot
1781		Death of Lord Mornington
		Wesley enters Eton
1787	7 March	Wesley enlists as an ensign
	25 December	Wesley promoted lieutenant
1789	17 June	The National Assembly takes power
	14 July	Storming of the Bastille
		Junot joins the National Guard
1790		Junot enlists in the French army
	30 June	Wesley becomes MP for County Trim, Ireland
1791		Junot transfers into 2nd Battalion of Volunteers, Dept of the Côte d'Or
	20 June	Flight of Louis XVI to Varennes
	30 June	Wesley promoted captain
1792	20 April	France declares war on Austria and Sardinia
	11 June	Junot wounded at Longwy
		Junot promoted sergeant
	19 August	Prussia invades France
	21 September	Establishment of the National Convention Government
	22 September	French monarchy abolished
1793	21 January	Louis XVI executed
		Committee of Public Safety established
	16 May	Junot wounded
	31 May	Reign of Terror begins
	27 August	Royalists in Toulon side with Britain
	7 September	Siege of Toulon begins
		Bonaparte makes Junot his military secretary
	30 September	Wesley promoted lieutenant colonel – fights in Flanders

	1 October	Junot promoted second lieutenant
	15–16 October	Battle of Wattignies
	16 October	Execution of Marie-Antoinette
	18 December	Toulon falls
1794	17 January	Junot promoted first lieutenant
	4 March	Bonaparte given command of artillery in the Army of Italy
	25 June	Jourdan defeats the Austrians at Fleurus
	27 July	*Coup d'état* of 9 Thermidor – fall of Robespierre
	21 September	Battle of Dego
1795	13 February	Junot promoted Colonel of 1st Hussar Regiment
	5 April	Peace of Bâle between France and Prussia
	24 April	Junot brings trophies to Paris and promoted *Chef de Brigade*
	4–5 October	*Coup d'état* of 13 Vendémiaire ('Whiff of Grapeshot')
	26 October	Bonaparte commands Army of the Interior
	1 November	Directory Government established
1796	2 March	Bonaparte appointed commander of the Army of Italy
	12–21 April	Battles between the Austro-Sardinians and the French at Montenotte, Millésimo, Dego and Mondovi
	3 May	Wesley promoted full colonel
	10 May	Battle of Lodi
	15 May	Bonaparte enters Milan
	2 August	First Battle of Lonato – Junot wounded
	5 August	Second Battle of Lonato
	8 September	Battle of Bassano
	15–17 November	Battle of Árcola
1797	14 January	Battle of Rivoli
	2 February	Surrender of Mantua
	4 September	*Coup d'état* of 18 Fructidor
	17 October	Treaty of Campo-Formio between France and Austria
1798	19 May	Bonaparte sails for Egypt
	10 June	Occupation of Malta
	May to August	Great Rebellion in Ireland
	21 July	Battle of the Pyramids
	1 August	Battle of the Nile

	2 September	The Sultan declares war on France
	21 October	Revolt in Cairo
	29 December	Second Coalition against France
1799	18 January	Junot promoted *Général de Brigade*
	8 February	Siege of El Arish
	1 March	War of the Second Coalition
	3–7 March	Attack on Jaffa
	19 March	Beginning of Siege of Acre
	25 March	Battle of Stockach
	8 April	Junot attacked near Nazareth
	16 April	Battle of Mount Tabor (Junot present)
	4 May	Seringapatam falls to Wellesley
		Death of Tippoo Sultan
		Wellesley appointed Governor of Mysore
	20 May	Bonaparte raises Siege of Acre
	4 June	First battle of Zürich
	17–19 June	Battle of the Trebbia
	25 July	Battle of Aboukir (Junot present)
	15 August	Battle of Novi
	25 Sept.–10 Oct.	Second battle of Zürich
	9 October	Bonaparte returns to France
	9 November	*Coup d'état* of 18 Brumaire
		Bonaparte becomes First Consul
	December	Junot taken prisoner by the Royal Navy
1800	15 May	Bonaparte crosses St Bernard Pass into Italy
	4 June	Genoa falls to Austria
	14 June	Battle of Marengo
		Junot returns to France
	27 August	Junot created *Commandant de le Place de Paris*
	30 October	Junot marries Laure Permon
1801	January	Junot promoted *Général de Division*
	1 January	Act of Union in Ireland
	9 February	Peace of Lunéville between France and Austria
	14 March	Prime Minister William Pitt resigns
		Viscount Henry Addington becomes Prime Minister
	23 March	Tsar Paul I dies – succeeded by Tsar Alexander I
	14 September	French evacuate Egypt
1802	25 March	Peace of Amiens between Britain and France
	29 April	Wellesley promoted major general
	4 August	Bonaparte created First Consul for life

1803	16 May	Great Britain declares war on France
	6 August	Second Mahratta War
	12 August	Ahmednuggur falls
	23 September	Battle of Assaye
	29 November	Battle of Argaum
1804	7 April	Execution of the Duc d'Enghien
	10 May	Addington resigns – Pitt becomes Prime Minister
	18 May	Napoleon I declared Emperor of France
	19 May	Eighteen generals created Marshals of Empire
	1 September	Wellesley awarded Order of the Bath
	2 December	Napoleon's Coronation at Notre Dame
1805	March	Junot appointed French Ambassador to Portugal
	10 March	Wellesley leaves India
	13 April	Junot arrives at Lisbon
	9 August	Third Coalition against France
	19 October	Mack surrenders at Ulm
	21 October	Battle of Trafalgar
	28–31 October	Battle of Caldiero
	2 December	Battle of Austerlitz (Junot present)
	26 December	Treaty of Pressburg between Austria and France
1806	19 January	Junot appointed Governor General of Parma and Piacenza
	23 January	Death of William Pitt
	1 April	Joseph Bonaparte created King of Naples Wellesley becomes MP for Rye, Sussex
	10 April	Wellesley marries Kitty Pakenham
	3 July	Junot appointed Governor of Paris
	15 September	Prussia joins Anglo-Russian Coalition
	14 October	Battles of Jena and Auerstädt
	21 November	Napoleon issues the Berlin Decrees
1807	7 January	Britain declares French ports and colonies under blockade
	8 February	Battle of Eylau
	3 April	Wellesley appointed Chief Secretary of Ireland
	14 June	Battle of Friedland
	7–9 July	Treaty of Tilsit between France, Russia and Prussia
	29 July	Napoleon orders troop concentration around Bayonne

11 August	Portugal instructed by France to sever diplomatic relations with Great Britain
2 September	Copenhagen bombarded by the British
4 September	Dutch ports closed to trade with Britain
5 September	Junot takes command of the Corps of Observation of the Gironde
7 September	British take Copenhagen and seize Danish fleet
25 September	Portugal offers to join the Continental System
1 October	French and Spanish ambassadors withdrawn from Lisbon
12 October	Junot ordered to prepare for invasion
17 October	Corps of the Gironde enters Spain
20 October	Portuguese Royal Charter issued closing ports to Britain
22 October	Secret agreement between Portugal and Britain concerning the evacuation of the Portuguese Court and the occupation of Madeira
27 October	Treaty of Fontainebleau between France and Spain
28 October	Carlos IV holds a public investigation into his son's alleged treachery
7 November	Russia protests over the bombardment of Copenhagen Russian Ambassador recalled from London
10–13 November	Fleet under Admiral Siniavin enters port of Lisbon
11 November	British fleet under Admiral Sir Sidney Smith leaves Plymouth for Portugal
12 November	Junot's army concentrates around Salamanca
13 November	Second Corps of Observation of the Gironde under General Dupont enters Spain
16 November	Fleet under Sir Sidney Smith reaches the Tejo
18 November	Portuguese ports blockaded by Royal Navy
22 November	Lord Strangford presents an ultimatum to the Braganças
23 November	First Decree of Milan ordering British vessels impounded Kingdom of Etruria is annexed by France
23–24 November	Junot's army reaches Abrantes
25 November	Privy Council established by the Braganças
27–29 November	Portuguese Court sails for Brazil

	30 November	Junot's vanguard enters Lisbon
	1 December	Spanish division under General Solano enters southern Portugal
	3 December	Herman appointed President of the Royal Treasury and Director General of Finances
	4 December	Confiscation of British property in Portugal Firearms and hunting prohibited
	12 December	King and Queen of Etruria abdicate Convention on the Anglo-Portuguese occupation of Madeira
	13 December	Spanish division under General Taranco enters northern Portugal
	15 December	Rioting in Lisbon
	17 December	Second Decree of Milan orders neutral vessels travelling through British ports seized
	22 December	Junot disbands sections of the Portuguese army Marquis of Alorna appointed Inspector General and Commander-in-Chief of the army in Trás-os-Montes, Beira and Estremadura
	23 December	Napoleon imposes 100 million francs indemnity on Portugal
	26 December	General Dupont's army enters Vitoria in Northern Spain
1808	1 February	Junot created Governor General of Portugal
	25 April	Wellesley promoted lieutenant general
	2 May	Revolt in Spain – begins widespread insurrection
	6 June	Rebellions at Porto and Vila Real against the French Joseph Bonaparte proclaimed King of Spain
	8 June	Revolt at Braga
	9 June	Revolt at Bragança
	12 June	Loison occupies Fort Concepción
	15 June	General insurrection throughout Portugal
	16 June	First Siege of Zaragoza begins
	17 June–1 July	Loison's abortive mission to Porto and return to Almeida
	18 June	Fortress of Faro taken by Portuguese
	19 June	Bishop of Porto appointed head of the Supreme Junta
	21 June	Loison repelled at Teixeira by Portuguese under General Silveira

25–26 June	Vila Vizosa and Beja sacked by the French
27 June	Fort of Santa Catarina at Figueira da Foz taken by the Portuguese
29 June	Loison reduces Fort Concepción's defences, garrisons Almeida and marches his main force back to Lisbon
5–6 July	General Margaron attacks and takes Leiria – retires upon Lisbon
12 July	British troops under Wellesley sail from Cork
16 July	Portuguese militia and insurgents surround Almeida
20 July	Dupont surrenders at Bailén
29–30 July	Portuguese and Spanish defeated before Évora Évora stormed and sacked
1–8 August	British land at Mondego Bay
11–12 August	Wellesley meets General Freire at Leiria
14 August	First Siege of Zaragoza ends
15 August	Skirmish at Obidos – Junot marches north from Lisbon
17 August	Battle of Roliça
21 August	Battle of Vimeiro
	Sir Harry Burrard assumes command
22 August	Sir Hew Dalrymple assumes command
	Armistice agreed at Vimeiro
30 August	Convention of Sintra
Sept.–October	The French evacuate Portugal
21 September	Wellesley sails for England
11 October	Junot disembarks at La Rochelle
27 October	General Moore leaves Lisbon for Spain
5 November	Napoleon takes command of the Army of Spain
4 December	Napoleon occupies Madrid
20 December	Second Siege of Zaragoza begins under Marshal Moncey
29 December	Junot arrives to command siege operations
1809 16 January	Battle of Corunna
22 January	Marshal Lannes takes over Siege of Zaragoza
20 February	Zaragoza falls to the French
9 March	Second French Invasion of Portugal under Marshal Soult

	April	Wellesley resigns as Chief Secretary of Ireland and sails for Portugal
	6 April	Archduke Charles invades Bavaria – war between France and Austria
	20–23 April	Battle of Eckmühl
	12 May	Battle of Porto
	13 May	Napoleon enters Vienna
	17 May	Napoleon annexes the Papal States
	20–23 May	Battle of Aspern-Essling
	5–6 July	Battle of Wagram
	6 July	Pope Pius VII arrested by the French
	27–28 July	Battle of Talavera
	July–September	British expedition to Walcheren
	4 September	Wellesley created Viscount Wellington
	September–October	Construction of the Lines of Torres Vedras
	4 October	Spencer Perceval becomes Prime Minister
	14 October	Treaty of Schönbrunn between France and Austria
1810	2 April	Napoleon marries Archduchess Marie-Louise of Austria
	17 April	Massena commands Army of Portugal
	9 July	Ciudad Rodrigo falls to Massena
	24 July	Combat on the Côa
		Third Invasion of Portugal
	27 August	Almeida surrenders
	27 September	Battle of Busaco
	3 October	Massena enters Coimbra – Junot's troops sack the city
	8 October	Wellington enters the Lines of Torres Vedras
	10–14 October	French halt before the Lines of Torres Vedras
	14 November	Massena withdraws to Santarém
1811	19 January	Junot wounded at Rio Mayor
	5 March	Massena begins to retreat
	11 March	Badajoz falls to the French
	22 March	Massena dismisses Marshal Ney
	3 April	Battle of Sabugal
		French leave Portugal
	3–5 May	Battle of Fuentes de Oñoro
	10 May	Massena relieved of command
	16 May	Battle of Albuera

1812	19 January	Wellington takes Ciudad Rodrigo
	9 February	Junot leaves France to command IV Corps of the *Grande Armée*
	6 April	Wellington takes Badajoz
	11 May	Prime Minister Spencer Perceval is murdered in the House of Commons
	24 June	Napoleon invades Russia
	22 July	Battle of Salamanca
	30 July–7 August	Junot takes command of VIII Corps
	17–19 August	Battle of Smolensk – Junot reprimanded
	18 August	Wellington created Marquess of Wellington
	19 August	Junot reprimanded for failing to cut the Russians off at Valutino
	7 September	Battle of Borodino (Junot present)
	14 September	Napoleon enters Moscow
	22 September	Wellington created Generalissimo of Spanish Armies
	29–30 September	Junot establishes his headquarters at Mojaisk
	14 October	Junot ordered to evacuate wounded and join the retreat
	27–29 November	French retreat over the Beresina
	14 December	French rearguard reaches the River Niemen
1813	12 February	Junot appointed Governor of Venice
	20 February	Junot appointed Provisional Commander of the Illyrian Provinces
	16 March	Prussia declares war on France
	3 May	Battle of Lützen
	21–22 May	Battle of Bautzen
	21 June	Battle of Vittoria
	28 June	Lieutenant Poiré submits reports to the Viceroy about Junot's erratic behaviour
	6 July	Napoleon removes Junot from office
	20–30 July	Battle of the Pyrenees
	29 July	Death of Junot
	12 August	Austria declares war on France
	31 August	San Sebastian falls to Wellington
	16–19 October	Battle of Leipzig
1814	1 March	Treaty of Chaumont
	31 March	Allies enter Paris
	10 April	Battle of Toulouse

	11 April	Napoleon abdicates
		Treaty of Fontainebleau
	26 April	Louis XVIII proclaimed King of France
	3 May	Wellington created Duke of Wellington
	4 May	Napoleon reaches Elba
	20 May	First Treaty of Paris
	5 July	Wellington appointed Ambassador to the French
		Court
	1 November	Congress of Vienna begins
1815	26 February	Napoleon escapes from Elba
	1 March	Napoleon lands at Golfe-Juan
	20 March	Napoleon enters Paris
		Beginning of the Hundred Days Campaign
	16 June	Battles of Ligny and Quatre Bras
	18 June	Battle of Waterloo
	22 June	Napoleon's final abdication
	7 July	Allies enter Paris
	5 October	Napoleon reaches St Helena
	20 November	Second Treaty of Paris
1821	5 May	Death of Napoleon
1830	9 April	Death of Sir Hew Dalrymple
1852	14 September	Death of the Duke of Wellington

List of Plates

Maps

Preface

Surprisingly there are few recent books dealing specifically with the Duke of Wellington's first Peninsular War campaign. Although it is often alluded to in general works about the war, subsequent campaigns are usually covered in far greater depth. Yet this great commander's entry into the conflict, which made his name a household word in Britain, is of considerable interest as it reveals much about his strategic and tactical thought during the first stages of the war. One reason for its relative obscurity is perhaps the manner in which it ended with the controversial Convention of Sintra, which illustrated the weaknesses of Britain's antiquated military command system and tested the strength of the Anglo-Portuguese relationship.

Yet the first French invasion of Portugal is even more obscure, at least in English language books about the Napoleonic Wars. This invasion, the rebellion of the Portuguese that followed and French moves to repel British intervention in Iberia have received little recent coverage and the enthusiast is obliged to refer mainly to primary source material with so few recent studies available. Though Junot is known as one of Napoleon's closest friends and fought in many campaigns, his tenure as the de facto ruler of Portugal has attracted little attention in English language studies. I hope to address these omissions and shed some light on what was undoubtedly an interesting and remarkable campaign.

In this prequel to *Wellington Against Massena*, it should be borne in mind that Sir Arthur Wellesley had yet to assume the ducal title by which he is commonly known. Nevertheless, in keeping with the spirit of the series of which this book is a part, he is referred to as Wellington in the title. To give the author further excuse there are other precedents such as Jac Weller's *Wellington in India*, Charles Grant's *Wellington's First Campaign in Portugal*, Ian C Robertson's *Wellington at War in the Peninsula 1808–1814* and others, detailing events prior to Wellesley becoming the Great Duke.

Regarding the interpretation of foreign words and spelling, I have tried to use modern Portuguese words in preference and discard Anglicization when possible. For example, instead of referring to the River Tagus I have adopted the Portuguese spelling of Tejo. In similar fashion, Oporto becomes Porto and Cintra becomes Sintra; being more akin to Portuguese usage. Nonetheless, I have left such words unaltered in contemporary quotations as their writers intended.

I have received valuable assistance from many individuals and organizations during the writing of this book and would like to thank the following. Even the best of manuscripts is prone to errors and inaccuracies so I would like to thank Pamela Covey of Pen & Sword Books Limited, who not only checked through this text but assisted me during the proofreading process for my previous books. Having worked in advertising for many years, I appreciate the work of good proofreaders, whose efforts go a long way to ensuring accuracy and quality. I would also like to thank Pauline Buttery, A E Godley and Stuart Hadaway, who also checked through this script for me. Stuart's knowledge and enthusiasm about the Napoleonic period has also been of particular value during our frequent discussions and I am grateful for the loan of several useful volumes from his collection.

I am grateful to Cynthia Howell who helped with the translation of French sources and to Patricia Richards who assisted with the translation of Portuguese material, notably the *Canto Patriotico*. This songbook, published in 1812, is written in a very old style of Portuguese which made translation particularly difficult, so I am doubly grateful to Patricia in that regard. Jorge Estrela, Architect and Museum Director of the Casa Museu – Centro Cultural João Soares in Leiria, kindly gave me a copy of the *Canto Patriotico* during my second visit to Lisbon, which was much appreciated.

Many libraries and archives have been used in this study and I would like to acknowledge the assistance of David Charlton and the staff of the University of Leicester's David Wilson Library in particular. I also thank the staff of the National Army Museum, British Library, Colindale Newspaper Archive and Worcester Regiment Museum for their co-operation.

I am obliged for the support that I received at Lisbon's famous Museu Militar. I particularly thank the Director, Lieutenant Colonel Alberto Borges da Fonseca who carried out a search for relevant material prior to my arrival including several Portuguese and French sources. I would also like to give my special thanks to Maria Fernana Nunes whose patience and excellent English language skills in the Arquivo Histórico Militar proved invaluable.

I must thank my travelling companions on my last two forays into Iberia including Sharon Whitmore, who helped record the events around the release of *Wellington Contra Massena*, the Portuguese language version of my first book. David Williams of the CWRS also deserves my gratitude for driving us around central Portugal on my last trip, which involved some locations that were difficult to reach.

Finally, many thanks to all those wonderful people I met in Portugal who gave me an insight into the Portuguese view of the Peninsular War. Foremost among these are Jorge Estrela, Rodolfo Beghona, Helena Rafael, João MacDonald (whose skill as interpreter proved invaluable), José Sardica, Rui Ribolhos Filipe (of the Battlefield Centre at Vimeiro) and his partner Dina Spencer da Graça along with many others. Their hospitality and kindness made my research visits to Portugal a great pleasure. I hope that they enjoy this book and feel that I have shown their nation and people due respect in this work.

David Buttery
April 2010

Chapter 1
House of Bragança

Towards the end of the eighteenth century French society was convulsed by the Revolution that overthrew the Bourbon monarchy and saw King Louis XVI executed on the guillotine. Appalled by the anarchy and violence in France, and fearful that radicalism might spread, the foremost European powers gathered to avenge the Bourbons and crush the young French republic emerging in their midst. Yet the Revolutionaries not only withstood military efforts to oust them but went on to take the offensive against the old monarchies who hoped to destroy them. Republicanism had taken root and Europe would never be the same again.

Napoleon Buonaparte was the most important figure to rise from the turmoil of the Revolution. He was born in 1769 on the isle of Corsica, which had only become part of France the year before. The Buonaparte family were impoverished but respectable, if not as highly placed in Corsican society as some would later claim. In the absence of aristocratic patronage, Napoleon's rise to power was due to his own exceptional talents and the opportunities that, but for the Revolution, would have been denied to him. His brilliance as a general made him very useful to a succession of revolutionary governments, though his popularity, determination and ambition soon began to trouble his contemporaries. Being both a natural leader and politically adept, Buonaparte rapidly overtook his rivals and seized power.

After the *coup d'état* of Brumaire, Bonaparte (who had changed the spelling of his name to appear more French) became the First Consul of France in 1799. Briefly sharing power with two other consuls, he swiftly gained ascendancy – the French being prepared to tolerate a dictatorship due to a widespread desire for stability after revolutionary chaos. A remarkable series of military triumphs secured Bonaparte's position sufficiently for him to be crowned Emperor Napoleon I on 2 December 1804. While the French were momentarily satisfied with their new Continental status, much of Europe was appalled by the sight of a military adventurer ruling France, many condemning him as a usurper.

Observers had been stunned by the success of the French revolutionary armies. With unusually large numbers of men raised through conscription, their use of massed infantry columns against mostly linear defensive formations proved very effective. The sight of these huge columns often had a ruinous effect on enemy morale and the sound of their advance was intimidating as soldiers roared revolutionary slogans in time to the drummers beating a steady rhythm to inspire and drive them onwards. This was one of the first occasions when common men strove for a cause in which they had a clear personal interest and they often fought with fanatical courage. A cannonade usually prepared the ground for their assault and columns were preceded by lines of skirmishers who would try to unsettle the defenders' lines before the main body came into contact with the enemy. Only well trained and disciplined infantry were able to resist these shock tactics.

Napoleon inherited an efficient military machine from the Revolutionary armies and perfected it to form his own *Grande Armée* during the Imperial period. Although Napoleon was effectively a monarch and rapidly created a new royal dynasty, France still represented a radical new ideology that terrified the old order who felt their social hierarchy was menaced. Therefore, despite a brief pause with the Peace of Amiens 1802–1803, the French would remain at war for over twenty years during 1792–1815. Most influential states were unwilling to make a permanent settlement until the balance of power in Europe was restored and the threat of revolutionary change subsided.

In 1806 when Prussia declared war against France, Napoleon conducted a lightning campaign that devastated the Prussian army and appalled those who witnessed it. Considered one of the foremost military forces in Europe, the twin victories of Jena and Auerstädt were so complete that they crushed the Prussian will to resist and Napoleon entered Berlin less than two weeks later on 27 October. On 21 November 1806, Napoleon issued the Berlin Decrees, announcing the start of commercial sanctions against Great Britain.

The land war continued against Russia, who enjoyed limited Prussian support, and hostilities spread into Poland. The battle of Eylau 7–8 February 1807 saw the first check to Napoleon's run of success as both sides fought to a bloody stalemate amidst great slaughter. In contrast, the battle of Friedland on 14 June was a conclusive French victory, forcing Tsar Alexander I of Russia to seek terms with Napoleon.

Napoleon met the Tsar on 25 June 1807 aboard a raft moored symbolically in the middle of the river Niemen. The subsequent Treaty of Tilsit was negotiated between 7–9 July, which saw the Russians abandon former allies such as Britain. Since the collapse of Prussia, Russia had faced the military might of France almost single-handed. Alexander published statements announcing his dismay at the way the British had acted, claiming that they had failed to fulfil their obligations in the Coalition against France.[1] During years of conflict, Britain had largely confined her efforts to naval warfare and financial support for her allies. Beyond limited coastal incursions, her actual military commitment had been small.

There had been no British troops present at the Battle of Austerlitz 1805 while thousands of Russians and Austrians had perished. The same had also been true of the land campaigns of 1806–1807 and the Tsar felt that the British allowed themselves to be distracted by minor objectives, deliberately failing to commit to a Continental land war, declaring: 'He was astonished that in her cause she did not act in union with him; but coolly contemplating a bloody spectacle, in a war which had been kindled at her will, she sent troops to attack Buenos Ayres.'[2] Furthermore, he claimed that all Europe was horrified by the later British assault on Denmark shortly after Tilsit. Following the British naval triumph at Trafalgar 1805, Napoleon contemplated the seizure of the Danish fleet to assist an invasion of Britain but the British forestalled this by bombarding Copenhagen and taking possession of it themselves. As Denmark was a neutral state, many observers were shocked by this ruthless act of self-preservation, which violated the rules of war.

The Tsar now felt obliged to make peace with France and form an alliance with her. As to his former ally: 'His imperial majesty, therefore, breaks off all communication with England, he recalls the whole of the mission which he has sent thither ... That (there) shall from henceforth be no connection between the two countries.'[3] Officially Russia was now at war with Great Britain, though it remained to be seen if this would break out into open conflict.

Napoleon and Alexander drew up plans for the future of Europe between them. Though King Frederick-William III of Prussia was present, he was treated with disdain by Napoleon and the agreement was essentially a Franco-Russian entente. Tilsit represented the summit of Napoleon's power and achievements. By the end of 1807 three of the Emperor's brothers were kings: Joseph in Naples; Louis in Holland; and Jérôme in Westphalia. He bestowed dukedoms and other titles on many French soldiers and statesmen and France became the most powerful nation on the Continent with a range of allied and satellite states to support her.

Yet the impression that France's position was now unassailable was a deceptive one. Russia had been brought to the negotiating table only by force of arms and Prussia, who had defied Napoleon twice, had been treated with such deliberate contempt that she would not be a willing French ally for the fore-seeable future. At best Tilsit was only a temporary settlement and much would depend upon how events developed over the next few years.[4]

Though France was victorious on land, Britain still dominated the oceans and, until the Royal Navy was overcome, she was beyond Napoleon's reach. Trafalgar may have crippled the fleets of France and her allies, but Napoleon hoped to assemble enough warships to challenge the British at sea through the construction of new vessels and the seizure of foreign navies. However, this would take time to achieve and meanwhile he would damage Britain's commercial interests by imposing a far-reaching trade embargo.

This policy had begun with the Berlin Decrees but at Tilsit he persuaded Alexander to adopt his Continental System thereby supporting a total trade ban against Britain throughout Europe. He believed that British power rested on her commercial interests and closing all European ports to her commerce should weaken if not ruin her. For example, the Royal Navy was reliant on trade with Russia for the wood it used in ship-building. Yet this would damage European trade simultaneously and the embargo was certainly not in Russia's long-term interest. Nevertheless, Napoleon hoped that it would quickly take effect, bring his enemies to the negotiating table, and its imposition would be short-lived.

Even as early as January 1808, observers were speculating over how enthusiastic Russia would prove as a French ally. *The Times* newspaper believed that the Tsar, and even Napoleon himself, might still consider coming to terms:

> ... if the secret stipulations of the Treaty of Tilsit only went so far as to declare the new system of maritime law, and to pledge the Emperor ALEXANDER to assist BUONAPARTE in the enforcement of it, that must have been considered as a measure highly prejudicial to this country, though not sufficient to provoke immediate hostilities ...[5]

However, Napoleon rapidly set about compelling Europe to adopt his blockade of British goods. Some countries were more amenable than others and even Prussia, smarting from her recent humiliation, agreed to comply. Not only were ports to be closed to British shipping and merchants from her colonies, but neutral ships, which had passed through British harbours, would be denied admittance 'on pain of the goods being confiscated and other punishment inflicted ...'[6] He was determined to inflict as much damage as possible on his strongest remaining enemy, regardless of the cost. He issued proclamations threatening reprisals against those who flouted the ban:

> Any functionary or agent of government who shall be convicted ... shall be prosecuted in the criminal court of the department of the Seine, which shall be formed into a special tribunal for this purpose, and punished, if convicted, as if guilty of high treason.[7]

Yet the Continental System was an ambitious policy and Napoleon over-estimated his power to enforce it. Its imposition could never be complete since it clearly damaged the trade interests of nations who had adopted it only through French diplomatic pressure. The sheer extent of the coastlines involved from the North Sea to the Mediterranean also meant that it would require a host of customs officials to oversee it, even if the governments involved were compliant. Though the British were unpopular on the Continent, business with them was profitable, while severing trade with them was not. The crucial flaw in Napoleon's grand strategy was that he underestimated European reliance on this commerce and he offered few incentives to compensate for its loss. Britain's trade with her own colonies was also increasingly lucrative and just how much damage the embargo could actually inflict against the British was questionable.

Until 1806 it is possible to argue that Napoleon's actions had been dictated by the need to defend France's borders and preserve her republican government. Yet after 1807 his wars took a more sinister turn, revealing a desire for personal glory and advancement. After Tilsit, France dominated the Continent and all Napoleon had to do was outwait his remaining enemies, who would probably sue for peace eventually. From a diplomatic point of view, it was time to play the magnanimous victor and heal the rifts that had divided Europe, allowing the Continent to become accustomed to French supremacy.

Yet the Emperor had always been impatient and never favoured adopting defensive or passive strategies. Ever on the attack, offensive action typified his approach and whenever he achieved an objective, he simply selected another goal, however unattainable it might seem. A more pragmatic man might have been satisfied with such achievements up to 1807 but Napoleon's ambition was limitless. Molé, then Napoleon's Minister for Finance, neatly summarized the Emperor's weakness: 'It is strange that although Napoleon's common sense amounted to genius, he never could see where the possible left off.'[8]

Commercial sanctions were not enough for Napoleon for he wished to strengthen his position even further. Spain had been an ally of dubious worth to France and Napoleon believed her monarchy, government and society were riddled with corruption and inefficiency. Neutral Portugal, Spain's nearest neighbour, plainly had little intention of being drawn into the Continental System and he believed that this could be used as an excuse to interfere in the affairs of both countries.

Historians are divided in their analysis of Napoleon's motives for intervening in the Iberian Peninsula. Some, such as Oman and Fortescue, tend to emphasize Napoleon's dissatisfaction with Spain and allege that he harboured great enmity against the Bourbon dynasty. After all, the people had overthrown them in France with great violence, this fact alone making Napoleon doubtful of the sincerity of their alliance. The Emperor was also intent on further conquests, believing that his power relied on military glory, which could only be upheld by a continuous succession of victories. Talleyrand, Napoleon's Minister of Foreign Affairs, believed that this was his Emperor's design but judged action against Spain to be dangerous:

> Napoleon, sitting on one of the thrones of the house of Bourbon, considered the princes, who occupied the other two thrones as natural enemies whom it was in his interest to overthrow. But it was an undertaking where he could not fail without ruining his own plans, and without perhaps losing himself as well. Therefore he must not attempt it without being entirely certain of success.[9]

In contrast, some pro–Bonaparte historians claim that political idealism lay at the heart of Napoleon's strategy. After the demise of her empire, Spain was in decline and her social system was both antiquated and oppressive to the people, the nobility and the church wielding incredible power. Though hardly a model of enlightenment, the political system Napoleon wished to impose on Spain would undoubtedly be fairer than the Bourbons' style of government.

French action against Spain was also partly dictated by strategic necessity since influential royal favourite Manuel de Godoy, acting on behalf of the Spanish King Carlos IV, had shown signs of disloyalty. In 1806 he had ordered the mobilization of Spanish forces, intending to side with Prussia against France, only to rescind these orders when Prussia's armies were unexpectedly defeated. Godoy's apologies and excuses did nothing to placate the outraged Napoleon who was astounded by this treachery.

Had it not been for the rapid success of Napoleon's 1806 campaign, a Spanish army could have crossed the border into southern France and wrought great destruction. Since the bulk of the French forces were deployed in the north, there would have been few troops there to oppose such an invasion. He had almost been outmanoeuvred and the Emperor confided in Talleyrand that he could never allow this to happen again. His problem was to find a legitimate excuse to take action:

> Spain therefore seemed to him as completely isolated as he could wish. But by attacking it openly, he had two dangers to fear. Since the Peace of Basle between France and Spain eleven years earlier, Spain had been the ally of France, and her faithful ally. Spain had committed money, vessels and soldiers to be disposed of by France; Spain had given them all generously ... How could he declare war on Spain? What pretext could he allege? Could he divulge the motives for his dynastic ambition? In making these known, he risked raising the feelings of his own subjects against him; and all his scorn for the human race did not stop him understanding that he should take proper account of the strength of public opinion.[10]

Talleyrand opposed Napoleon's plan to annexe Spain, believing it might cripple France by dragging his already overstretched nation into a prolonged

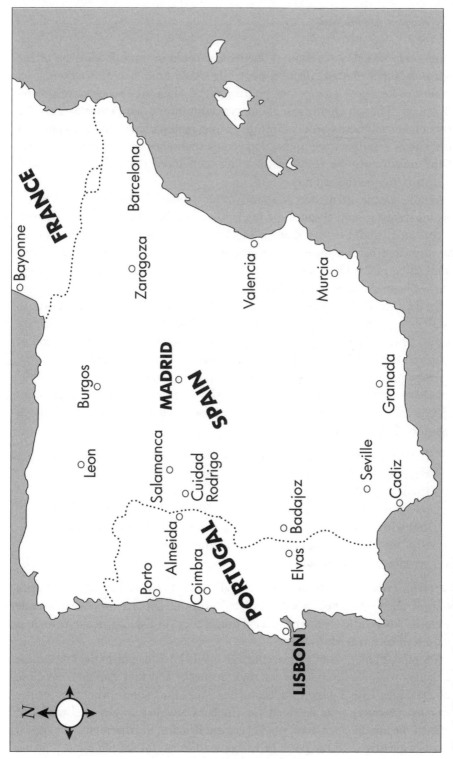

Map 1: The Iberian Peninsula 1807–1808

conflict. He was also uncertain if such a war could be won. Regardless of the approach Napoleon took, turning on an ally would be seen as a treacherous act by most of Europe – a dangerous political move when the French were already unpopular. Though Godoy's duplicitous actions meant that France would have to watch her southern borders carefully, Talleyrand preferred to seek a political rather than a military solution. Napoleon's insistence on the latter was one of the reasons why he resigned his office, convinced that this course would eventually topple the regime.

Another factor often cited as a motive for Napoleon's interference in Spain was his desire to find thrones for his family. Placing a Bonaparte in Madrid, he reasoned, would ensure that his blockade was enforced. Again this invites the suspicion that Napoleon's boundless ambition lay at the heart of his plans, culminating in the idea that he could become Emperor of Europe,[11] presiding over a Bonaparte dynasty of allied monarchies.

On 19 July 1807 Napoleon demanded that Portugal close all her ports to the British, imprison British expatriates, confiscate their property and declare war on Britain. Without waiting for a response, he ordered a concentration of troops on the Spanish border shortly afterwards. Alarmed at how events were developing, the Portuguese government played for time. On 3 September 1807 Napoleon attended an official function where numerous foreign dignitaries were present, including a Portuguese minister. Here he loudly voiced his disapproval of Portuguese policies:

> If Portugal does not do as I wish the House of Braganza will not be reigning in Europe in two months' time. I will no longer tolerate a single English envoy in Europe; I declare war on any power that has one two months from now ... I have 300,000 Russians at my back, and with this powerful ally I can do anything. The English declare that they will no longer respect neutrals at sea; I will no longer recognize them on land.[12]

Napoleon's open hostility placed Portugal's royal house of Bragança in a grim political dilemma. Their small, outdated army meant that opposing France militarily stood little chance of success but, if they turned against the British, it could lead to financial disaster.

Adopting France's commercial embargo would be damaging to the Portuguese as British trade was important for their economy and they had enjoyed close political links with London for centuries. Most Portuguese wine, one of her foremost products, was destined for England and her colony of Brazil had recently begun to open new markets with Britain. Furthermore, the Royal Navy frequently used the ports of Lisbon and Porto for supplies and refitting on voyages to Africa, the Mediterranean and to maintain their blockade of French ports like Toulon and Marseilles.

The Braganças were an absolutist monarchy but there had been few recent signs of discontent among the people. During the eighteenth century, reforms introduced by the Marques de Pombal had seen the influence of the nobility and the Catholic Church vastly reduced, in contrast to neighbouring Spain. Though her economy had suffered in the last fifty years when the production of gold, tobacco and sugar fell in Brazil, the Braganças had reason to hope that this would change. The discovery of diamonds in this colony, along with increased production of cotton, meant that Portuguese fortunes were likely to improve.[13]

Portugal had been hostile to France in 1793–1797, but the wars had hardly touched the country itself except for the brief War of the Oranges 1801 against Spain. The fighting had largely been confined to the border region, particularly around the fortress town of Elvas, and peace had been secured with a loss of Portuguese territory and the promise of an indemnity to Spain, which remained unpaid. The Portuguese government knew that neutrality was their wisest national policy but it now seemed that this was no longer an option.

Despite the fact that Spain was their only land neighbour, the Portuguese conducted very little trade with the Spaniards and were reliant on seaborne commerce. Since the Royal Navy was virtually unchallenged at sea, maintaining Britain's friendship was vital. If the British declared war against Portugal, communication with her colonies would be lost, her vessels waylaid on the high seas and their goods impounded.

Napoleon had decided to annexe both Portugal and Spain using subterfuge and duplicity as much as military force. The age-old enmity between the two nations meant that the Spanish would look favourably on any move made by France against the Portuguese, particularly if they stood to gain by it. The Emperor wrote to Carlos IV outlining his plans to invade Portugal:

> Portugal offers the spectacle of a power that has been in the English pay for sixteen years. In Lisbon England has possessed an inexhaustible spring of wealth, and a constant resource, both as a port of call, and as a base for naval expeditions. It is time that Porto and Lisbon were closed against her.[14]

Though negotiations with the Portuguese were still proceeding, Napoleon had already ordered General Jean Andoche Junot to concentrate an army at Bayonne with the seemingly innocuous title of the 'Corps of Observation of the Gironde'. The Spaniards were suspicious about this force but were reassured when told that they were destined for an invasion of Portugal.

Napoleon had already demanded that 15,000 of Spain's best troops be sent under La Romana to the Baltic in March 1807, revealing his displeasure at

Godoy's recent activities and his intent to weaken the Spanish military. He now entered into negotiations with Godoy asking Spain to provide troops to accompany Junot's forces. In fact the mere presence of Junot's army would probably have been sufficient to persuade the Portuguese Prince Regent to come to terms with France. There was little that Portugal's small army could do to oppose both Spain and France if they marched against them.[15]

The secret Treaty of Fontainebleau was drawn up by Duroc (Napoleon's Marshal of the Palace) and Godoy's agent Eugenio Izquierdo. In return for allowing French troops to march through Spain, Portugal was to be divided among the victors. Godoy was promised southern Portugal as a principality with the title Prince of the Algarves. As the Spanish Queen's favourite and the instigator of unpopular reforms, this proposal appealed to Godoy because securing a place of refuge was advisable due to his precarious political status. Lisbon and central Portugal would initially be occupied by French troops but eventually come under Spanish control. Northern Portugal was earmarked for the Etrurian ruling house to compensate for their loss of the Tuscan provinces, which Napoleon had annexed to allow better French access to the Papal States, relations with the Vatican having begun to deteriorate. When Portugal fell, Carlos IV planned to style himself 'Emperor of the Two Americas'.

It is unlikely that Napoleon ever intended to honour his promises to the Spaniards, the main purpose of the treaty being to distract them while he massed troops on the border. General Dupont was permitted to garrison towns along Junot's proposed route through northern Spain with French troops. This was explained as a necessary precaution in case of British raids along the coast to sever his communications. With similar threats to Junot's rear, Napoleon also proposed to concentrate a further 40,000 soldiers at Bayonne, though in fact he assembled 100,000.[16] By the time the treaty was agreed and signed on 27 October 1807, Junot's army had already crossed the frontier.

Meanwhile Portuguese diplomats were desperately trying to placate both France and Britain, the Chief Minister António de Araújo de Azevedo being foremost among them. Dom João (later King João VI) had been Prince Regent in Portugal since 1792 after his mother, Queen Maria I, became mentally ill. Though dismissed by some British historians, such as Chandler and Oman,[17] as being weak-willed and slow-witted, he was a reasonably capable man. Yet even the greatest ruler would have blanched at Portugal's diplomatic predicament, caught between two superpowers with France poised to invade and Britain threatening a blockade. Love of good food and wine had seen Dom João become rather stout but he took a keen interest in affairs of state and was deeply religious, spending much of his time at the Convent-Palace at Mafra. He had married the Spanish Princess Dona Carlota Joaquina but they became increasingly estranged and usually lived apart.[18]

Dom João told the British Ambassador that while he might be forced to close his ports to British ships, he would continue to permit trade with Brazil and offered to lease the island of Madeira to Britain. He also suggested dispatching the Portuguese navy to Brazil where it would remain out of French reach until the end of the war. However, the pathetic failure of Britain's move against Buenos Aires persuaded the Portuguese to offer concessions to the French instead.

They proposed conceding to three of Napoleon's demands: closing the ports, seizing all British subjects in Portugal and declaring war against Britain. Privately the Portuguese assured London that the war would be in name only and actual fighting was out of the question. However, they still refused to confiscate British property within Portugal. Such an unjust measure went against Portuguese principles as it belonged to civilians whose trade had assisted them in the past and whose surety was guaranteed by the government.[19] Despite Portuguese concessions, Napoleon cynically used the refusal to confiscate British property as justification for war. It did not matter what the Portuguese offered – he was determined to invade. The seizure of Portuguese merchant ships was a sure sign that hostilities were impending: 'In Holland, all the Portuguese vessels have been embargoed. We are assured that M. de Berzana, Ambassador from Portugal to the King of Holland, is preparing to depart.'[20]

By 1807 Britain's war effort against France was flagging. Although Prime Minister William Portland and his Tory administration wanted to continue the war, the Whigs' demands for peace were gaining ground. Conflict with France had dragged on since 1792 with only a year's relief, and Britain's military expeditions had achieved little. Napoleon's Continental System was seen as a significant threat and Whigs like Earl Grey and Lord Holland were beginning to suggest making a treaty with France. Though King George III loathed Bonaparte as a revolutionary upstart, ruinous ill-health rendered his support tenuous and even firebrands like George Canning in the government were not enough to ensure the continuation of hostilities.[21]

Now that Russia, Austria and Prussia had made peace, Britain was increasingly isolated. Her only allies, Sweden and Sicily, could offer little in the way of military support and required assistance merely for their own defence. The prospect of Portugal, England's oldest ally, joining with France was therefore a strong possibility. Britain threatened to intercept Portuguese ships and blockade her ports if the Regent declared war upon them. It was also clear that Britain might attempt to take the Portuguese navy by force, just as they had seized the Danish fleet at Copenhagen. It was too valuable a prize to be allowed to fall into French hands as every warship added to the French fleet increased the possibility of an invasion of Britain. Though sympathetic to Portugal's plight, the British could not afford to compromise.

By mid-October, British sources were receiving conflicting reports over whether the Braganças had come to an agreement with Napoleon. Some members of the Court hoped that, even with an army approaching their frontier, such an agreement could still be reached. Lord Strangford, the British *Chargé d'Affaires*, wrote that the Prince Regent had received a letter via extraordinary courier from Paris, which implied that it was not too late. He stated that the Regent 'appeared in great spirits after the communication with France'.[22]

One of the problems for the Regent was that political opinion in the Portuguese middle and upper classes was divided. Although Dom João's monarchy was not unpopular, many high-ranking Portuguese saw political developments in France as the way forward. António Araújo de Azevedo proposed an alliance with France and Spain in order to avoid war, despite the loss of trade with Britain that would be involved. The liberals argued that the war would not continue forever and France now possessed a great empire and would offer trade concessions to allied powers.

Opposed to the liberals was a staunchly pro-British faction led by João de Melo e Castro and Dom Rodrigo de Sousa (a member of the powerful Sousa family). Despite occasional disagreements with London, they reasoned Portuguese interests were so closely intertwined with British commerce that breaking links forged over centuries was folly. A convincing argument in their favour was that, for all her revolutionary bombast, France seemed to be offering very little in any potential alliance while asking for a great deal. Her military success on land could hardly guarantee Portuguese seaborne trade, for example. As conservative reactionaries, they were also alarmed at proposals of French-style reforms.

Nevertheless, while he continued to debate his options with his counsellors, the Regent was still making preparations for flight. The situation was fraught with uncertainty:

> We still continue here in a state of suspense. Never was the fate of the country more seriously at stake. The PRINCE REGENT is resolved, should BUONAPARTE put his threats in execution, and invade the country, to embark for the Brazils. The ships for that purpose are preparing with all possible dispatch. The people are at work night and day, and do not relax in their exertions even on Sunday.[23]

If the Regent stayed he would probably become a mere vassal of the Emperor or be deposed; yet conceding to Napoleon's demands would undoubtedly alienate the British. Portugal's maritime economy meant that the nation would undergo severe hardship if the Continental System was adopted, even in the short term, and British supremacy at sea meant that contact with her colonies would be lost.

When news that Junot's army was on the move reached the capital, Dom João became increasingly worried as British entreaties were combined with implied threats. Strangford claimed that he openly ridiculed Portuguese duplicity in their dealings with France, declaring the Emperor would see straight through such efforts. The Regent must take a side he argued, urging that '. . . the sword must be entirely sheathed, or entirely drawn'.[24] Just before Sir Sidney Smith's fleet arrived off the Portuguese coast, he hinted that His Majesty's government might be forced to adopt stern measures to ensure that the Portuguese navy remained out of enemy hands.

The Regent's last desperate effort to placate Napoleon was to send Don Pedro Vito de Menezes, the Marquis of Marialva, with further concessions to Paris. These included a proposal of marriage between the 9-year-old Prince of Beira and one of the daughters of the Grand Duke of Berg (Marshal Murat). However, the Marquis was detained by the Spanish at Madrid. Officially he lacked travel permits, but the Spaniards were well aware that Junot had now marched against Portugal and the likelihood was that Napoleon would have spurned his offer in any case.

The Portuguese were in a terrible position. Their oldest ally was unwilling to help defend the country and reluctantly threatened to take measures against them if they sided with France. Yet worst of all a French army, part of the awesome military machine that dominated Europe, marched against them. It was time for the Braganças to take sides.

Chapter 2

The Tempest

Napoleon had chosen General Jean Andoche Junot to command his invasion of Portugal, reputed to be one of the fiercest fighting men in the French army. Though a committed revolutionary, he was also devoted to the Emperor, the pair having become great friends during the early years of the Revolution. Junot was a celebrated firebrand who tolerated no insult to his friends, family or regiment. He had demonstrated his willingness to back up his principles many times with his fists, sword or pistols – sometimes at the slightest provocation. Wounded many times in battle, he had seen extensive campaigning and was known to be fond of gambling, drink and women. He was a fighting soldier first to last and his appointment signified that Napoleon was willing to drag Portugal into his Continental League by force if necessary.

Jean Andoche Junot was born on 24 September 1771 in the village of Bussy-Legrand, a few miles from Dijon. His second name was unusual and chosen because his birthday fell upon the feast day of Saint Andoche and throughout his life he preferred to be known by his second Christian name.[1] He was the third of four children born to Michel and Marie Junot, who were of respectable middle-class origin. Although he worked in local government and was of the bourgeoisie, Michel Junot was a republican and happily served the succession of revolutionary governments that ruled France after the fall of Louis XVI. Marie Junot had several influential relatives, including a brother who ultimately became Bishop of Metz, but she shared her husband's republican beliefs.

They sent young Andoche to a respectable school at nearby Montbard where he received a liberal education. Although intelligent, he was a lazy and inattentive scholar, constantly at odds with his teachers by his own admission in later life. Physically fit, he excelled at sports and rapidly grew to be tall and well-built. Being blond-haired and good-looking, he soon attracted female attention and developed a taste for the company of women, occasionally writing love poetry for his amours. His quick temper frequently got him into fights and he was prone to throwing noisy tantrums when he failed to get his way.[2] Nevertheless, he did well enough at school to continue his education, later studying law at Chatillon-sur-Seine. Here he met Auguste Marmont, who eventually became a Marshal of Empire, the pair becoming lifelong friends.

The old French society was dying and in 1789 Andoche embraced revolutionary idealism. Setting aside his studies, he travelled to Paris and listened to radical speeches delivered at political gatherings. Caught up in the revolutionary fervour spreading like wildfire through the streets and salons, he publicly swore many oaths proclaiming his dedication to the cause.[3] He enlisted with the National Guard on his return, later transferring into the 2nd Battalion of Volunteers in the Department of the Côte d'Or in 1791 aged 20.

The violent demise of the monarchy plunged France into a series of conflicts and Andoche's regiment was swiftly sent to defend French borders during the Revolutionary Wars. Formerly the mostly aristocratic generals of the eighteenth century had fought campaigns with relatively small, professional armies, concentrating on seizing strategically important cities and regions in the hope of forcing a peace settlement. Though heavy casualties were occasionally inflicted, the limited scale of these conflicts usually ensured that widespread death and destruction were avoided. Throughout the Revolutionary and Napoleonic Wars, the increasingly large numbers of men deployed heralded a change in emphasis, the destruction of enemy armies becoming paramount. The carnage that ensued during this era exceeded anything that had gone before.

Junot had joined the infantry, which was the backbone of any army during the period. The smooth-bore, flintlock musket was the infantryman's main weapon and its accurate range was limited. It was a heavy, muzzle-loaded, single-shot weapon that could only be loaded comfortably while a soldier was standing. Even in well-trained hands, its rate of fire was unlikely to exceed three shots per minute with the need to separate, insert and push down cartridge and musket-ball with a ramrod. Though capable of killing at 200 yards or more, an infantryman was unlikely to hit the man he aimed at beyond 50 yards. To compensate for this, soldiers were deployed in linear formations, the men standing virtually shoulder to shoulder, so that a heavy volume of fire could be concentrated against the enemy. When firing his musket against a similarly close formation, a soldier might not hit the man he aimed at beyond a certain distance but there was a strong likelihood that his musket-ball would strike another man within a few feet of his intended target.

Rifles were becoming more common during the period and were capable of reliably hitting a man-sized target at ranges of 200–300 yards. However, they were much slower to load than muskets and, with the dense smoke produced by the gunpowder of the time, it was difficult to utilize their full range and accuracy on the battlefield during heavy engagements. Longer training was needed to use them compared to the musket and their application was largely confined to elite units, usually deployed as sharpshooters and skirmishers.

If the fighting was at close quarters, the musket was equipped with a bayonet, whose threat alone was often enough to deter one side from standing and fighting after suffering casualties. Therefore, after an initial exchange of fire, the advance of the side who were gaining the upper hand was usually enough to persuade their foes to flee. The bayonet was also a vital defence against cavalry, who could decimate infantry once they became disordered or gaps were made in their ranks. To counter this, infantry formed square formations several ranks deep, which presented a wall of bayonets to dissuade cavalry from pressing a charge home. Though this tactic was highly effective, squares were vulnerable to enemy infantry or artillery who could concentrate their fire on such a closely-packed target.

While often considered the elite in European armies, cavalry's use on the battlefield had diminished after the adoption of gunpowder. Though cavalry charges could be devastating, they had to be well timed or risk suffering great losses for little gain as cavalry presented a large target to enemy firepower. While infantry squares were not invulnerable, they were well protected against cavalry and enemy artillery could wreak bloody ruin upon cavalry unless attacked from the flank or rear. The cavalry's most effective use in battle was in conjunction with other arms or when an enemy was on the verge of retreating. As the arm with the greatest mobility, cavalry excelled in pursuing a defeated foe after a battle had been won. They were also essential for scouting, foraging, protecting armies on the march or in camp, screening an army from enemy observation, providing a commander with intelligence and discouraging their counterparts from doing the same. For a commander-in-chief, their actual combat role had become one of their less important duties now that gunpowder dominated the battlefield.

Artillery was a devastating force on the battlefield. While it required protection against cavalry and careful deployment, cannon enjoyed the longest range of any weapon during the early nineteenth century. Most European artillery used two kinds of projectile: roundshot and shell. Roundshot consisted of a solid iron ball capable of inflicting horrific wounds or instant death. Ideally it would be fired at a point just before its target and the cannon ball would bounce many times along the ground hitting numerous targets as it went until its energy was spent. When fired against infantry columns or squares, a single roundshot could strike down as many as ten men. Even against thinner line formations, it could still hit several men at a time. In siege warfare the impact damage of roundshot, especially from large calibre guns, was vital for battering down stone walls and ramparts.

Shells looked similar to roundshot but were fused and packed with gunpowder. They would explode and shower the surrounding area with fragments of their iron casing. When bursting within a body of men or horses they could be devastating. Although they usually detonated shortly after landing, they occasionally exploded in flight, which made them more effective by showering metal splinters over a wide area. The British were experimenting with a new shell, designed by Major Henry Shrapnel, which exploded above a target to shower those below with musket-balls. If attacked by cavalry or infantry at close range, artillery fired canister or case-shot (better known by the naval term grapeshot). This consisted of a canister packed with musket-balls that would break up when fired, producing a hail of projectiles capable of striking many targets with one discharge.[4]

The tactical use of infantry was being modified by the French because they had little time to train men to fight in line formation making the best use of their firepower. Conscription added large numbers of volunteers enabling the French to field large armies but conscripts stood little chance of matching the rate of fire that professional, disciplined troops could deliver. This placed them at a significant disadvantage during a fire fight, especially when they were attacking.

Consequently, the French often used large assault columns for offensive operations. These oblong-shaped formations presented a narrow frontage against men in line but were able to discharge fewer muskets, as those in the rear ranks were unable to fire over the heads of their comrades. Yet it was easier for novice soldiers to adopt, march in and maintain this formation under fire. To compensate for lessened firepower, the French used large numbers of skirmishers to engage the enemy as their columns marched into range. These were the best shots in a battalion who would target officers and NCOs. They were difficult to counter without wasting large amounts of ammunition or deploying skirmishers to match them. They were also capable of inflicting sufficient casualties to create gaps in a formation prior to the column engaging the enemy.

When coming into close or actual contact with an enemy line, it would enjoy a tremendous local advantage, either with firepower or the bayonet, and was intended to break through the enemy formation and exploit its success on either flank. Since a column presented a large target, vulnerable to artillery and massed musketry volleys, it had its limitations. Napoleon favoured a combination of line and column formations in adjacent units known as *ordre mixte*, thereby gaining the advantages of shock tactics and concentration with columns while supported by the firepower of men in line.[5]

The French usually preceded column attacks by concentrated artillery fire on the areas they were about to engage, inflicting casualties and damaging enemy morale to improve the column's chance of success. In later years, Napoleon became adept in massing numerous batteries of artillery and setting their combined firepower against weak points in an enemy army. Although France's enemies would eventually identify and counter these tactics, their early use brought France considerable military success.

Junot served as a grenadier in his battalion, seeing action with the *Armée du Nord* in the fighting around the fortresses near Verdun. On 11 June 1792 he was seriously wounded in the head by a musket-ball, at Longwy. He rapidly won the respect and admiration of his comrades and, in true revolutionary fashion, they elected him as sergeant shortly after this incident.

While recovering from wounds, he was posted to guard the frontier and was involved in the capture of the Countess of Brionne who was trying to flee France. Junot was appalled at the rough treatment the Countess received at the hands of his superiors and, according to his wife's revelations years afterwards, connived in her escape. Mistakenly believing him to be a secret royalist, the Countess thanked him profusely but was surprised when Junot responded that, as a committed revolutionary, he was acting merely out of natural gallantry.[6]

He loved army life and actively sought combat. He was also winning some repute as a skilled card-player and was a hard drinker, carouser and womanizer. He became popular and could be a generous and loyal friend but his readiness to engage in violent disagreements made him a terrible enemy. When his battalion was transferred to the *Armée du Rhin*, he was wounded again on 16 May 1793, being both shot and sabred in the action. His bravery and stormy temper became famous in the army and comrades nicknamed him 'The Tempest'.[7]

It was during the siege of Toulon that Junot first met Captain Napoleon Buonaparte, the man who would shape his destiny. Royalists in Toulon had rebelled against the government and invited the Royal Navy, carrying British troops, into their port to assist them on 27 August 1793. Toulon was a vital seaport for French access to the Mediterranean and the government ordered the army to retake it at all costs. Initially General Carteaux's efforts enjoyed little success. Junot took part in the first attempt to storm the city defences, charging through an artillery embrasure of an outlying fort to seize a gun, shooting and bayoneting two artillerymen. Yet the assault was repulsed and the siege continued for months.

On one occasion, Junot and his comrades were eating in a tent near the siege lines when a shell burst through the canvas, rolling on the ground, its fuse spluttering and fizzing:

> Everyone had risen and was running away when Junot, seizing a glass, exclaimed, 'To the memory of those of us who are going to perish!' How far the wine had any influence on the effect his words produced, I know not; but all stopped, took up their glasses and remained motionless till the shell exploded. One fell dead, and the others tossing off their bumpers cried, 'To the memory of a hero!'[8]

When Captain Buonaparte of the 4th Artillery Regiment arrived, he enjoyed the support of some political officers, or 'Representatives of the People', monitoring the siege forces. His formidable talents, naked ambition and influential political allies allowed him to gain great influence during the operation. Toulon proved the making of Buonaparte, enabling him to rise swiftly in rank. With his keen interest in all aspects of the siege, he soon learned of Junot's reputation and asked him to perform a dangerous task as a courier. Advising him to don civilian clothing, as British gunners would fire upon a man in uniform, he was astounded at the sergeant's curt refusal: 'I will never shrink from the chance of being killed by a cannon-ball, but I will not run the risk of being hung as a spy.'[9] Impressed by such bravado, Buonaparte agreed and Junot returned from the mission unscathed.

Discovering that Junot was well-educated, Buonaparte made him his military secretary. During a dangerous survey of Toulon's defences, the pair were showered with earth as a roundshot slammed into the wicker gabions protecting the trench they stood in. Casually dusting the soil from the notes Buonaparte had dictated to him, Junot casually murmured: 'Well, now I will not need sand.'[10] Inspired by his sergeant's bravery and competence, Buonaparte managed to get him a promotion to second lieutenant but:

> On receiving it, without a word he tore it up and threw down the pieces. 'What are you doing?' said his chief. 'What a man ought to do that is not the sort to take his epaulettes from those beggars. When you are a general, give me them if you think I deserve them.'[11]

Buonaparte's patronage ensured that by 1 October Junot received an officer's commission and transferred into the artillery. When the city fell on 17 December 1793 it was largely due to Buonaparte's careful strategy, orchestrating the seizure of outlying forts commanding the Royal Navy's anchorage and rendering further defence untenable. Having already gained rapid promotion during the siege, he was finally promoted *général de brigade* for his conduct during the operation.

Junot realized that Buonaparte was destined for high office and possibly greatness but his father was unconvinced and enquired why he had left the infantry to ally his fortunes with such a man, asking: 'Who is this General Buonaparte? Where has he served? No one knows anything about him.' Junot replied, 'I will respond as Santeuil: "to know him is to be him …"'[12], going on to explain how much he admired his chief's talent, determination and ambition. After Toulon Junot's career became closely combined with Buonaparte's and he became his devoted friend and follower.

Nonetheless, Buonaparte's career was seriously threatened when the Coup of Thermidor saw Maximilien Robespierre and other members of the Committee of Public Safety arrested and tried for their crimes. They had instigated the reign of terror in which thousands had been executed and their excesses could no longer be tolerated. Buonaparte's association with Robespierre resulted in his arrest and imprisonment. Outraged at his friend's plight, Junot, Marmont and other officers planned to break him out of gaol and were only dissuaded from this wild enterprise by the prisoner himself, who said it would make him look guilty. Fortunately for Buonaparte, he still had influential friends and Salicetti, who had supported him at Toulon, got the charges dismissed for lack of evidence while Robespierre and others went to the guillotine.

In 1794 Buonaparte became Commander of the Artillery in the Army of Italy. He now changed his name to 'Bonaparte' to make it appear more French than the previous Corsican pronunciation and spelling. Junot followed his chief to Italy, acting primarily as an aide-de-camp and military secretary, but Bonaparte knew that he lacked the mathematical skill and patience necessary for the artillery and in early 1795 obtained a cavalry command for him with the 1st Hussar Regiment.[13] This meant that Junot had the unusual distinction of having served in all three military arms.

Yet in May 1795 Bonaparte had been dismissed and returned to Paris to endure a period of unemployment while seeking a new command. Fraternizing with Marmont and Junot, the trio became inseparable friends frequenting the bars and salons of the capital and spending a great deal of time at the Hôtel de la Liberté in Montmartre. Though Junot's successful run of gambling yielded a limited income, they were living on half-pay and became reliant upon the money sent by Michel Junot to support his son. According to Thiébault, Junot's father even sold some land to meet the young general's debts.[14] Though Junot became a firm friend of the future Emperor's at this time, in many ways he knew too much about his poverty-stricken early years and no great man likes to be reminded of such experiences. In later years Bonaparte may well have discouraged Junot's reminiscences of this time and frequent indiscreet references to this period may have been held against him.

At this time Junot met the 11-year-old Laure Permon, his future wife. She was captivated by the charms of this good-looking cavalryman whose company was sought by many women. He also formed a romantic attachment to Napoleon's sister, Pauline Bonaparte. For a while, Junot was smitten and asked his friend's permission to marry her, their father having died some years before. Though he gave his cautious approval, Bonaparte counselled him to wait as the couple lacked money, but he probably recognized the transitory nature of Junot's affections, believing his friend would soon find solace elsewhere. Junot reluctantly agreed to wait and never raised the subject again, revealing Bonaparte's insight regarding this matter.

In October 1795 when Bonaparte saved the Convention Government by brutally putting down a revolt in Paris (the infamous 'Whiff of Grapeshot'), he was restored to favour with the establishment. The grateful Paul Barras had him promoted to *général de division* and made commander of the French Army of the Interior. On 2 March 1796, he became commander-in-chief of the Army of Italy and Junot joined him with the promotion of *chef d'escadrons* for the 3rd Dragoons.

Junot divided his time between the cavalry and acting as an aide to Bonaparte, often reprising his role as military secretary and leaving subordinates to act in his stead. The 1796 campaign displayed Napoleon's brilliance as a commander and his mastery of swift manoeuvre saw the Austrians suffer a series of defeats and Europe was stunned at the speed and scale of French success. It was an excellent chance to observe one of the leading generals of the age at work in all the facets of a commander's role.

Junot was sent to Paris bearing twenty-one captured enemy standards as war trophies, conveying Bonaparte's enormous trust in him. He was given a rapturous welcome, being fêted as a hero and made *chef de brigade* by the government. Secretly, he was also tasked by Bonaparte to persuade his wife Josephine to join him in Italy. Junot managed to convince Josephine to leave despite her liking for Paris and the distracting love affair she was engaged in with Captain Hippolyte Charles. Nevertheless, he offended Josephine by seducing one of her female attendants.[15] Josephine was hardly a prude concerning romantic liaisons and her anger must have been provoked by a considerable lack of respect on Junot's part.

Returning to Italy, Junot discovered that he had missed several months of important campaigning, but was present at the Battle of Lonato where he performed one of his most famous exploits. While leading a cavalry charge, he was cut off and attacked by a large number of the enemy. Refusing to panic or surrender, Junot laid about him with his sword killing six enemy cavalrymen. He was wounded at least six times by sabre cuts, mostly to the head and upper body, but cut his way out of the mêlée and captured his opposing cavalry commander, Colonel Bender. His wounds were serious and might have killed a lesser man. Indeed, some head wounds were so severe that he never truly recovered and his scalp bled periodically for the rest of his life.[16] Nevertheless, at the Battle of Rivoli 14 January 1796, he had recovered sufficiently to lead another cavalry charge.

After the occupation of papal land, there was limited action as the papal troops were reluctant to fight and the Pope rapidly came to terms with the new Directory Government. Along with his compatriots Junot showed little compunction in looting the church's wealth in Italy, being a strong opponent of religious influence in politics.[17] Numerous treasures and works of art were brought back from the Italian states and the Vatican was forced to pay a huge indemnity of 30 million francs.

Junot was involved in the fighting against the Austrians in the north and was also entrusted with a diplomatic mission to ensure the Italian state of Venetia disarmed and declared neutrality. Knowing that Bonaparte required a fast response, Junot became angry when the Venetian senators prevaricated, reacting with an impulsive tirade of threats and abuse, whereupon Venetia declared war against France. Although this proved to be more of a short-lived protest than a serious conflict, it was the exact opposite of Junot's purpose. Clearly his talents did not lie in diplomacy.

He accompanied Bonaparte on his invasion of Egypt but proved so dis-interested in the planning sessions conducted during the voyage that Bonaparte stopped insisting upon his presence as he set a bad example. He remained Bonaparte's first ADC but Junot's contemporaries were beginning to outstrip him in terms of promotion and some received field commands. He took part in the small-scale fighting when the fleet paused at Malta and carried Bonaparte's terms to Baron Hompesch, Grand Master of the Knights of St John, who ceded Malta to French control on 11 June 1798.

The French landed in Egypt where campaigning proved arduous as the difficult terrain and climate hampered operations. In addition to the Mamelukes who opposed them, nomadic tribesmen and brigands dogged the French on the march, attacking small units and stragglers. Torture, murder and reprisals became commonplace and many spoke out against what they considered an ill-advised campaign and poor performance by their commander-in-chief. Junot engaged in many arguments in defence of his chief but it was a quarrel with General Lanusse that caused the most trouble.

Despite efforts to separate them (by Lannes, Murat and Bessières), bitter insults were exchanged and Junot challenged Lanusse to a duel. They fought one evening by torchlight in the garden of a house on the Nile, requisitioned by Murat. Showing considerable gallantry, Junot turned down his opponent's suggestion that they fight with pistols as his personal marksmanship would give him an unfair advantage. They fought with swords, the extent of their enmity ensuring that the duel continued long after first blood had been drawn. Eventually, after both were wounded several times, honour was declared satisfied. Junot was incapacitated for a while having taken a severe thrust to the abdomen that left an 8-inch scar but nobly refused to bear a grudge during future dealings with Lanusse.[18] Publicly Bonaparte reprimanded all concerned due to his prohibition of duelling, but privately acknowledged that he was flattered by his friend fighting on his behalf.

Junot had recovered sufficiently to fight at Shubra Khit on 13 July. At the subsequent Battle of the Pyramids on 21 July 1798, the French deployed in vast square formations, incorporating whole divisions with artillery batteries placed at the corners, to fight the largely cavalry-based Mameluke forces. The Battle of the Pyramids broke the enemy's power and the French seized and occupied Cairo.

Bonaparte was elated by the victory but dismayed to hear of Josephine's scandalous affairs, which were public knowledge in Paris. It is thought that a careless remark of Junot's was either overheard by his commander or reported to him by someone else. He was not averse to keeping mistresses himself in later years but Bonaparte was surprised when he discovered that Junot maintained a private harem in Cairo and had fathered an illegitimate child by an Abyssinian slave girl named Xraxrane. To his credit, Junot ensured that the child was educated and cared for.[19]

Junot was dispatched on reconnaissance missions to consolidate the French occupation but was now increasingly overshadowed by the success of his friends, with Marmont newly created Governor of Alexandria. However, with Bonaparte absent in the old city to the south, he was the most senior officer present when a serious revolt broke out in Cairo. Captain Moiret recalled the extent of the violence:

> It was not long before we learned that ... the citizens of Cairo had gathered in their mosques in a state of tumult and then rushed to the houses in which the French were living; that General Dupuy ... had been murdered, together with his escort. We heard also that, in spite of very frequent patrols, French people were slain whenever they were found without protection.[20]

Bonaparte soon returned but Junot was able to put down the uprising. During the savage street-fighting, Captain Jozef Sulkowski, one of Bonaparte's ADCs, was dragged from his horse and torn apart by a mob when he tried to ride through them with ten cavalrymen. Bonaparte enforced harsh reprisals and the revolt was put down with what Junot considered excessive force.

He now began to receive independent commands and, shortly after he was provisionally promoted *général de brigade*, was ordered to take over the garrison at Suez on 18 January 1799. The following month, Bonaparte went to war against the Ottoman Turks, crossed the border into Sinai and marched on to invade Syria. Junot was given a brigade in General Kléber's division and was employed in a cavalry role, reconnoitring in the vanguard of the army, a task that eminently suited his abilities.

After Gaza and Jaffa fell, the advance halted outside the fortress city of Acre, which defied Bonaparte's siege efforts. While occupied with the siege, Bonaparte sent Murat and Junot on scouting missions to ascertain the strength of the enemy to the north and east of the city. Junot led a force of 200 infantry from the 2nd Légère and 125 of the 14th Dragoons. On 8 April, close to Nazareth, he was attacked by 3,000 Turkish cavalry under the leadership of

Ayoub-Bey, known as 'The Father of the Sword'.[21] The infantry were caught off guard by the speed of the assault but, despite being in line formation, managed to stand their ground and form square.

Recovering from his initial surprise, Junot swiftly formed his cavalry and attacked the Turks in the flank to relieve the pressure on his infantry. He knew he was vastly outnumbered but exhorted his dragoons by shouting: 'You must die, but we will kill as many as we can. Forward and long live the Republic!'[22] The charge was a stunning success, taking many of the Turks unawares and driving them off for a time. However, the situation was desperate and Junot dispatched a rider to inform Kléber of his plight and conducted a fighting withdrawal towards a better defensive position near Cana. Though harassed all the way by repeated attacks, the infantry retreated slowly and steadily, stopping periodically to fire upon the enemy or standing to receive their charges in square. Junot led several counter-charges and, by the end of the engagement, claimed to have inflicted around 600 casualties in return for twelve dead and forty-five wounded. He also captured five cavalry standards in the vicious cavalry mêlées that ensued.

Kléber responded to Junot's dispatch and they met at Nazareth on 9 April, but the Turks had also been reinforced and when Kléber attacked the Pasha of Damascus near Tiberias, the French were outnumbered by three to one. Junot commanded the second of the two brigade-sized squares they formed against the Turks and for an entire day the French withstood a series of assaults, Junot having two horses and a camel shot from under him. Only the arrival of Bon's division when they attacked the Turks again on 16 April enabled them to prevail, routing the enemy and capturing their baggage train. Junot's courage during these actions was used by Bonaparte for propaganda in dispatches sent back to France.

However, the French failed at Acre as the British seized the heavy guns Bonaparte had ordered to be brought from Egypt and the garrison withstood all attempts to storm the walls. The siege was raised and they retreated to Egypt where Junot fought at the Battle of Aboukir on 25 July and during the subsequent siege of Aboukir Castle. When Bonaparte abandoned his army to return to France on 23 August, Junot's wounds obliged him to stay behind.

He was unable to leave until December of that year and his reputation as a looter was such that some French soldiers rifled through his baggage as it was brought on board the *America*. Enraged at this, he immediately issued duelling challenges and it was with great difficulty that the Captain calmed the situation and set sail. That night they were waylaid by HMS *Theseus* and Junot became a prisoner of war. He would later complain that Captain Steel of the *Theseus* treated him poorly with no regard to his rank and demanded that he showed himself on deck before the victor of the Battle of the Nile:

Is this the way you address a general? You have the courage to address me with such impertinence? ... tell your Admiral Nelson, who is neither a hero nor a great man to me ... I am not his prisoner but a prisoner of his government ... if Admiral Nelson wants to see me, he knows where I am.[23]

Nelson was impressed by his defiance and sent him and his officers' presents of fruit and wine as a magnanimous gesture. Subsequently held captive by the British for seven months, Junot was eventually exchanged and landed at Marseille on 14 June 1800.

He had missed the *coup d'état* of Brumaire, in which Bonaparte overthrew the government and seized power, becoming First Consul of France. The future Emperor always favoured those who had supported him during Brumaire and, though Junot would undoubtedly have backed him, he had missed a chance to display his loyalty. However, Bonaparte was overjoyed to see his friend and asked him to accept the appointment of Commandant of Paris.

In his new duties Junot entertained foreign dignitaries and performed various civic functions but was also responsible for protecting the life and safety of the First Consul. Although he earnestly desired another field command, Junot accepted the assignment as it conveyed enormous trust and faith in his abilities. However, it also required close co-operation with Joseph Fouché, Bonaparte's sinister chief of secret police, and it came as no surprise that a fighting man like Junot developed a serious dislike of this new associate, whom he saw as little more than a glorified spy. As a result of Bonaparte assuming dictatorial powers, extremists from both sides of the political spectrum wished to eliminate him and Junot's role involved keeping a close watch on their intrigues in Paris.

Bonaparte stressed the need for respectability in his new diplomatic role and urged him to marry and, although Junot had a number of women in mind, he chose Laure Permon for his bride. He knew her family well, having frequented her mother's salon during the early days of the Revolution, and friends persuaded him to marry her to save her from an unfortunate betrothal her family had arranged to a man three times her age. However, Bonaparte did not favour the match as Laure was only 15 years old, her mother had royalist connections and the Permons were relatively poor.

The marriage nearly ended before it began when Junot refused to hold a religious marriage service and was only persuaded to conduct one in secret after the official republican civil ceremony. Bonaparte eventually gave his grudging approval and bestowed generous wedding gifts but revealed his displeasure at a ball held shortly after the marriage. Bonaparte was inclined to bully and browbeat people at such affairs and when Junot formally introduced his young wife he suddenly remarked: 'I suppose you have heard of the harem your husband kept in Egypt?'[24]

There were several attempts to assassinate the First Consul during Junot's period of office. The one that came closest to success occurred when Bonaparte visited the opera and an explosive device was detonated at the roadside, narrowly missing the carriage containing Bonaparte and Josephine. Twenty-two people were killed and fifty-six were injured in the blast and Bonaparte used the attempt on his life to persecute Jacobin extremists, hundreds of whom were exiled, despite the fact that Fouché identified Royalists as the culprits.[25]

Junot suffered nightmares because of this incident, finding the pursuit of a role that went against his nature stressful. He took to drinking heavily and gambling, running up many debts. Bad luck at the gaming tables exacerbated his violent temper and he was involved in several public brawls as a result, to Bonaparte's anger and dismay. On 5 January 1801, Laure bore him a daughter, naming her Josephine, but within a year of their marriage Junot was already seeing other women.

His relationship with Bonaparte was strained when Junot publicly denounced his acceptance of the consulship for life as being against revolutionary principles. While he might have accepted such criticism from an old friend in private, Bonaparte was incensed at this disloyalty and had the Junots thrown out of the palace. Yet it was Junot's reluctance to arrest British subjects and enforce a ban on their goods in Paris that proved the final straw for his master. He had many British friends among the expatriate community in the capital and the fact that he kept an English mistress became scandalous when war between the two nations recommenced on 16 May 1803.

By the end of the year, Bonaparte lost patience and transferred Junot to Boulogne to help organize the army that was massing there to invade Britain. Here Junot performed his functions well and was recalled to Paris to participate in Bonaparte's coronation as Napoleon I, Emperor of France. He attended the ceremony dressed as a Peer of France and carried Charlemagne's Orb of Justice during the procession. In acknowledgement of his many services he was granted a pension for life, membership of the *Légion d'Honneur* and made a Grand Officer of the Empire.[26]

However, he failed to be created a Marshal of Empire, a title he coveted and which many close friends and associates were honoured with in 1804. More a civic rank than a military one, it was designed to give the army increased political influence to support Napoleon, but most of the Marshalate went on to gain princely and ducal titles, great wealth and in some instances a crown as the First Empire expanded. Napoleon was aware that Junot felt left out but assured him that he would not be overlooked for long. He even joked that, had his name been anything other than Junot, he would have made him Duke of Nazareth.

With war impending, Junot had hoped for a divisional command and was bitterly disappointed when Napoleon announced his intention to send him to Portugal as French Ambassador instead:

> I am not made for diplomacy. Lannes told me that the court in Lisbon is a veritable bear garden. The Austrians menace us as we turn our backs and the Russians and Prussians too. While there is musket and cannon fire, I will be taking a siesta in Portugal![27]

Rarely were truer words spoken for Junot was plainly more at home on the battlefield than at court. Nonetheless, Napoleon wanted to appoint someone trustworthy who lacked political ambition. The Emperor was also determined to deny any concessions whatsoever to the Portuguese and a bluntly-spoken soldier would serve him just as well as an able statesman for political intimidation in Lisbon.

Junot took Laure with him to Iberia and stopped at Madrid on 18 March 1805 on an official visit to the Spanish Court. He found Manuel Godoy more agreeable than he had been led to believe and was presented to Carlos IV, relaying assurances of a rosy future for the Franco-Spanish alliance and even hinting that France was considering war against Portugal.[28]

Laure Junot found the trip through Spain disconcerting as the roads and accommodation were poor. On some occasions she refused to sleep in roadside establishments and spent the night in their coach. Near Badajoz on the Spanish border, they stayed at an inn where Junot was awakened by his wife's frantic screams when she discovered a corpse underneath her bed. Junot nearly killed the landlord in consequence when it transpired that he was also the village mortician.[29] A similar altercation occurred when their coachman foolishly attempted a steep hill on a wet and muddy road. After crawling out of the over-turned vehicle that contained Junot's daughter as well as his wife, the enraged Junot gave the unfortunate man a severe thrashing. It had not been the most pleasant of journeys.

They entered the capital on 13 April. As the first incumbent to be formally named as ambassador by Napoleon, he received a warm welcome from the Portuguese. Antônio de Araújo, Count of Barca and Portuguese Foreign Secretary, was of great assistance to him upon his arrival. Having some sympathy with the French, he helped with introductions and advised him on some of the difficult procedures that had to be observed at court. He made a good impression with Laure and became a firm friend of the couple.[30]

On presentation to Dom João, Junot donned his best hussar uniform of blue breeches embroidered with gold thread, white tunic, a red-faced dolman with nine well-earned chevrons on the sleeve and a white cavalryman's pelisse (a short jacket thrown cloak-like over the shoulder) bordered in fox blue. This was topped with a white shako adorned with a heron's feather that had become fashionable in Paris.[31] The five prominent sabre scars on Junot's handsome face also drew considerable attention and comment, revealing that he was an experienced fighting man and no mere peacetime soldier. The Regent was so impressed by his appearance that he promptly asked Junot to have a duplicate uniform made for his son. He also offered to present him with the Ribbon of the *Grand Cordon of the Order du Christ*, but Junot had to decline as he had no permission from Paris to accept it.

Though outwardly cordial to the Regent, Junot wrote to Talleyrand that he considered him '. . . a fallible man, suspicious, jealous, and disrespectful. He is dominated by priests'.[32] He soon discovered that there was little prospect of getting the Portuguese to sever their ties with England through diplomacy alone. The nation was dependent upon many British goods and, despite being a maritime power, could not hope to match the English at sea. He estimated that only four English ships of the line could effectively blockade the coast and prevent Portugal from trading with her colonies.

Yet the Portuguese were pleased to receive a new ambassador after General Lannes's stormy period in office 1802–1804. A soldier with a fiery temperament, similar in many ways to Junot, Lannes made a poor impression at court by resorting to insulting and tactless language. On several occasions he had threatened both the Regent and De Souza but eventually learned to conduct himself more fittingly and persuaded the Regent to sign a declaration of neutrality. Junot's hosts hoped he would prove more agreeable than his predecessor.[33]

Junot performed his duties surprisingly well but when a fleet under Admiral Knight, carrying 5,000 troops destined for Sicily, moored in the Tejo estuary for supplies, his official protest that this violated Portuguese neutrality was ignored. Although he managed to get some of the more obvious British agents removed from office he swiftly realized that the country was riddled with sympathizers, lamenting:

> All the province of Algarve and the coast to Porto are filled with agents disposed to inform the British of all that happens. Above all, the British pay well and in good time. They will always find help and protection here.[34]

Junot had hit upon a crucial point here in that the British offered good incentives to cement their alliance, unlike France. Nevertheless, both Napoleon and Talleyrand were pleased with Junot's efforts, perhaps realizing that furthering French interests in Portugal significantly was beyond his capability in the current political climate.

When he learned of Napoleon's march against Austria and Russia in 1805, Junot rushed to his Emperor's side and requested a transfer but, typically, acted before receiving a reply. When he arrived at Napoleon's command tent on the eve of the Battle of Austerlitz, both the Emperor and Berthier were astounded that he had covered such a vast distance in so short a time but there were no repercussions for this impulsive act and Junot joined Napoleon's staff just before his greatest victory.

In 1806 Napoleon appointed Junot Governor General of Parma and Piacenza to put down revolts that had taken place in these provinces. Working with Prince Eugène, who had been created Viceroy of Italy, he imposed marshal law, threatening to shoot rebels who were found carrying arms but while Napoleon urged him to impose harsh measures to pacify such large areas, Junot kept reprisals and executions to a minimum. Officially only twenty-four insurgents were shot and one village was burned as an example, though many other rebels were exiled or imprisoned.[35] Relative quiet returned and the collection of taxes resumed, testifying to Junot's success.

However, he acted in an increasingly autonomous manner in these provinces and his unauthorized restructuring of local government led to complaints and clashes with the Emperor's prefect, whom he eventually arrested, to Napoleon's fury. His performance in office was inconsistent and eventually Napoleon recalled him to resume the role of Governor of Paris, where he could keep a close eye upon him.

Despite his republican beliefs, Junot had a taste for luxury. Now that Laure had been made a lady-in-waiting for the Emperor's mother, she developed a liking for expensive jewellery and dresses, which matched her husband's flamboyant clothing and so, despite an annual income of 913,000 francs, their lavish lifestyle cost as much as 1,500,000 francs per year. Junot bought the château and estate of Raincy just outside the city and his high stakes gambling led them further into debt. Creditors called at Raincy several times only to be met by a sabre-wielding Junot in a drunken state, who chased them off his property yelling obscene oaths. No doubt remembering his father's previous generosity, Napoleon quietly paid off Junot's debts on several occasions.[36]

He was dismayed when denied the chance to join Napoleon on his campaign against Prussia 1806, the Emperor ignoring his repeated requests, and the miserable Junot had to satisfy himself by following events in the newspapers and letters that friends sent back from the front. Junot became even more distressed when his mother Marie died in his arms at Raincy on 14 November. His father was grief-stricken and retired from public life, much to Napoleon's disgust. Junot's discontent began to show in his work and there were complaints about his handling of the 1st Division, garrisoned in Paris. Even worse, the Governor still behaved like a drunken private soldier on occasion:

... he was not the man to play billiards in a public room in the
Champs Elysées, quarrel with the markers, and try conclusions with
them with a billiard-cue and get beaten – an adventure adroitly
turned to account with the Emperor.[37]

He found solace in the arms of Caroline Bonaparte. Ever manipulative and
power-hungry, she evidently wished to influence the Governor of Paris for
her own reasons, which sometimes conflicted with her brother's interests.
Though Laure was pregnant at this time, he continued the affair to the outrage
of Parisian society, one friend commenting: 'In general, Junot had no idea of
discretion.'[38] On one occasion the Junots drove Caroline home in their carriage
and he escorted Caroline into her residence. Waiting outside, Laure left in
disgust when he failed to reappear by 3:00 am and returned home in such a
despondent mood that she considered suicide.[39]

Napoleon's outrage when he heard of Junot's affair with his sister was
exceeded only by the towering rage of Marshal Murat, Caroline's husband.
The two old comrades were only prevented from fighting a duel over the
matter by the direct intervention of the Emperor, who wrote to Junot: 'You
must leave Paris ... It is necessary to destroy the rumours that are rampant
about my sister and you. Go, my faithful friend, the marshal's baton awaits
you.'[40] It is likely that Napoleon was far angrier than Madame Junot's memoirs
imply as Junot had engaged in romantic liaisons with two of his sisters, thereby
showing considerable disrespect for the imperial family, whether intentional
or not. Napoleon's tolerance of this reveals the strength of the bond between
them but Junot finally had what he wanted – the command of an army. He was
to take control of the 1st Corps of Observation of the Gironde, destined to
invade Portugal.

So what kind of man was Napoleon sending to command his expedition
against Portugal? General Thiébault gave a good brief description of his volatile
nature: 'Without being proud, he was vain; though good-natured, he could be
offensive; his quick temper was devoid of tact in handling people of rank and
authority. He was fanatically submissive to Napoleon, but recognized no other
subordination.'[41]

Napoleon appreciated his loyalty so much that he would forgive almost
any infraction. Unfortunately Junot was an extreme personality, occasionally
becoming a slave to his own passions and a danger to those around him.
Nonetheless, his civilian vices could be military virtues in combat, particularly
in an age where a cavalry officer was expected to lead his men from the front.
Failings such as excessive drinking, gambling and womanizing were not unusual
in the army and common traits of the characteristic 'devil-may-care' image
cultivated by cavalrymen. More than any other arm of the service, cavalry

officers had to take risks and make swift decisions, especially when faced by their enemy counterparts – the first to make an aggressive move often proving the victor. Junot's quick reflexes and contempt for danger helped to make him an accomplished cavalry commander, a role where restraint could be a weakness.

Few would disagree that the Emperor needed a renowned soldier to demonstrate the seriousness of his intent and, since speed was of the essence, a cavalry general seemed a sensible choice. One officer wrote:

> France had no longer an enemy on the Continent, yet an army was assembling at the foot of the Pyrenees. If there could have been any doubt in the public mind as to the destination of this army, it must have been removed on hearing the name of the general to whom the Emperor had confided the command.[42]

Although Junot was undoubtedly a good soldier and leader of men up to brigade level, the question remains was he capable of commanding an army? Though obviously intelligent, he could also be arrogant and lazy, as witnessed by his lack of interest during Bonaparte's staff conferences on the voyage to Egypt. Despite having the advantage of closely observing Napoleon's method of waging war at many levels, he seemed to have learned very little from the experience. He lacked the self-discipline and studied dedication a commander needed to plan and execute effective strategy during a campaign. Admittedly he was capable when it came to organizing and running a brigade, but whether he would be able to manage the complicated logistics to support an army corps remained to be seen.

Thiébault visited Junot shortly after he had received his new assignment to offer his congratulations. He believed that Napoleon had given Junot the command both as a reward and as a punishment for various offences. During his time in Paris, he had offended many powerful men, such as Savary, Le Marois and Clarke, and the fact that they all resented his hold over the Emperor undoubtedly meant they would be pleased to see him out of the way. The object of their derision was not unaware of this but Junot tried to avoid giving this impression:

> The more furious he was, the more pains he took to make believe he was glad. 'It is a fine errand,' he said, 'and highly confidential. There is not a marshal who did not want to have it, and there is not a general who could not get a marshal's *bâton* out of it.'[43]

Despite Thiébault's belief that the appointment might be a poisoned chalice, he accepted the position of chief-of-staff from Junot readily enough.

Few full biographies of Junot exist and Dubreton's work, being the main French language study, perhaps overemphasizes his undoubted heroism, republicanism and loyalty to Napoleon, playing down his character flaws. MacKay gives a more balanced view but suggests that Junot would never have risen further than a senior cavalry officer had he not met and been befriended by Napoleon. Essentially he was promoted beyond his abilities for friendship's sake,[44] a view backed by considerable evidence from Junot's career. Oman's opinion corresponded with this, assessing him as an exceptional fighting soldier but hardly an accomplished strategist in the style of commanders like Massena or Davout. He considered him a lacklustre general who owed this assignment largely to his recent experiences in Lisbon.[45]

Throughout his career, Napoleon ensured that Junot was kept on a short leash and often struggled to find him suitable employment. Friendship aside, the Emperor seemed to value Junot primarily for his loyalty and lack of long-term or political ambition, since all dictators fear talented subordinates who could potentially replace them. He had denied him field commands many times but now at last Junot had a real chance to prove himself.

Chapter 3

Junot's March on Lisbon

On 18 October 1807 Junot's army began to move towards the border and marched over the mountain passes of the Pyrenees into Spain. Few guessed that hundreds of thousands of soldiers would soon follow in their footsteps as the war they were about to begin would escalate out of control, plunging Iberia into years of strife. Writing to Champagny, recently appointed Minister of Foreign Affairs, Napoleon made his intentions crystal clear:

> I consider that we are in a state of war with Portugal; I expect my troops to reach Burgos on the 1st of November; if Spain wants more troops, she has but to ask ... As the English may possibly send troops to Lisbon, I would like to know what number of troops Spain is placing in the field. But make it clear that this must not be like the last war; we must push straight for Lisbon.[1]

Colonel Maximilien Foy marched with Junot's army and wrote a memorable account of the invasion. Estimates of the size of the Corps of Observation of the Gironde vary but Foy believed that about 25,000 infantry and 3,000 cavalry and artillery marched with Junot. These would be supported by an auxiliary corps under General Caraffa of 8,000 Spanish infantry, 3,000 cavalry and artillery with thirty cannon that would meet them at Alcantara. This force included one battery of heavy artillery and two companies of sappers in case siege operations were necessary.[2]

While predominantly French forces would occupy Lisbon and the central regions, Napoleon had arranged for Spanish troops to invade the north and south of the country with roughly 6,500 men set to enter the province of Entre Douro e Minho and 9,500 promised for the Alemtejo region. Technically the Spanish generals who commanded these forces enjoyed independent commands and even Junot was theoretically obliged to submit to the authority of Carlos IV or Godoy, in the unlikely event that they arrived in person.[3]

Arrangements had been made to supply Junot's corps as it marched through northern Spain and he was met at Irun by Lieutenant General Don Pedro Rodriguez who helped arrange food and lodging for the French. In 1801 he had provided the same service for General Leclerc and the fact that French troops had previously entered the Peninsula as allies partially allayed Spanish fears about their intentions. Many soldiers were elated at the welcome they received:

> Everywhere on its route the French army met with a favourable reception . . . The horror which, but a few years before, the Spaniards had manifested towards a people who had been represented to them as heretics and enemies of social order, had given place to feelings of hospitable kindness.[4]

Although the Spanish clergy had previously denounced the Revolution, it now appeared that Napoleon's partial restoration of Catholicism in French society had paid off. As they marched through Vitoria, Burgos and Valladolid, priests came out to greet the French and inquisitive peasants thronged the route to see the troops reputed to be the best soldiers in Europe. Celebrations were put on and Thiébault commented: 'If our march seemed like a holiday for them, it was a triumph for us.'[5] He speculated that it was not only the fame of French arms which led to this reception but the Spaniards' approval of a conflict against their traditional enemy. However, attitudes began to change when troops following Junot to guard his supply lines were garrisoned along the route in larger numbers than expected.[6]

On 8 October, the Emperor wrote to Junot, urging him to hurry: 'I assume that as a result of my last dispatch you have quickened your march; it was too slow; ten days are precious; all the English troops and the Copenhagen expedition have returned to England.'[7] By this Napoleon was not only referring to possible raids by the Royal Navy but the urgent need to establish a strong presence in Portugal to deter a possible counter-invasion by the British. Even if Junot was successful, he knew it would take time to secure the conquest.

Napoleon advised him to take the road to Abrantes rather than going by way of Ponte Murcella. According to his maps, it was shorter than the usual route to Lisbon and would avoid the Portuguese frontier fortress of Almeida. Though Napoleon considered serious resistance unlikely, Junot's progress would come to a sudden halt if he was obliged to conduct siege operations. Furthermore, the Emperor wanted the army's cartographers to study the area as current maps were unreliable and required updating. Unfortunately the Emperor's maps did not reveal how mountainous and impenetrable the region of the Tejo valley actually was, especially for a large force of men with horses and artillery.

Ever since Portugal's formation, turbulent relations with Spain had resulted in numerous disputes and conflicts. Though clearly dominant in terms of manpower, invading Portugal by land posed a dilemma for Spanish kings. Although Portugal is a long, narrow country with a lengthy frontier, there were few practical invasion routes for a large, well-equipped army to use. Most of the

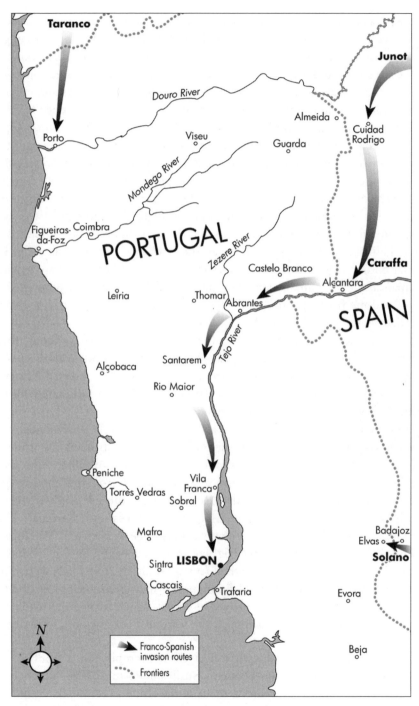

Map 2: The French Invasion of Portugal 1807

frontier was mountainous and sparsely populated, presenting many obstacles to an invading force and making supply lines difficult to maintain. The rugged terrain gave a natural defensive advantage and many of the preceding wars had been confined to border areas. Furthermore, few decent roads existed capable of allowing the passage of large numbers of men or supporting artillery and wagons. For centuries these factors had helped maintain Portuguese independence.

Due to mutual antipathy between Portugal and Spain, even the main highway between Bayonne and Lisbon bypassed Madrid. Few commercial links existed between the two nations and the Portuguese relied largely on seaborne trade, Foy commenting: 'Nature and state policy have conspired together to prevent any roads of communication being made, between Portugal and Spain.'[8] He continued that the army was almost totally ignorant of the local geography and lacked adequate maps for the expedition. They intended to enter the principality of Beira and even the Portuguese knew little about the central border region, few having reason to visit it. When the army reached Salamanca, the only intelligence they could gain about the route Junot wished to follow came from 'ignorant muleteers', being the only people who regularly travelled there.[9]

At Salamanca, further dispatches from Napoleon arrived ordering them to ignore the temptation to gather supplies as it would lead to unacceptable delays. Citing his own experience on campaign, the Emperor asserted: 'Twenty thousand men ... can live anywhere, even in a desert.'[10] Unfortunately for the French, he was about to be proved wrong.

Prior to reaching Salamanca the army had been well provisioned with Spanish assistance but, bound by his orders, Junot instructed the army to continue without securing supplies and set out on 12 November. The army marched in brigades, separated by almost a day's march from one another and, when the vanguard reached Ciudad Rodrigo, they turned south marching parallel with the frontier instead of taking the road west into Portugal. They were heading for the Tejo river valley via Puerto de Perales and Moraheja.

The weather deteriorated and baggage carts had begun to fall behind in the mud even before the army reached Ciudad Rodrigo. The roads were often little better than farm tracks, a condition made worse by incessant rain and the passage of large bodies of men, horses and guns, which turned the roads into quagmires. Though official foraging parties were sent out, pickings were scarce:

> ... and it was impossible to collect them promptly on a frontier
> depopulated by former wars between Spain and Portugal. The soldiers,
> having nothing to eat, roamed about in the rear and on the flanks of
> the columns, lost themselves in the woods, and alarmed the peasants.[11]

Tired from forced marches and lack of food, the army was in a miserable condition when Junot reached Alcantara, Foy recalling: 'The van of the army arrived on the Tejo in a state of wretchedness and confusion ...'[12]

Alcantara was an important border town having a small fort and guarding an old Roman bridge across the Tejo. Junot had hoped to find supplies for his men but thousands of Spanish troops under General Caraffa were already stationed there to rendezvous with his army. They had been there for a week, so the town had little to offer new arrivals. The fortress stores provided fresh musket cartridges, a welcome bonus since many had become sodden and useless in the rains, but Alcantara's stores could not meet their needs. Those who received one day's rations felt themselves lucky.

Yet Junot was determined to press on, especially as it seemed increasingly unlikely that his progress would be opposed. However, he ordered Adjutant-Commandant Bagneris to pause at Zarza-la-Major, so that he could assemble stragglers. Junot wrote proclamations to be given to travellers and distributed among the Portuguese peasantry when they crossed the border. In these he urged the people to remain quiet and not impede their march, claiming that the French were coming as liberators having '... a common cause against the tyrant of the seas'.[13]

On 19 November 1807 leading elements of Junot's army entered Portugal, crossing the Erjas River over the bridge at Segura. A company of light infantry quickly took up positions in Segura village followed by the 70th Regiment and two companies of Catalonian sappers; 300 Spanish hussars of the Maria Louisa Regiment then rode over to scout ahead, the command of the vanguard being given to General Maurin.[14] Next day the 1st and 2nd Divisions crossed along with elements of Caraffa's division.

Junot recorded that the inhabitants of most villages they passed through were friendly but knew nothing about recent events, adding: 'They are extremely poor and the area can offer almost no resources ...'[15] When the army reached Castelo Branco they found the town totally unprepared for their arrival. The town authorities were aware that a French army was heading towards Portugal but everyone had assumed it would take the easier route to Lisbon to the north, rather than struggle through this mountainous area. Furthermore, they had received no instructions from the government and were uncertain whether they should regard the French as invaders or welcome them as allies.

Junot's weary men increasingly began to fall upon isolated hamlets, desperate for food and shelter. Foy put it succinctly: 'Woe to the humble cottage that fell in the way of these famished marauders! The terrified families immediately took flight. Many soldiers of the infantry were killed by the peasants, who were driven to despair.'[16]

Castelo Branco, whose storehouses were unable to cope with demand, was looted unmercifully and excesses against the townsfolk took place in the resulting chaos. Soldiers seized anything edible including maize, unripe olives and even the acorns set aside for cattle fodder. With the loss of their winter supplies, the people reacted violently. Hoping to avoid alienating the population, Junot had some of the worst offenders tried and hanged. Yet these examples failed to deter his increasingly wretched soldiers, many of whom had not eaten for days.

Rain still lashed down upon them as they continued their march. Though mountain tracks proved better than anticipated, their narrowness obliged the troops to march in narrow formations, or even in single file, slowing their progress. Several tributaries of the great River Tejo lay in their path and were difficult to cross, many flowing through high-sided gorges. The broken terrain and the constant need to cross rivers and large streams broke up the columns and large numbers of exhausted stragglers fell behind. Thiébault considered this part of the journey across Beira to be the worst part of the march and claimed that Caraffa's division '... lost 1,700 or 1,800 men from hunger or fatigue, drowning in torrents or falling down precipices'.[17]

Even veterans who had fought in the mountain campaigns in Switzerland and Austria were surprised at the hazardous terrain with men sometimes having to descend almost vertically to shore level when rivers flowed through gorges. Makeshift rafts and boats acquired locally were necessary to cross the Ocreza and other rivers but with so few river craft available, progress slowed to a crawl and accidents were commonplace. Foy lamented: 'The soldiers straggled along at random; and, ceasing to be restrained by the tie of discipline ... they had no longer the appearance of an army, but rather of a medley of individuals exasperated by distress.'[18]

The artillery fell further and further behind, even though the oxen and mules dragging the guns coped with the broken country better than anticipated. Cannon were very difficult to handle and the gunners resorted to separating the barrels from their carriages and dragging them along on sleds. Naturally, winching cannon piece by piece over rivers or down cliffs proved a lengthy and dangerous operation.

The army now approached Abrantes but the weather and the rigours of the march had taken a horrendous toll. Even Junot's renowned endurance began to fail him and Thiébault recalled that his chief abruptly seized his lodgings at Sobreira-Formosa, collapsing onto a peasant's humble bed and instantly falling asleep. Meanwhile: 'General Delaborde and I, in spite of our exhaustion, went to work to have the big drum beaten and fires lighted, and set men to shouting to collect the poor fellows who had gone astray in the mountains.'[19] Nonetheless, the arrival of Junot's vanguard in Abrantes marked a turning point in French fortunes as it became apparent that there was little prospect of serious resistance and the way to Lisbon was open.

Realistically there had never been much chance of Portuguese military opposition to the invasion, yet even as late as 11 November, Principal Sousa recorded that various nobles had agreed to raise regiments or donate money towards clothing and arming *ordenanças* (local volunteer units). He wrote that the main problem was continued uncertainty over who the forthcoming hostilities were likely to be against.[20] Their ambassador spoke belligerently but previously good relations with Britain made actual fighting with their old ally seem unlikely, especially as there was an understandable fear of French expansionism in both countries. France was openly hostile and another short conflict with Spain, who might enjoy limited French support, seemed the most likely consequence of these troubles. Many were reassured by such reasoning and considered an actual French invasion unlikely.

In addition, the Portuguese army was poorly armed and discipline was lax due to inadequate leadership, training and low pay. Its command system was disorganized and, because of remarkable French military success in recent times, many of its officers harboured pro-French sympathies. Their defeat during the War of the Oranges 1801 naturally had a demoralizing effect and, despite the reorganization of the army into three districts in 1806, it was seriously under strength, having as little as 50 per cent of its official establishment under arms.[21]

At the time of the invasion, around 14,000 men were concentrated in and around Lisbon, possibly to defend the capital against a British rather than a French incursion or at least to give the impression of being prepared to do so. Another large body of troops had been sent to Alemtejo in the south as Spanish troops were massing near the border.[22] Therefore there were few regular soldiers available to oppose Junot in the central regions. There were about forty-three militia regiments in addition to *ordenança* available but they were no match for regulars. However, even 5,000 men could have caused Junot problems by mounting delaying actions along his route, defending rivers, cliffs and defiles but the French military reputation alone was enough to discourage the *ordenança* from attempting this. In any case the Regent had appealed to his people not to resist the invasion.

When his men entered Abrantes, Junot sent Captain Mezeur of the engineers to the town of Punhete where, accompanied by a detachment of infantry, he was to use a company of Catalonian sappers to restore the boat bridge across the Tejo. At this point the Tejo broadened as it approached the ocean and no longer flowed within a gorge as it did towards the east. The boats comprising the bridge had been used for other purposes but Mezeur was to replace them and guard this important strategic point.

Abrantes was the last major city on the way to Lisbon and, when French troops staggered painfully through its gates, Junot requisitioned and distributed sorely-needed supplies. As well as food, many were in great need of clothing with their uniforms torn and ragged after enduring weeks of hardship. Adequate footwear was in particularly short supply and was fought over as warehouses were broken open. Junot recorded the loss of many troops from fatigue and instances of men being killed by the inhabitants while looting.[23]

Yet Thiébault claimed that his commander-in-chief was selfish when issuing new equipment. As chief-of-staff he assumed that Junot would provide mounts for him and his aides after requisitioning all the saddle horses in the area. Junot's response baffled him when he requested this: 'No,' he said, 'you are big enough to look after yourself.' When he asked where he was supposed to obtain horses as Junot had seized all those available in Abrantes, he angrily retorted: 'Get them where you like,' he said; 'for my part, I have not so much as a dog to give you.'[24]

He took Junot at his word, ordering Captain Vidal de Valabreque to cross the Zezere river with twenty-five men and requisition horses from Santarém. Valabreque did so but Junot was furious when he heard about it. The unfortunate Valabreque protested to Thiébault saying that the General had ordered him to return alone to Castelo Branco as its 'governor'. With the countryside in uproar after the destructive passage of the army 'going alone meant ten chances to one of being murdered, he sent word that if I was not off in an hour he would have me shot'.[25] Thiébault only persuaded Junot to relent after a lengthy argument in which he pointed out that Junot's own actions had obliged him to take this course. Furthermore, having poorly-mounted aides made it difficult for him to fulfil his role and made his command a laughing stock.

The army spent two days at Abrantes reorganizing and issuing new supplies. Because the bulk of the army was incapable of fighting, Junot took the best of the light infantry and grenadiers from his 1st and 2nd Divisions and formed four battalions of picked men. He intended to press on with this small yet cohesive force ahead of the main army as he was unwilling to sacrifice the time necessary for it to reassemble. He felt confident enough to write a dispatch to the government in Lisbon, stating: 'I shall be at Lisbon in four days,' said he. 'My soldiers are quite disconsolate that they have not yet fired a shot. Do not compel them to do it. I think you will be in the wrong if you do.'[26]

On 24 November, the day before Junot reached Abrantes, the Prince Regent received a British emissary confirming the news that he had long feared. Admiral Sir Sidney Smith presented him with an issue of *Le Moniteur* in which Napoleon declared: 'The House of Braganza has lost Portugal: it experiences the fate of all the Powers who have put their confidence in England.'[27] None of the threats and entreaties Dom João had received from British, Spanish and

French envoys, or the advice of his own ministers, was as effective as this blunt statement of Napoleon's intent. He had made contingency plans for months but this decided the issue – he would flee the country.

Yet the Portuguese Court had been considering a move to Brazil for many years. As early as 1779 Dom Rodrigo argued that: 'Portugal is not the best and most essential part of the monarchy.'[28] Admittedly Dom Rodrigo could be accused of self-interest, owning extensive property in Brazil, but with the Portuguese economy in decline and new markets developing in South America, there was some truth in his claims.

The Regent had always hated the idea of abandoning his homeland but there was a possibility that, should Portugal side with France, the British might seize their colonies in South America. The enmity between his nation and Spain, who was a French ally, was also an ominous sign for Portugal's future standing in Napoleon's Europe. Deserting the mother country of the Empire was a humiliation but it need not be permanent and the British would support him if the government was re-established abroad, promising to grant trade concessions to Brazil. After months of preparation, it was finally time to act and Dom João issued a proclamation to be read to his people:

> Having tried by all possible means to preserve the neutrality hitherto enjoyed by my faithful and beloved subjects, having exhausted my royal treasury, and made innumerable other sacrifices; even going to the extremity of shutting the ports of my dominions to the subjects of my ancient and royal ally . . . thus exposing the commerce of my people to total ruin . . . I find that troops of the emperor of the French . . . are actually marching into the interior of my kingdom . . .[29]

Dom João went on to state that he was appointing a government to act on his behalf, making the Marquis de Abrantio Governor and Regent and listing the appointment of a series of ministers and officials, but it was how his people would react to the following statement that concerned him most: 'I have resolved, for the benefit of my subjects, to retire with the queen . . . and all my royal family, to my dominions in America, there to establish myself in the city of Rio de Janeiro until a general peace.'[30] He hoped the people would understand the reasons for his departure. Certainly Napoleon had contemptuously rejected his government's best efforts at compromise, but he feared that his subjects would see his flight as an act of desertion. For this reason, news of the royal departure was delayed until just before the embarkation, though the extent of his preparations had made Dom João's intentions obvious.

The scale of the Braganças' evacuation was awesome. Many officials had either guessed or been informed that a move to Brazil was imminent months beforehand but despite this, a vast number of people and possessions needed to be ferried across the Atlantic in an evacuation that required complicated planning. The Palaces at Quelez and Mafra were stripped of paintings, furniture, carpets and valuables of all kinds and wagon-loads of royal treasure were hurried to the docks. Hordes of palace servants crowded the quaysides, many hoping or expecting to be taken on the voyage. For months gold and silver plate had been melted down and cast into ingots and coinage for easy loading. Cases of government documents were packed and readied for stowage. Cristiano Müller, the archivist charged with keeping ministry records, had thirty-four crates of paperwork ready for shipping, after packing them for months.[31] Large numbers of onlookers impeded the operation, Eusebo Gomes, the Royal Storekeeper recalling the pandemonium:

> Everyone wanted to board, the docks filled up with boxes, crates, trunks, luggage – a thousand and one things. Many people were left behind on the quay while their belongings were stowed on board; others embarked, only to find that their luggage could not be loaded.[32]

There were not enough places for everyone on the crowded vessels and those without permits were denied berths. Seeing the extent of the confusion, some returned to their homes rather than endure the chaos.

Many onlookers were aghast at the scale of the desertion. It rained heavily during the days it took to load, causing delays and exacerbating the entire process as small craft ferried stores to ships anchored offshore – the quayside being too crowded for all of them to moor alongside. When the Regent arrived it was in a plain carriage. His advisors had urged him not to make impassioned speeches or provide any kind of spectacle, fearing the reaction of the watching crowds. Many observers were tearful at the sight of their monarch leaving but others were angered, the authorities taking the precaution of spiking some of the guns in the batteries overlooking the embarkation.

The inhabitants of Lisbon were indeed very angry and Araújo was waylaid in the street and the windows of his house 'were broken by the mob, in resentment for his having, in their opinion, concealed from them the perilous and desperate situation of the country. He was obliged to escape secretly on board a frigate.'[33]

Queen Maria I added to the excitement when she was driven down to the docks from the Quelez Palace. Mentally unstable and now in her seventy-third year, she gave vent to several outbursts during the journey, shrieking that they should not leave without putting up a fight and repeatedly yelled at her coachman: 'Not so fast,' said she, 'it will be thought we are running away.'[34]

The Prince Regent made a quiet and dignified departure: 'Dom João was visibly shaken throughout the ordeal, and was holding back tears as he boarded a skiff in the driving rain.'[35] Backed into a corner by states far more powerful than his own, Dom João cut a tragic figure. Ultimately it was better to make this strategic withdrawal than become a French puppet ruler or be deposed and exiled. In his wake were dozens of carriages abandoned on the docks. Many cases, heavy bales, trunks and boxes had been abandoned and lay scattered around. Among the items left behind in the rush, or discarded for lack of stowage space, were 60,000 volumes from the Royal Library of Ajuda and fourteen carriages of church silver and other treasures.

The weather began to clear on 29 November and the Royal Fleet began to sail down the estuary, towards Sir Sidney Smith's ships, some of which waited to escort them on their long voyage. It had been an ignominious and hurried departure, if not quite the panicked flight that is sometimes depicted.

The British were elated at the decision to transfer the Court to Brazil as it relieved them of the awful strategic necessity of seizing the Portuguese navy had the Regent decided to stay. This was an act that His Majesty's government hesitated to commit against a long-term ally. As much as they wished to intervene on land, they doubted that such action would be effective at this time and, even if successful, whether the nation would resist further invasions. The chances of defending Portugal effectively were slight and, in the current political climate, the Portland administration could not afford to take the risk. As far as the British were concerned, Portugal might fall to the French but the government-in-exile would provide a rallying point for loyal subjects, a far better outcome than seeing the Braganças exiled to some distant principality by Napoleon. The Royal Navy would escort the fleet to the Americas and in return the Braganças had granted the British the right to temporarily occupy the island of Madeira.

Meanwhile at Abrantes, Junot continued his preparations for a lightning march on the capital. He also dispatched General Caraffa to occupy Thomar and stock provisions for the army there. Due to heavy rainfall, the waters of the Tejo had risen alarmingly and prevented the engineers from rebuilding the boat bridge at Punhete. Nevertheless, Junot ordered them to continue to requisition and construct boats in order to transport the artillery and the sick downriver into Lisbon.

Colonel Grandsaigne commanded the advanced guard, which marched through Punhete on 26 November and crossed the Zezere by ferryboat. Junot was with the vanguard when they met a deputation under José Oliveira de Barreto (the Commander d'Araújo) on the riverbank. He informed him that the Braganças were embarking for Brazil and requested that Junot halt his army so a settlement could be agreed without the sight of foreign soldiers aggravating the people.

The Braganças were a political obstacle to Napoleon's grand scheme for Iberia and, once the country was secure, Junot was under orders to remove the royal family as a potential rallying point for dissent. His instructions regarding their fate were unequivocal:

> Inform the Prince Regent that he must go to France; and try to induce him to do so willingly. Assign him officers whose overt instructions are to escort him, but whose real duty will be to keep him prisoner ... Treat all claimants to the throne in the same way, and send them off, without troublesome restrictions, to Bayonne.[36]

Accomplishing these ends without inciting violent Portuguese opposition would have been a diplomatic nightmare. While the Portuguese might eventually side with France, mishandling this abduction could provoke serious trouble and thus damage French interests. Therefore, Junot received news of Dom João's departure with a mixture of relief and disappointment. Napoleon had lost a propaganda coup but Junot had been saved a politically sensitive and unpleasant task. However, the loss of the fleet was a serious blow as Junot knew how eager Napoleon was to deny its use to the British and to seize warships and crews for his own navy. His instructions regarding the fleet's capture were now redundant:

> If (as I expect) the Portuguese do not oppose your entry, this is how you should proceed: occupy the harbour, encamp your troops in good positions, seize the fleet, hoist the French flag, put 200 infantrymen on board every vessel, and distribute among the fleet the naval officers I am sending you.[37]

Yet, even had he wished to, Junot could not halt his army's march at this point. Still short of provisions and liable to get out of hand, it had to be re-supplied and garrisoned as quickly as possible. Sending former French Consul François Herman with the Marquis, Junot sent assurances to the Regency Government that Lisbon would be spared if his army was unopposed.

The French still had another difficult march to endure before they reached Lisbon. The rain continued and many of the rivers were in spate, breaking their banks and inundating the floodplains. The vanguard crossed the plain of Golegao struggling through water that was knee-deep in places. Further provisions had been secured at Santarém but the troops were bedraggled and in an ugly mood after the hardships they had suffered over the last two months. Foy recorded that, when they reached isolated villages, rape and murder were not uncommon.[38]

At the village of Sacavém, roughly 6 miles from Lisbon, Lieutenant General Martino de Souza e Abuquerque met Junot with a deputation from the Regency

Council. Royal Navy ships were still present in the estuary and a fleet carrying General Moore's troops from Sicily (destined for Sweden) was expected. He cautioned the General that these troops might disembark to occupy Lisbon.[39] Junot was well aware that his tiny vanguard could easily be denied entry into the city by a determined force and his main army was dispersed, poorly supplied and would take days to assemble. Even when this was achieved, it was doubtful how efficient they would be as a military force after the terrible march they had endured. He decided that a display of force was necessary to demonstrate French resolve.

Four French infantry battalions entered Lisbon on 30 November 1807. Junot's artillery was far behind and the Portuguese themselves provided him with a small cavalry escort drawn from the Royal Police Guard. At the Belém Docks, Junot observed that some ships of the Royal Fleet still remained within the Tejo estuary and ordered the river forts to open fire, compelling some vessels to put back into port. Crowds had gathered to watch the triumphal French entry which, after such a hazardous march, was a considerable achievement, Thiébault remarking: 'As everyone knows, Junot took possession of Lisbon, of the army that was there, and of the entire kingdom, without having at hand a single trooper, a single gun, or a cartridge that would burn …'[40]

Yet the Portuguese were shocked by the vanguard's appearance. Many firelocks were rusty and the majority of their powder and cartridges were too damp to use. Exhaustion showed on every face and it was all many could do to keep marching in step. Were these the men who had humbled Europe? A poorly provisioned eighteen-day march in terrible weather had taken a heavy toll. Even high-ranking officers had suffered, Thiébault recording:

> The state we were in when we entered Lisbon is hardly credible. Our clothing had lost all shape and colour; I had not had a change of linen since Abrantes; my feet were coming through my boots; and in this guise I took possession of one of the handsomest suites of rooms in the capital.[41]

Nonetheless, his commander felt obliged to

> by way of demonstration, walk the poor wearied wretches all over the town, in pouring rain, for six hours. The rest of the army dropped in at intervals of one or two days in still worse condition, some even falling down dead at the gates.[42]

Thiébault was lodged with Monsieur Ratton, a Burgundian merchant, and was extremely grateful when his host clothed and fed him. As chief-of-staff, he was relieved that the rains had prevented many Portuguese from witnessing his tattered appearance. Onlookers were unimpressed by the sight of their conquerors, Foy remarking: 'The Portuguese had been prepared to feel terror; the only feeling which they now experienced was that of vexation, at having been astounded and brought under the yoke by a handful of foreigners.'[43]

The Spanish armies, supposed to act in concert with Junot, failed to match his determination and speed. General Taranco marched south from Galicia and occupied Porto on 13 December with 6,500 men, while General Solano crossed the border near Badajos, arriving at Elvas on 2 December with 9,500 men. Ostensibly the invasion had been a great success with Lisbon taken and other areas of the country falling under Spanish occupation. There was little immediate prospect of serious British intervention and Portugal's fall also furthered Napoleon's ambitions in the Peninsula for future conquest.

Yet the French occupation was only just beginning and the startling speed of the operation, which had caught France's enemies off guard, had been bought at great cost. Would it have been better to wait for spring before marching? Certainly the weather had greatly restricted Junot's movements and exacerbated the problem of provisioning his army. Losses in men and equipment had been substantial and with hindsight it may have been better for Junot to have waited outside Lisbon for a few days for his army to reassemble and rest before entering the city. It now seemed unlikely that the British had really intended to make a landing, so little would have been lost by the delay.

Admittedly the *Grande Armée*'s fierce reputation was far-reaching, helping to deter the Portuguese from resisting the invasion. Nevertheless, most Portuguese had never seen France's best troops and had only these exhausted men by which to judge them. Junot's decision to display his tired and dishevelled soldiers before a resentful city was ill-advised and those Portuguese prepared to embrace the French cause were disconcerted by the spectacle and began to question the usefulness of such allies.

Junot's invasion was portrayed in Paris as a heroic triumph. Indeed, with only the vanguard of a small army, he had taken a capital city without a fight. Yet considering the condition in which his army had arrived, the invasion could be viewed as the action of an adventurer who owed as much to luck as strategic forethought and planning. Had the Portuguese resisted, would Junot's men have prevailed? In many ways the main deterrent for the Portuguese had been the fear of forces that France might subsequently have sent against them rather than the sight of Junot's army. Consequently it remained to be seen just how long-lasting the French presence in Portugal would be.

Chapter 4

Brought Before Maneta

Now that Portugal had fallen, Napoleon turned on Spain hoping to bring the entire Peninsula under his control. Recent intrigues within the Spanish court saw Crown Prince Ferdinand and his associates charged with conspiracy against Godoy by Carlos IV, who feared his son wished to seize power. Though pardoned by his father, the inquiry discredited Ferdinand, giving Napoleon the excuse to claim that he had forfeited his rights to the succession. Yet Ferdinand was still enormously popular with the people, partly due to Godoy's unsavoury reputation, many seeing him as venal, corrupt and promoted above his station. This political uncertainty in Spanish society made Napoleon's plan to undermine the Bourbons far easier.

Napoleon now sent substantial reinforcements into Spain, ignoring the Treaty of Fontainebleau, which stated that he should secure Spanish permission first. While Junot was still on the march, the Second Corps of Observation of the Gironde crossed the frontier, ostensibly in his support. This force consisted of around 25,000 men but, since most of its soldiers were recent conscripts, it implied that the Emperor considered serious fighting unlikely. Alarm grew in Spain as the Corps of Observation of the Ocean Coast under Marshal Moncey crossed the border a few weeks later. Rather than marching towards Portugal, these forces lingered in Spain establishing large garrisons in Burgos and Valladolid. Rumours that further armies were being assembled at Bordeaux and Poitiers did little to allay Spanish fears.

Urgent entreaties were dispatched to Napoleon, who was touring the Italian provinces. He feigned lack of interest and failed to respond to Spanish queries about his intentions. Meanwhile he formally annexed the Kingdom of Etruria, depriving the last surviving Bourbon monarchy (except Spain) of its throne. Neither Carlos IV nor Godoy would risk war, believing they had no chance of success against France. Godoy guessed that Napoleon had imperial designs on Spain and, hoping to dissuade him, proposed a royal marriage between the Bourbon and Bonaparte dynasties to cement their alliance. Napoleon contemptuously spurned this offer.

On 10 February 1808 General Duhesme crossed the Pyrenees with 14,000 men. Marching through Catalonia towards Barcelona, all attempts at subterfuge were abandoned. In mid-February the border fortresses were seized by treachery, assisted by the number of French troops already stationed in the area. Similar events occurred at Barcelona on 29 February and the fortresses of San Sebastian and Figueras were occupied in early March. Some resistance was encountered but orders arrived from Madrid instructing the Spanish army not to oppose the French.[1]

Napoleon's intentions were now brutally clear and, after weeks of regal indecision, Godoy persuaded the royal family to move to Seville, away from the main concentration of French troops. The Bourbons now contemplated fleeing to their colonies, such as Mexico or Buenos Aires, as the Braganças had done, but the Spanish people would not allow this.

Anticipating Godoy's plan, hundreds of people converged on Aranjuez where the Royal Guard was preparing to escort the king to Seville. Riots ensued and the guards refused to fire on the mob when they broke into the palace, demanding Godoy's head. They tore through the corridors, smashing furniture and looting valuables in their search for the queen's favourite. Hiding in an attic, Godoy narrowly avoided being murdered and the Royal Guard arrested him for his own safety when he finally emerged. Terrified by the upheaval, Carlos IV abdicated in favour of his son, which was welcomed by the crowds who roared their approval of the new sovereign at the palace.

Marshal Joachim Murat had entered Spain at the head of more French reinforcements and, acting in the capacity of 'Lieutenant of the Emperor', headed for Madrid. A total of 100,000 French and allied (mostly Polish or Italian) troops were now stationed in Spain. Murat was renowned as one of the greatest cavalry commanders in Europe but, though celebrated for his flamboyance and bravery, he was no diplomat. He arrived to occupy the capital on 23 March, bringing 20,000 infantry and a large body of cavalry. The next day he was astounded when Ferdinand rode into Madrid accompanied by hordes of ecstatic people loudly proclaiming him as king. Murat and the French ambassador acted coolly towards the new monarch and refused to acknowledge his accession, entering quickly into talks with his parents. Carlos and Maria Luisa roundly condemned their son, claiming that the abdication was made under duress.

Showing great naïveté, Ferdinand appealed to Napoleon who offered to mediate and resolve the dynastic squabble and invited the Bourbons to France for talks. Yet many Spaniards feared treachery and implored them to turn back on their way to Bayonne. Some crowds even tried to prevent the royal carriages from passing through Vitoria on their journey to France.

Napoleon gave them a cordial reception but, after a brief interlude, abruptly demanded that both father and son renounce their claims on the throne. He argued that Carlos no longer enjoyed the support of his people and alleged that Ferdinand was little more than a usurper who had conspired against his family. When they protested that Spaniards would oppose their deposition he remarked scornfully:

> 'Countries full of monks, like yours,' he said, 'are easy to subjugate. There may be some riots, but the Spaniards will quiet down when they see that I offer them the integrity of the boundaries of the monarchy, a liberal constitution, and the preservation of their religion and their national customs.'[2]

The Spanish monarchy had effectively been abducted and Napoleon had them at his mercy in Bayonne. They had little choice but to give in, Ferdinand and Carlos agreeing to abdicate in early May in favour of Napoleon's brother, Joseph Bonaparte. The Bourbons would remain under Napoleon's 'protection' and Ferdinand was sent to Valençay where he remained for the next six years.

Meanwhile, General Junot had been busy establishing a French presence in Portugal. He appointed General Delaborde as Governor of Lisbon and energetically set about repairing the damage suffered by his army during the invasion. Portuguese army barracks were in poor repair, so many soldiers were billeted in convents and government buildings. This misuse of religious buildings in a devout nation did little to endear the French to the Portuguese. Yet Junot did his best to allay Portuguese fears, issuing decrees such as:

> Inhabitants of Lisbon ... remain quiet in your houses; neither fear my army nor myself; we are only terrible to our enemies and to the wicked. The Great Napoleon, my Master, has sent me to protect you – I will protect you.[3]

Napoleon was pleased with Junot for his swift and successful invasion, granting him the title of Duke d'Abrantes to honour his achievements. Junot now believed that a marshal's baton was almost within his grasp. If a just and impartial government was set up in Lisbon he might work wonders in Portugal and a royal crown was not out of the question. These notions made him complacent and he remarked arrogantly: 'This people,' he continuously said, 'is easily managed. I am better obeyed here, and more expeditiously, than ever the Prince Regent was.'[4]

Loison's 2nd Division quickly posted garrisons at Sintra and Mafra and French troops were stationed along the coast as far as the Mondego estuary. The majority of the cavalry and artillery were garrisoned at Lisbon but a sizable presence was established at Santarém, Abrantes and Almeida. Peniche was an important fortress on the west coast and General Thomières was ordered to garrison it with French troops as soon as possible. Well positioned to monitor the coastline, it was set upon an eminence and reached only by an isthmus covered by the sea at high tide. Possession of this strongpoint was invaluable to deter British naval intervention and it would be difficult for a landing party to attack successfully without a major siege operation.

Securing the capital was Junot's main priority. It was vulnerable to naval assault and the Tejo was extremely wide and difficult to command at the point where the city lay without the possession of both of its banks and a substantial naval presence within the port itself. On the northern bank, forts such as São Julien were quickly garrisoned by Travot's 3rd Division along with defences at Estoril, Cascais and other towns along the coast guarding the approaches to Lisbon. The island-based Fort of São Lourenço do Bugio was garrisoned and the heights of Morfacem on the southern bank were occupied. Possession of these coastal forts was vital to prevent an enemy naval force attempting to sail up the estuary and assail Lisbon.

The French were assisted in this task by the supplies stored at the *Fundicão* arsenal in Lisbon. Further cannon were brought up and placed in the forts from this armoury and decaying or obsolete gun carriages were replaced. French engineers and sappers began repairing and modernizing fortifications, clearing firing lines of obstructions, thickening parapets and creating new artillery batteries. Furnaces were constructed in many forts to heat and contain red-hot roundshot for use against shipping, Foy remarking: 'These instruments for the destruction of naval forces, were unusual among a people accustomed to live under the protection of England.'[5]

Previously the Portuguese army had garrisoned these strongpoints and now Napoleon was keen to remove them, ordering Junot to disarm and disband most Portuguese soldiers. Nevertheless, he wrote:

> You can go so far as to mobilise a body of 5–6,000 officers and men from the Portuguese army, and to send them off towards France in columns 1,000 strong, telling them that I am taking them into my service. Make them take the oath; draft a few French officers among them ... and I really will take them into my service. By this means you will get rid of a crowd of undesirables. Be careful to send them off by different routes.[6]

Napoleon hoped that this would make the French seem more like allies than conquerors but he had no illusions as to where the soldiers' present loyalties lay. Because the army could provide the backbone of a rebellion against the occupation it had to be demobilized. Those who had seen more than six years' or less than a year's military service were disbanded but many were transferred into the French army and marched off to France.[7]

Napoleon's instructions for taking over the country are remarkable for their lucidity and practicality. Yet they also reveal his overconfidence in what could be achieved, a cynical disregard for Portuguese interests and a casual willingness to dispossess a legitimate ruler to further his own imperial ambitions. Admittedly his purpose was to introduce a new European order that promised to be more enlightened than previous regimes but Portugal had been dragged into his Continental League with threats and intimidation. Even though the Braganças had conceded to nearly all his demands, he had still seized their country by force – hardly the act of a benevolent ruler.

The possibility of naval raids and, ultimately, a landing in force by the British was difficult to counter without French naval support. As early as 22 November 1807, Admiral Sir Sidney Smith had declared Lisbon under blockade, proclaiming: 'It being notorious that the ports of Portugal are shut against the British flag, and that his Britannic Majesty's Minister has quitted the capital, the mouth of the Tagus is declared to be in a state of rigorous blockade.'[8] The Royal Navy was almost unchallenged at sea, making the arrival of a French fleet to help defend Lisbon a remote possibility. However, about twenty warships remained in harbour after the departure of the Braganças. The largest of these were frigates and the Royal Fleet had depleted the naval stores and taken most of the experienced sailors with them, but Captain Majendie of the French navy was able to form the nucleus of a small fleet for defensive purposes.

A Russian fleet, under Admiral Siniavin, also lay at anchor within the port. They had been sailing towards the Baltic when hostilities between Russia and Britain were declared. Principal Sousa, of the Portuguese government, had speculated about Russia's intentions in November, believing they wished to use the protection of a neutral port until their nation's political position became clear. He thought that they were unlikely to sail into the Mediterranean, adding that the presence of a British squadron off the coast undoubtedly influenced Siniavin's decision to remain in port.[9] Although the presence of this fleet appeared to favour the French, the Russians refused to make commitments and, though they entertained French emissaries and Junot dined aboard Siniavin's flagship on several occasions, they emphasized that they were not at war with Portugal and felt unable to offer any assistance without orders from the Tsar.

Admiral Cotton, who commanded the fleet blockading the coast, concentrated his efforts on the ports of Lisbon and Porto, but the British were not prepared merely to prevent ships from entering or leaving but mounted small raids on a regular basis. As early as January 1808, marines were landed on the small islands off the coast near the Peniche fortress, capturing the Portuguese invalid soldiers manning the small defensive works there, who offered no resistance, and the British left a garrison. There were some ship-to-ship actions fought in or near the mouth of the Tejo estuary and an attempt to board the corvette *La Gavotte* by marines in small gunboats was repulsed with difficulty.

Yet Junot's efforts to involve the Russians in the port's defence were still rebuffed:

> More than once, he pressed Admiral Siniavin, whose fleet was stronger than that of Admiral Cotton to quit the Tagus with some ships; but it was all in vain. Neither for the purposes of attack nor of defence, could the French reckon upon the aid of any force but their own.[10]

Though ostensibly at war, the Russians were acting more as a neutral power after years of hostility towards France, so the British were very cautious about provoking their former ally. Siniavin was well aware that the Tsar was waiting to see which side gained the upper hand before committing Russian forces again and was equally reluctant to initiate any unfortunate incidents. Nevertheless, the mere presence of a Russian fleet at anchor at Lisbon reduced the prospect of a serious Royal Navy attack on the port.

The Marquis d'Alorna commanded the border fortress of Elvas south-east of Lisbon and closed the gates to the Spanish forces that approached the city. As d'Alorna had raised 3,000 militiamen to supplement the garrison's regular troops, Elvas could have held out for some time but, upon receiving orders from the Prince Regent not to resist, he handed the city over to General Solano. When he returned to Lisbon, the Marquis witnessed the first signs of serious discontent in the capital.

On 13 December Junot paraded 6,000 men in and around the Rossio Square, presenting a very different appearance to the tattered soldiery that had marched into the capital only weeks before. Thousands of people watched as a cannonade was fired from the Castle of São Jorge, which rose above the city. The Portuguese royal standard was then lowered and the French tricolour hoisted in its place. Acknowledging the gravity of the incident, Foy wrote:

> If there be any veteran warriors, who, after their lives have been spared by war, have dragged out existence long enough to see the banner under which their blood was shed, insulted by hostile hands, they can imagine the anguish which was now felt by the faithful sons of Lusitania.[11]

The standard was believed to have been consecrated and presented to the first king of Portugal, making it not only a patriotic but a religious symbol, and many observers were deeply offended by the spectacle.

Groups of people remained in the Rossio as the troops were dismissed and marched back to barracks and ominous sounds of discontent were heard throughout the square. The appearance of the Marquis d'Alorna, a popular though ironically pro-French soldier[12] excited the crowd and wild shouts and scuffles broke out. Insults were hurled at remaining soldiers, French émigrés and those Portuguese known to support the French. The Marquis was almost dragged from his horse and several fights broke out as French soldiers were set upon by the crowd.

Many cried 'Portugal for ever! Death to the French!'[13] as infantrymen hurried back into the square and formed firing lines under a hail of bottles and stones from the crowd. Shots were fired at the French and Junot threatened severe consequences unless the Regency Councillors still present after the ceremony helped him restore order. Addressing the mob, the appeals of these officials partly pacified the crowds but it was not until Junot brought up some squadrons of cavalry and a few guns along the waterfront that they dispersed. Some French officers believed that this incident represented the true fall of Lisbon rather than the moment when their army had entered the city two weeks beforehand.[14] In correspondence with Napoleon, Junot wrote that raising the tricolour had ignited the crowd's passions but believed that British agents were behind the disturbances:

> ... I am concentrating on the restoration of tranquillity in the city of Lisbon. The vilest rabble flooded into the streets of the capital and, not wishing to see the tricolour flying, yelled insults at our soldiers and some shots were fired before a military committee managed to restore calm. I cannot ignore the fact that tempers here are easily provoked and suspect they were strongly encouraged by British agents, though proof of this is very difficult to find. I learned yesterday that a fishing boat brought two Englishmen into Lisbon and immediately set the police to searching for them; they have not been found but, if they are arrested, they shall be shot as spies.[15]

The authorities had already taken steps to reduce the threat of disorder. Junot issued a military decree banning firearms within the city limits without permission from the city's military commandant. Those violating the ban 'shall be considered as a vagrant and highway assassin, and tried as such by a Military Committee ...'[16] The Count of São Pais, in the Regency Council, announced the imposition of a curfew for all soldiers (regardless of nationality) frequenting taverns after 7:00 pm. Tavern-keepers would be fined 100 crusados for a first offence and 400 for a second along with a month's imprisonment. Furthermore, he announced the 'prohibition of firearms, and Arms of every description, especially at night'.[17]

At first Junot allowed the members of the Regency Council to assist him in ruling Portugal and kept military influence to a minimum. Former Consul Herman, who was popular in Lisbon, worked well to ensure that most civil government was conducted by Portuguese magistrates and local dignitaries.

Public money was left alone and the arrears of the troops, many of whom had not been paid for months, were settled. The Emperor had ordered Junot to act justly:

> One thing I insist upon; you must be as correct in your conduct as I should be myself, and set an example of absolute incorruptibility. It is better to have a fortune you have won by your merits ... than one made by illegitimate and disgraceful means. Portugal is not a country in which you are likely to win much military renown: so you must acquire the reputation of an honest and blameless administrator. And, to do that, you must set a good example.[18]

He had also given orders for taxes to be collected in his name and made Herman the Administrator-General of Finance, promising to send an official tax collector to act under him. Yet in spite of these noble ideals, Napoleon allowed Junot to retain General Thiébault in his position although he considered him dishonest.[19]

However, as much as 50 per cent of the nation's wealth had been taken by the exiles to Brazil and the currency had depreciated in value by as much as 30 per cent because of recent upheavals. The government therefore froze the prices of basic commodities on 4 December 1807 in Lisbon.[20] As the weeks passed, the value of Portuguese currency rose by about 12 per cent and the economy began to recover slightly.

The Emperor insisted on imposing harsh measures. The Regent's flight to Brazil may have been a propaganda coup but his continued freedom provided a focal point for Portuguese disaffection and resistance to French rule. Napoleon had never really expected Junot's army to arrive in time to seize the Portuguese fleet but its loss, along with most of the country's elite and national wealth, greatly angered him. Despite his previous declarations, Napoleon scorned Junot's wish to rule benevolently as he anticipated the hatred of the Portuguese, seeing them as a minor ally of his greatest enemy. His priorities were the acquisition of fighting men and revenue, which could be swiftly obtained through oppression and strict rule. Denying Britain the advantages of her alliance with Portugal was even more important but granting the benefits of republicanism to this nation was a low priority for Napoleon, very low indeed.

Henri Clarke, Minister for War, conveyed his Emperor's thoughts in a letter to Junot:

> ... of what use is it to make promises which you will not be able to perform? No doubt nothing can be more laudable than to gain the confidence and affection of the inhabitants. But do not forget that the safety of the army is paramount.[21]

Continuing along these lines, he emphasized the need for the strict domination of the Portuguese with a view to preventing strong leaders from emerging. The Spanish troops could not be relied upon and British intervention was inevitable at some stage. He cautioned Junot to keep these factors in mind, with the proviso that keeping the people in a state of fear was the best way to ensure their obedience.

Napoleon still believed in the old revolutionary adage that war should pay for itself and, to make up for the loss of potential revenue that had disappeared overseas, he imposed an extraordinary tax upon Portugal of 100 million French francs. This colossal sum would be extremely difficult to extract from a small nation, already deprived of its colonial revenue and foreign trade. Junot, his officers and civil officials realized that it was bound to cause resentment and the chances of collecting it were negligible. Everyone would have to contribute and Foy remarked 'it was necessary to lay hands on the most sacred objects of public veneration, by seizing the church plate'.[22] Though this statement could be taken as an excuse for the looting which took place later, it is difficult to believe that a man as intelligent as Napoleon believed such a vast sum could be gathered. Naturally the idea that their nation should effectively pay for its own invasion was taken as an insult by the Portuguese.

On 1 February 1808, Junot informed the Regency Council that he was assuming supreme authority and they were effectively dissolved. Though some Portuguese officials retained their roles, Paris sent considerable numbers of civilian administrators to take up government positions. Virtually all Portuguese dignitaries were removed from senior office and symbols of the old regime were removed from public buildings and replaced with the Imperial French Eagle.

Increasingly, acts of defiance against the occupation began to take place and were dealt with harshly. In Mafra, a man who shouted insults against France in public was tried by a military tribunal and executed. Likewise a brawl between Portuguese soldiers and French infantrymen of the 58th Regiment saw the Porto Regiment disbanded, which was an overreaction since it had been misrepresented to Junot as a near uprising. A formal execution of six men in the main square at Caldas was also mishandled as it incensed the already sullen townspeople rather than frightening them into submission.[23] Deeply resentful over the occupation, the Portuguese were enraged at what they saw as arrogant and high-handed behaviour by the French. Nevertheless, Junot felt sufficiently secure to begin arrangements to reinforce French forces in Spain as war had erupted there. Marshal Bessières was pacifying Galicia and Old Castile and General Dupont was marching into Southern Spain. Both needed support and Junot was ordered to help.

Napoleon had seriously miscalculated if he thought that the Spaniards would submit quietly to foreign rule. Discontent had spread like wildfire through

Spain after the monarchy had been deposed and isolated acts of violence and robbery had been committed against the French even before the royal family took the road to Bayonne. Many French encampments found that sentries had had their throats cut in the night and had to double the guard.

Yet hostility and disorder were not limited to rural areas. When it was learned that the Bourbons were virtual prisoners in France, many Spaniards were outraged. As a proud nation, they were greatly angered by the planned imposition of a foreign king and the fact that Napoleon had chosen his own brother revealed his dynastic ambitions. City dwellers were increasingly resentful of the French presence, which was viewed as an army of occupation rather than allied support. Local customs regarding Spanish women and religion were often carelessly flouted or openly ignored, provoking the disgruntled population even further.

Serious disturbances began on 1 May (and continued into 2 May) when remaining members of the royal family were sent to France by the Regency government. The sight of the tearful young Prince Francisco de Paula being forced into a waiting carriage infuriated the watching crowds and a riot ensued. Pelted with stones and assaulted with knives and staves, a detachment of the Imperial Guard sent by Murat as an escort opened fire on the mob, killing or wounding at least ten people.[24]

News of this spread rapidly through the city and people armed themselves with makeshift weapons, knives, swords, pistols and fowling pieces. Hundreds of furious people came out onto the streets during the riot that became known as the *Dos de Mayo*. It began with attacks on single or small groups of soldiers in Madrid and many were beaten or murdered. Some soldiers joined in the fighting and Daoíz and Velarde, two junior Spanish army officers, led a group who seized one of the main artillery parks in the city and attempted to turn the guns on the French.

Murat's men soon began to drive the crowds through the streets with few rioters prepared to stand before a disciplined line of soldiers presenting a row of levelled bayonets. However, they hurled bricks, tiles and furniture from the upper floors and rooftops as the soldiers forced them back. In the *Puerta del Sol*, a central square, infantry deployed and fired volleys into the mob. Murat sent cavalry into the square and the dreaded Mamelukes (incorporated into the French army during Bonaparte's invasion of Egypt) galloped into the crowds, riding people down and slashing at the frenzied rioters with their razor-sharp scimitars.

Eventually French discipline prevailed and the crowds fled into alleyways and houses where many were hunted down and shot or bayoneted. At least 200 Spaniards lay dead on the streets and artillery was brought up and placed in the squares to help restore order. Arbitrary executions followed over the next few days and around 300 more were shot before firing squads as examples to deter further unrest.[25]

Despite limited military involvement, this had been a spontaneous uprising by the common people and the savagery of the *Dos de Mayo* was a foretaste of what would follow over the next few years as Spanish resistance and defiance of French rule increased. The serious nature of the disturbances appalled the authorities and news spread rapidly throughout Spain, along with lurid tales of brutality, which grew in the telling as they progressed.

Portuguese society was also turning against the French. Even those who initially welcomed the prospect of change switched their allegiances or kept their own counsel as the atmosphere became increasingly charged. One resident of Porto wrote to friends in London about the evils of French rule: '... their behaviour in Lisbon has rendered them very obnoxious to the Portuguese; and it is the general opinion, that if they do not conduct themselves with more propriety here, a deal of bloodshed will be the consequence.'[26] The writer added that, once he could be sure of transporting his property overseas, he meant to charter a vessel for Brazil rather than risk financial ruin with the prospect of serious revolt. Over the following months, *The Times* reported the arrival of large numbers of emigrants from Portugal, fleeing the French regime and hoping to settle in England or sail on to the Americas.[27]

British newspapers carried vitriolic articles criticizing the French occupation, *The Times* commenting that Junot's regime was mercilessly persecuting a people that Paris claimed were allies. One journalist wrote:

> Even the national enmities between the Portuguese and the Spaniards are forgotten; and the latter are held up deservedly to our applause ...
> (France had imposed) nothing but a system of violence and rapine, which can serve no other end than to swell the stores of the conqueror's agents, and confirm and spread the despotism of their master.[28]

Although British press sources should be assessed in the knowledge that they were criticizing an enemy power, it should be borne in mind that the British and Portuguese had formed close links after centuries of commercial partnership. Significant numbers of British subjects owned property and businesses in Portugal, especially in the wine industry, and were naturally concerned over the fate of the Portuguese. Portugal's plight troubled British society far more than the defeat and occupation of any other European state by France during the wars.

After the *Dos de Mayo*, major revolts took place in Valencia, the Asturias and Seville. A junta was established at Seville, which sent appeals via Gibraltar for the British to intervene. Many *afrancesados* (pro-French Spaniards) and

French expatriates were murdered and, with dissent spreading rapidly, Spanish generals like Joaqúin Blake and Antonio Cuesta began to gather troops in the unoccupied regions of the country to oppose the French, who soon realized that serious military force was necessary to repress the uprising.

News of fighting in Spain soon spread to Portugal. The confiscation of royal and government property to meet Napoleon's extraordinary tax was taken as an affront to Portuguese honour but it was the seizure of money and goods that caused major resentment, as all sections of society suffered from this. The lucrative wine industry faced catastrophic ruin and colonial trade links were severed by the British blockade. French arrogance and callous treatment exacerbated the situation and open revolt erupted in the Northern provinces of Tras os Montes and Minho.

When he learned about fighting in Spain, General Taranco led a mutiny in Porto, where General Quesnel (the French governor) was arrested and the small detachments of dragoons and artillery under his command were swiftly surrounded and surrendered. Portuguese patriots declared a Junta of Insurrection on 6 June and Taranco allowed the Portuguese flag to be raised above the city. However, he had no intention of staying to support the insurgency and soon marched his 6,000 men towards the frontier to fight for Spain.

Colonel Francisco de Silveira was made a general by the insurgents on the same day at Via Real and General Manuel José de Sepulveda was also persuaded to join the insurgency on 9 June. Many other officers, such as General Andrada and Colonel Coutinho, had retired from the army and returned home rather than serve under France and the majority of these officers needed little persuasion to volunteer their services. Rebellions began in the south at Braga and Melgaço over the following days but the patriots desperately needed a political leader of some standing. By 16 June they had found one when they proclaimed the Supreme Junta of the Kingdom, declaring the Bishop of Porto, Don Antonio de São José de Casto, as City Governor and President of their government.[29]

The Bishop of Porto was a descendant of João de Castro, renowned for his work in India, and the natural son of the Count de Reizende. Since King João I of Portugal had himself been illegitimate, such a background was viewed as no disgrace in the country. He had entered the Order of Saint Bruno at an early age and rapidly became Principal Superior. He was popular with all classes of Portuguese society and lent the junta an aura of respectability.[30] One of his first acts was to open negotiations with the Spanish Junta of Galicia in the expectation of receiving support.

The Bishop made the following somewhat premature announcement on 20 June 1808:

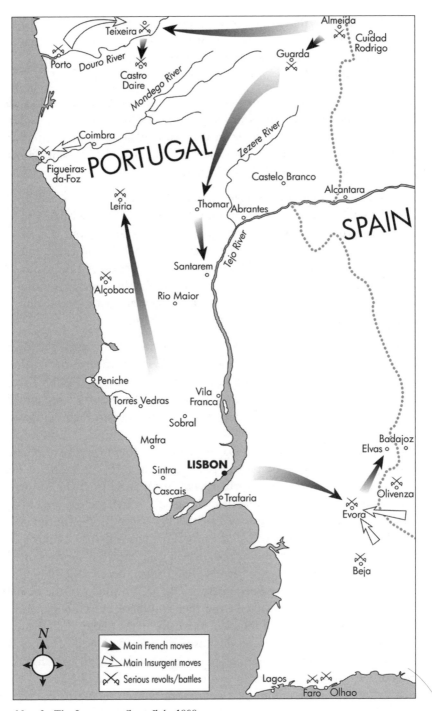

Map 3: The Insurgency June–July 1808

> In the name of the Prince Regent of Portugal, the Junta of the
> Supreme Government of the city of Oporto makes known ... that
> the French government is entirely exterminated from the country,
> and the royal authority of our legitimate sovereign is restored ...[31]

He declared that symbols of Portuguese royalty should be restored to public
buildings and monuments and issued an edict on 19 June that veteran soldiers
should travel to Porto and re-enlist in the two regular army regiments being
raised there. He also cautioned the people who, though understandably jubilant,
should refrain from wild acts of indiscipline:

> Portuguese! Listen to one who loves you. The French intend to strike a
> blow, fatal to you, and you are lost if you are guilty of insubordination,
> or disregard the councils of your governor. Your firing, your beat of
> drum, your bells, give to your enemies, the knowledge of where you
> are, where your force (is), and where your weakness (lies). From your
> enemy conceal your power, that you may strike the blow with more
> success; and that you may encounter him when he least expects your
> approach. By these means you may conquer him.[32]

In fact, the Bishop's call to arms merely lent legitimacy to what was already
happening. Hundreds of disbanded regular soldiers returned to their colours,
after enduring months of occupation, and were eager to oppose the French.
The majority of Portuguese regulars remaining in the country were attached
to French or Spanish units and many now deserted to join their compatriots
at Porto.

Junot's administration used propaganda in an effort to improve relations
with the populace, saying that the French had their best interests at heart
and claiming '... the present disturbances in Spain arose from the Emperor's
refusal to consent that Portugal be dismembered'.[33] Nonetheless, anti-French
feeling was rife and few were deceived by this half-truth. In the south Colonel
José de Sousa tore down one of Junot's proclamations nailed to a church door
in Olhao, loudly exhorting the crowd, which had gathered to view it: 'Do
not believe these falsehoods, my friends! The French deceive us, plunder us,
degrade us. We are no longer Portuguese ... we are unworthy of the name!'[34]
Sousa's dramatic rhetoric provoked a riot then and there, even though the men
of the Algarve were considered the most peaceable in the nation. Following the
Colonel, fishermen and sailors of the town plundered a local armoury and
rapidly seized Olhao. The southern coast was lightly held by the French and the
fortress of Faro fell to the patriots two days afterwards on 18 June.

Men previously in the militia had only recently been released from service
and it was an easy matter for the patriots to reassemble them, especially as the

state of the economy meant that few had any prospect of gainful employment. The French had unwittingly collaborated in raising such men by allowing General Antonio Henriquez to enlist five companies in Alemtejo for the Elvas garrison, the majority of whom immediately joined the rebellion.

Word of revolts in the north was received by 9 June and Junot swiftly convened a council of war. Shocked by this sudden outbreak of insurrection, he soon concluded that the northern provinces were temporarily lost and even entertained suggestions of withdrawal into Spain via Badajoz. However, the French position was still strong while the capital remained in their hands along with most of the major fortresses on the border and the west coast. Yet Junot only had about 25,000 men in Portugal and would have to weaken his major garrisons to concentrate a force large enough to dominate a significant province or match a substantial foreign incursion. He decided to send out columns of a few thousand men to attempt to subdue the main centres of the revolt.

The Spanish division under General Caraffa was soon isolated and disarmed. Since they had only just begun to receive news of unrest from Spain, the Spaniards were surprised and captured without serious bloodshed. Only the Reina cavalry regiment escaped the net, withdrawing into central Portugal and eventually fleeing over the frontier. Most were imprisoned on barges moored in the Tejo but Spanish officers who gave their paroles were permitted to stay in Lisbon. Junot then made efforts to suppress the insurgency, ordering General Loison to march from Almeida and retake Porto, with a second column marching north from Torres Vedras to combine with his force. In the south Junot planned to re-establish a French presence at Évora and Estremoz.

Despite his military accomplishments, Napoleon never formulated a successful approach to combat guerrilla activity. Professional soldiers invariably viewed those fighting out of uniform as bandits and treated them as such. Guerrillas usually responded in kind, rarely granting or receiving quarter. The greatest nineteenth-century military theorist Carl von Clausewitz termed this kind of conflict the 'people's war' and, during most instances of this period, a cycle of atrocity and reprisal was repeated many times. Napoleon's armies faced insurgencies in Egypt, the Austrian Tyrol, the French Vendée, Spain, some German states and Italy. The usual response was to dispatch flying columns to target centres of rebellion, and discourage resistance through intimidation and terror but these callous punitive actions were rarely completely successful and occasionally counter-productive.

Antoine-Henri Jomini, Clausewitz's greatest rival, believed that the Peninsular War should be studied at length for the lessons learned about this kind of warfare. Indeed, the word 'guerrilla' entered the English language from its use during the conflict, meaning literally 'little war' in Spanish. His solution was to

... make a display of a mass of troops proportioned to the obstacles
and resistance likely to be encountered, calm the popular passions
in every possible way, exhaust them by time and patience, display
courtesy, gentleness, and severity united, and, particularly, deal
justly.[35]

During the campaign in Portugal, where the swift suppression of rebellion
was paramount, introducing such a policy was difficult but Jomini correctly
identified that brute force and reprisals were unlikely to succeed against an
enemy whose main strategy was to strike swiftly from ambush and then elude
pursuit by hiding within the civilian population. However, the French response
in Portugal would concentrate on crushing rebellion rather than winning over
the people with displays of restraint and justice. Though many of the enemies
the French were about to encounter were uniformed militia, the *ordenança*
in particular often wore civilian clothes and so were classed as guerrillas and
treated accordingly. Yet there were also many instances where ordinary
Portuguese civilians assembled to form guerrilla bands against the French, who
fell outside the accepted rules of war.

Loison left Almeida on 17 June with two battalions of the 2nd and 4th Light
Infantry, a squadron of the 5th Dragoons and a detachment of artillery dragging
six field pieces. French sources claim this force was about 1,800 strong but
Portuguese historians maintain that it numbered as high as 2,600.[36] The force
was occasionally fired upon from the hills and sentries were attacked in the
night when they bivouacked but no organized resistance was encountered until
they reached the town of Régua on the river Douro on 20 June.

As Loison's men were ferried across the Douro, they observed large numbers
of Portuguese irregulars on the hills to the north. General Silveira had marched
down from Amarante with a large force composed mainly of militia. Though
these militiamen were armed predominantly with pikes and improvised weapons,
he had distributed muskets judiciously and had a small body of regulars as the
core of his hastily-raised army. Silveira had even managed to secure two small-
calibre cannon, served by regular artillerymen, and was confident of stopping
Loison or delaying his march on Porto at least.

The French marched along the riverbank to Mesao Frio and were shadowed
by the insurgents on the hills as they did so. The steep hillsides rose in tiers,
often covered with vineyards that would make ascending the slopes difficult for
men marching in formation. The region was famous for its fortified wine so the
collapse of the wine trade had heightened anti-French feeling locally, many
villagers rushing to join Silveira. On 21 June Loison found his march blocked
by the insurgents at Teixeira where Silveira had taken up a strong position on
the hillsides, his force having grown to approximately 10,000 men.[37]

After ordering a reconnaissance, Loison and his staff observed that most of the insurgents were poorly armed militia and concluded that a bold frontal attack up the slopes by disciplined regulars would scatter them. In two battalion-sized columns, the French set off up the broken slope preceded by a skirmish line of tirailleurs to weaken the insurgents' lines. At first they made good progress with the largely pike-armed militias unable to respond effectively when the French main body fired musketry volleys into their midst. Reluctantly the Portuguese fell back and their two guns inflicted only slight losses on the French toiling up the slope towards them.

However, as they advanced, the French columns received musket fire on both flanks from knots of irregulars positioned in the rocks and vineyards around them. Time and again the columns had to pause and deploy more skirmishers to deal with these troublesome groups. Firing from heavy cover, these men were well protected from supporting French artillery fire, already limited by the difficulty of firing uphill, and only skirmishers could dislodge them. Dealing with this harassment slowed the attack and the assault stalled. Heartened by the enemy's hesitation, Portuguese resistance before the columns intensified and the militia stood their ground despite their losses. Loison suffered a slight wound while urging his men onward and, seeing the attack was faltering, ordered a general withdrawal to regroup.

He then received unwelcome intelligence that regular Portuguese troops had been raised in Porto and were marching to reinforce Silveira. Though this rumour later proved untrue, additional news that an attack was taking place on his rear was even more worrying: 'the rearguard and the baggage ... were assailed by a discharge of musketry from among the vines, and behind the walls, and by stones hurled from the high points of the rocks.'[38] Two companies of infantry dispatched to skirmish with the ambushers were enough to drive them off and they took a few prisoners, some of whom proved to be former soldiers.

Meanwhile, Loison could see no rearward movement or depletion in the numbers of the enemy. The French were heavily outnumbered and likely to encounter stubborn resistance should the patriots be reinforced. With the prospect of being cut off with a large river to his rear, Loison decided to retreat knowing that Junot could not afford the loss of two infantry battalions. The French retreat could be traced by pillars of smoke as Loison ordered villages along the route put to the flames, knowing that many villagers had aided or joined the insurgents. Régua was viciously sacked as they withdrew and Silveira followed the retreating French, his irregulars harrying the rearguard at every opportunity.[39]

Always distrustful of the French after what the church had suffered during the French Revolution, Catholics in Portugal and Spain felt a renewed sense of hostility after recent excesses. Foy remembered many monks and clergymen taking up arms and joining the insurgency. Some fought at Teixeira and joined in the pursuit:

> Father José Joachim de l'Assomption, a monk of the order of Black Friars, marched at the head of this multitude, with his gown tucked up, and firing his musket, like the rest. Another monk, father José Bernardo de Azevedo, went to Coimbra, with a party of the militia of Aveiro, and a crowd of peasants, to slaughter some French soldiers who were in the hospital of that city.[40]

As acts of atrocity multiplied on both sides, they bred fanaticism and the war began to escalate, with tales of the murder of prisoners and civilians becoming commonplace.

During the retreat to Almeida the majority of the French baggage and loot, seized in Régua, was lost along with two howitzers as the French struggled back to the fortress. Loison reached Almeida on 1 July having suffered several hundred casualties but claimed to have inflicted far more damage on the insurgents.

Meanwhile defiance grew in the south with a series of revolts breaking out. At Vila Vizosa, a company of the 86th Ligne was hemmed in at the fortress there and only saved by the timely arrival of a column under General Avril. An even more serious outbreak occurred at Beja where two town officials, Francisco Pesagna and Antonio Cermasao, were set upon and killed by the townsfolk as collaborators. Other officials fled Beja as a French force under Colonel Maransin came to restore order, only to find the town gates barred to them. Maransin stormed Beja, his men scaling the ramparts with siege ladders and his pioneers cutting down the gates with axes before the town's defences were breached. Furious close-quarter fighting took place in the streets and the French lost eighty men killed putting down the revolt. As many as 1,200 Portuguese were killed, with anyone found carrying arms or even suspected of being an insurgent, put to the sword. In reprisal, Beja was put to the flames.

Junot had decided to pull back Loison's force to the capital and concentrate on putting down the southern rebellion. Leaving a strong garrison at Almeida, Loison destroyed some of the defences of the nearby fortress of La Concepción before taking the road to Lisbon. His forces comprised the 32nd Ligne, 4th Swiss Regiment, the 2nd and 4th Light Infantry and all the cavalry and field artillery at his disposal. During his journey he encountered resistance with guerrillas firing on his men as they marched and harassing the rearguard. Infuriated by such attacks and the surly or openly hostile attitude of the villagers, Loison ordered many summary executions of alleged sympathizers and hanged many peasants from trees at the roadside. According to Portuguese accounts, he ordered the entire population of Atalaya village massacred as an example. When some militia offered serious resistance at Guarda, he stormed the town and allowed his men to sack it. Chasing the inhabitants through the streets and breaking into houses, the soldiers bayoneted even old men, women and children in their fury.[41]

Although the murder of civilians is always inexcusable, historians like Napier suggested that the French, subjected as they were to constant hit-and-run attacks and treachery, were not wholly accountable for the escalating violence. Constant attacks from guerrillas, who disappeared back into the hills whenever they retaliated, made French soldiers eager for revenge against an enemy who refused to stand and fight. Often their officers were unwilling or powerless to prevent their cruel excesses. Napier argued:

> In such a combat it is difficult to say where fighting ends and massacre begins. Peasants are observed firing and moving from place to place without order; when do they cease to become enemies? More dangerous single than together, they can hide their arms in an instant and appear peaceable, the soldier passes and is shot from behind.[42]

Fighting uniformed militia was one thing, but the poorly equipped *ordenança* often fought out of uniform and consequently French soldiers were unlikely to make the distinction between them and guerrillas if they were taken prisoner. Civilians taken under arms could expect little mercy as, under the current rules of war, they were considered bandits and usually put up against a wall and shot. Often unable to strike back at irregulars, it was a simple thing to fire a cottage or farmstead on the pretext that the owners 'must' be guerrilla sympathizers and had to be punished. Tempers flared under these circumstances and torture and atrocities became more frequent.

Loison was met at Santarém by forces under Generals Kellerman, Thomières and Brenier and began to form a mobile column of all arms to suppress the rebellion. Knowing the importance of securing strongpoints in Portugal, they dispatched a battalion of the 4th Swiss Regiment to Peniche and a battalion of the 32nd Regiment to Abrantes to reinforce their garrisons.

On 5 July General Margaron encountered significant resistance at Leiria while marching towards Coimbra. The militia there were crushed when the French broke into the city and Margaron allowed his soldiers to run riot in an orgy of murder, rape, looting and destruction. Although Kellerman and Loison took Alcobaça, resistance was intensifying and, believing that advancing further north without reinforcements was futile, they returned to Lisbon.

Coimbra seemed out of reach to Junot for the moment so he decided to delay a move against the city until the south was pacified. Throughout June and July there had been constant rumours and false alarms of landings by the British, which excited the population and renewed riots occurred in the capital during the procession of Corpus Christi on 16 July. Nevertheless, Junot felt able to allow Loison to take a large force of 7,000 men (in two brigades under Solignac and Margaron) over the Tejo. The city of Évora had formed its own junta and was considered a focal point of resistance by the French, making it Loison's primary objective.

Évora was held by General Francisco Leite who had been the military governor of the Alemtejo region before the invasion and, now that the Algarve had risen, had been reappointed by Évora's junta. The city walls were rebuilt in places and four of the five gates were barricaded and blocked up with earth and stone. Évora was full of willing volunteers who eagerly joined Leite who also had regular Portuguese cavalry, artillery and infantry at his disposal. He was heartened to receive the assistance of Spanish Colonel Moretti who marched to support him bringing the Maria Louisa Hussars, two regular Spanish infantry battalions, a Legión Extranjera battalion and numerous militia units collected en route. Moretti also brought two batteries of artillery and between them the Hispano-Portuguese force fielded ten cannon and two howitzers. Perhaps the arrival of these reinforcements made Leite overconfident when he heard the French were approaching and, instead of preparing for a siege, he marched out to oppose them.

Loison crossed the Tejo on 25 July. Unlike most of Portugal, which is often mountainous or hilly, the land beyond the river largely comprises rolling plains dotted with groves of cork oaks and olive trees. Known as the *terra do pão* (land of bread) this part of Alemtejo broadens out into vast fields planted with wheat or oats. Marching through this countryside, turned the colour of burnt ochre by the summer heat, the French trudged along dusty roads towards their goal as the hot July sun beat down upon them.

From the very outset the peasantry opposed the French, after hearing lurid tales of atrocities committed in the north. Many fled at their approach and soon the French were short of food and especially water. Hatred of the repressive French regime meant that soldiers desperate for water were often directed towards stagnant or even poisoned ponds or wells. Thiébault recorded that stragglers were often set upon by vengeful guerrillas, occasionally when they were only a few hundred metres behind the main body and within sight of their comrades.

On 29 July the French came within sight of Évora but found their way blocked by an opposing army. Unlike the high ground they had previously fought through in the north, Alemtejo's flatlands allowed them to deploy and use the French army tactics tried and tested on many European battlefields. Both sides sent skirmishers forward who began a brisk exchange of musketry as the Hispano-Portuguese artillery began to fire on the French. Loison reconnoitred his enemy's position and decided to send Solignac's brigade around their flank while Margaron's brigade made a frontal assault. Should the attack on the enemy centre prove successful, he hoped to use his cavalry to assault the opposite flank and connect with Solignac's brigade in a pincer movement.

As his infantry advanced in assault columns, Loison saw the Portuguese infantry in the centre waver and break as Colonel Lacroix led his 86th Battalion straight into them. The Maria Louisa Hussars and the Portuguese cavalry turned and fled without engaging as the centre broke in a near rout. Only the Spanish infantry units under Major Grallejo put up determined resistance, firing volleys at the oncoming French and retiring slowly to cover the retreat. Their tenacity saved five cannon as the army broke leaving seven guns on the battlefield. However, General Leite and much of the army fled towards Olivenza in relatively good order.

Many of the men were still full of fight and Colonel Lobo rallied large numbers of fugitives and put up a spirited defence of Évora. With cannon placed in a battery to defend the Rocio Gate, the town presented a formidable obstacle with hundreds of peasants and militia crowding the ramparts shouting defiance at the victorious French who now approached.

Flushed with victory, the French were determined to engage the insurgents. 'The soldiers pressed forward in the badly repaired breaches. Some stuck their bayonets into the walls, to serve as ladders. Others got into the city through drains and old posterns.'[43] The defenders met them with a hail of bricks, rocks and other objects cast from the ramparts and laid down a heavy fusillade of musketry. Lieutenant Spinola of the Engineers was killed in the assault and the French suffered losses, but Loison resolutely continued the attack, training artillery against the four walled-up gateways. Sappers were then sent forward to haul the remnants of these barriers aside as the Portuguese fired down at them. Columns of infantry then charged through into the city.

Once the French broke in, the majority of Spaniards abandoned the fight for Évora and fled. Though French dragoons were sent to cut them off, large numbers of fugitives reached the Estremoz Road before the cavalry and managed to evade pursuit. In contrast, the bulk of the Portuguese fought for their city as the French fought laboriously through the streets as bricks, tiles and stones rained down at them from the rooftops. Bitter fighting took place as the militia matched their pikes against French muskets at close quarters. Breaking down doors with musket butts, the French carried the fight into the houses and dreadful carnage ensued.

After losing many of their comrades killed or wounded during the storming, atrocities against civilians were predictable. Even women and children who took refuge in the churches were slain and reports of the massacre spread terror throughout Alemtejo.[44] The French entered the town at around 4:00 pm but the merciless sacking of Évora continued until 11:00 am the next day when the soldiers, many now drunk, were finally brought under control by their officers: 'at length, the archbishop, Father Manuel do Canacolo Villas Boas, obtained mercy from the victor.' After severely reproaching this prelate with the dreadful consequences of a revolt which his episcopal character had authorized and sanctioned, General Loison entrusted him with the administration of the city.[45] Foy recorded that the French lost about a hundred dead with double that number wounded in the battle and subsequent storming of Évora. The Portuguese suffered between 3,000 and 4,000 casualties with approximately 4,000 men taken prisoner.[46]

The brutality at Évora shocked Portugal, being the bloodiest clash of the insurgency, and Valente later wrote: 'Loison's Alemtejo campaign was without doubt the most brutal part of the first invasion.'[47] General Loison earned an unenviable reputation as a butcher for his eagerness to put men to the sword, execute suspected guerrillas and enact reprisals throughout 1808. Loison had lost a hand in combat, which led to his unflattering Portuguese nickname 'Maneta', or 'One Hand'. To this day the saying *Ir pro Maneta* is used by the Portuguese to tell someone that they are in trouble or are about to pay the price for an infraction.[48] It translates literally as 'go to Maneta' but signifies the act of being brought before the notorious general for judgement, the implication being that most men ended up before a firing squad or swinging from a hangman's rope by nightfall.

Loison's decision to abandon the advance on Coimbra earlier that month proved to be a fateful one. Once Coimbra had declared for the Prince Regent, it became a hotbed of dissent and students from its famous university, reputedly the oldest in Europe, enlisted en masse. Even the university buildings were used to support the insurgency, with one science laboratory converted into a gunpowder factory and the professor of metallurgy turning his talents to the repair and manufacture of firearms.

Led by the engineer Don Cibrao and artillery Sergeant Bernardo Zagalo, a large militia force marched downriver to Figueira-da-Foz. This town lay at the mouth of the Mondego and along the bay there were several miles of wide beaches, protected by the fortress of Santa Catarina. Only a single company of French infantry were in the area and they rapidly took refuge in the fort at the insurgents' approach. The besiegers had no cannon to batter a breach but surrounded Santa Catarina, its garrison having too few provisions to hold out for long.

Informed by their besiegers that Loison had returned to Lisbon, they surrendered on 27 July with the promise of being allowed to rejoin their army. Foy claims that the patriots reneged on the terms and triumphantly marched their prisoners to Coimbra instead. Though a small fort, Santa Catarina was strategically important, its cannon covering beaches that would make ideal landing sites for the British. The insurgents rapidly contacted the Royal Navy, whose ships constantly patrolled the coastline, and Admiral Cotton landed a detachment of 100 marines to man the fortress.[49]

Further inland, the frontier fortresses of Almeida and Elvas were also surrounded by insurgents. Portuguese militia, backed by hundreds of civilian volunteers, hemmed them in and while they were unlikely to storm these strongholds, as they lacked siege guns, there was the prospect of starving the garrisons out. Even though they were well stocked with provisions, the defenders could do little but man their walls and pray that they would be relieved. The neutralization of these fortresses cut Junot off as he could no longer communicate with French forces in Spain.

Despite the efforts of the French, Portugal was still in a state of serious unrest. Had he been able to send a strong force north to retake Coimbra and Porto, it is possible that Junot may have broken the back of the rebellion but he was crippled by lack of numbers and his desire to retain the capital and strategic fortresses. General Dupont had been defeated at Bailén on 21 July in southern Spain. News of the catastrophic defeat of an entire French army corps appalled the French in Portugal and encouraged the people of Iberia to resist. With pardonable exaggeration, Foy remarked: 'Thus the insurrection burst forth in all quarters at once. The earth could not be stamped on without enemies to the French starting up from it.'[50]

The insurgency had drastic effects in Lisbon with many people leaving to seek refuge with friends or family in the hinterland. Landlords did not receive rents and workers went unpaid as rebellion in the countryside doubled food prices and roads to the city became prey to brigands and guerrillas. Junot imposed movement restrictions on the population and insisted that those leaving the city had to have permits. However, Lisbon was a huge city by the standards of the day, with suburbs sprawling out into the hills, and the lack of city walls made preventing people from leaving virtually impossible.

The difficulty of defending Lisbon against a British army approaching over-land was a cause of deep concern for Junot's chief-of-staff. With no city walls and few fortifications beyond the old Moorish castle above the city, Thiébault advised his commander to create a fortified enclave where the French could retire should the capital fall. He considered Lisbon so indefensible that an army could theoretically march straight into its streets unless opposed by a sizable military force.

As early as February 1808, Thiébault dispatched Lieutenant Vallier, an engineer officer on the staff, to make a survey of suitable areas between 15–20 miles from Lisbon for this purpose. He chose the Setúbal Peninsula to the south of the capital as capable of supporting large numbers of men and dominating much of Alemtejo. A large camp constructed across the Tejo would be near enough to support the fortress of Bugio and so partly command the estuary if the enemy gained possession of the forts on the opposing coastline. The great width of the river at this point was a major obstacle to forces approaching from the north. Transferring the contents of the main Lisbon arsenal, a year's supply of provisions and the construction of earthwork redoubts, would probably suffice and allow this enclave to hold out for a few months, he reasoned. He also believed that such a strategy would allow Napoleon time to send another army to relieve them.[51]

Thiébault believed that his proposals were ignored due to lethargy on his commander's part, yet, in fairness to Junot, he was beset on all sides by strategic dilemmas during the insurgency. The plan demanded the use of large numbers of men and resources but, with hindsight, had he adopted this approach it would have allowed him another option towards the end of the campaign.

Although the French were still strong enough to maintain their hold on Portugal, Junot desperately needed reinforcements from Spain to put down the revolt and pacify the north. From the patriots' point of view, while they could harass the forces of occupation they needed a regular army to defeat them. Napier argued:

> There was an essential difference between the Spanish and Portuguese insurrections. The Spaniards had many great and strong towns, and large provinces in which to collect and train forces at a distance from the invaders, while in Portugal the naked peasants were forced to go to battle the instant even of assembling.[52]

Peasants armed with pitchforks, scythes and hunting firearms had no chance of matching regular French soldiers in the field and even trained militia could rarely hold their own against them. They could mount ambushes or a stubborn defence of towns and cities but to win an offensive campaign required a well-trained regular army. As reports of further revolts reached him in Lisbon, Junot must have likened his regime to a storm-battered ship, sailing on an ocean of dissent. Just as it seemed that the French were finally making progress, news reached him that a British army had landed on the western coast.

Chapter 5

The Lion Awakes

Joseph Bonaparte was declared King of Spain on 6 June 1808. He had been browbeaten by his brother into abdicating the throne of Naples and only accepted the Spanish crown against his better judgement. Though overshadowed by his younger brother, Joseph had considerable diplomatic experience and harboured genuine liberal impulses. He intended to govern his new kingdom justly but realized that Spanish anger over recent French policies and a habitual distrust of foreigners meant gaining their approval would be difficult.

Numerous provincial juntas had declared their allegiance to the Bourbons and on 10 June the Supreme Junta of Seville sent a direct appeal to the British government via Gibraltar, requesting arms and money for a war against France. Regional juntas were gathering all the regular troops they could find, along with local militias, to form armies. When the Aragonese city of Zaragoza rebelled, a garrison composed largely of townspeople and militia withstood a vigorous French siege. Such defiance from ordinary people inspired Spaniards to resist the occupation.

Despite being caught off guard by the scale of the revolt, Napoleon ordered a swift response, targeting the destruction of the two armies forming in Galicia and Andalusia as priorities. Marshal Moncey led 10,000 men against Valencia while General Dupont marched south with 13,000 men against Seville. Although confident of matching the regular forces ranged against them, both columns were waylaid by guerrilla ambushes and resistance by the common people, leading to many reprisals. Though professional soldiers also participated in the resulting atrocities, the large proportion of conscripts in these armies meant that discipline was difficult to enforce and magnified the problem. Compelled to enter the army, many were resentful of their predicament and lived in a state of fear in this hostile environment. Consequently they were easily provoked into violence and brutality.

On 14 July Marshal Bessières defeated the combined armies of Blake and Cuesta at the Battle of Medina del Rio Seco but Dupont's southern march had encountered major difficulties due to widespread popular resistance and the number of inexperienced conscripts in this army slowed their march. Though the cities of Gerona and Zaragoza were now under siege, the French were meeting unexpectedly high levels of opposition.

King Joseph's suspicions that his rule would be unpopular were reinforced during his journey to Madrid. The enthusiasm of local dignitaries who met him at towns along his route was decidedly muted and news of serious discontent was confirmed when he entered the city on 20 July 1808 to a very sullen welcome, hearty cheers at the roadside coming predominantly from French soldiers. This was an inauspicious beginning for French rule.

In London Portland's government was still uncertain how to pursue the war with France or whether hostilities should continue at all in light of increasing Whig opposition to the conflict. In June 1808 two Spanish noblemen, the Viscount Materosa and Don Diego de la Vega, arrived in England seeking British intervention in the Peninsula. Their deputation represented the juntas of Galicia and Asturia and Lord Canning, then Foreign Secretary, entered into tentative negotiations with them.[1]

The British government had already contacted many of the juntas opposing the occupation but most of these bodies had very specific requirements and vehemently opposed direct military intervention by a nation that had so recently been their enemy. In essence the Spaniards were happy to accept money, provisions, arms and ammunition but hesitated to allow troops to land in Spain, particularly if they were under British command. The Junta of Cadiz even denied Spencer's brigade permission to land in their support.

January 1808 witnessed a great scandal in both Houses of Parliament after the seizure of the Danish fleet at Copenhagen. Politicians from all parties were outraged by this action, which had alienated much of Europe. The Danish crown prince had made a clear declaration of neutrality and as one speaker rose to point out 'nothing short of a hostile design in the government of Denmark could justify the demand of her fleet, or the bombardment of Copenhagen, to enforce the surrender of it'.[2] Debate still raged over this matter as news emerged that the government was negotiating with the Spanish and concerns were raised at the prospect of another ill-advised foray. By July military preparations were obvious:

> The Earl of Suffolk rose to call the attention of the house to the critical situation in which we now stood with respect to Spain. It was generally understood that a large armament was to be sent to assist the patriotic exertions of that nation in resisting the tyranny that would oppress its liberty, and in enabling it to assert its independence. Who was to command that expedition?[3]

He not only referred to the Denmark expedition, which had been politically disastrous, but reminded the House of Lords that the mission to Buenos Aires under General Whitelocke in 1807 had also been a dismal failure which 'tarnished the honour of the country ...' Although Whitelocke was cashiered for his incompetence: 'No minister had as yet pleaded guilty to the charge of that appointment.'[4] He argued that, judging by their previous mistakes, Parliament had the right to know the government's mind over who would command this new mission.

Suffolk failed to receive convincing answers to his questions but the Lord Chancellor rose and delivered a speech revealing his majesty's unequivocal support of Spain and her recently deposed royal house. A clearly harassed Lord Castlereagh also spoke in favour of the Spanish cause and Mr Wilberforce MP confidently stated that support for Spain was universal, despite that nation's recent hostility towards Britain.[5] The Whigs, who sometimes claimed that Bonaparte was merely misunderstood, had consistently opposed the policy of mounting small-scale raids, which had made little impression on France's empire. Yet even they found Napoleon's manipulation and treachery at Bayonne repugnant. Indeed, the newspapers stirred up a surge of patriotic feeling attracting considerable public support.[6] For once, both sides of the House agreed and the government decided to take advantage of this to distract attention from their recent failures. Sending a sizeable force overseas might achieve this and the proposed expedition appeared to stand a good chance of success.

The government's choice of commander was a wise one. Sir Arthur Wellesley was selected to lead an expeditionary force that had been destined for South America but was now redirected towards Spain. Yet he was a young lieutenant general and, with the political situation so uncertain, the cabinet hesitated to consider his appointment as permanent.

Sir Arthur Wellesley would later win fame as the Duke of Wellington, a title he received in 1814. He subsequently won a decisive victory at Waterloo 1815, became Prime Minister and was even seen as the father figure for Victorian England along with a virtually unchallenged position as Britain's greatest general. Yet in 1808 his future was unclear in an army containing many officers of general rank who lacked appointments but enjoyed seniority over him. His experience and talent did not guarantee his prospects of gaining an important command. Indeed, many of his contemporaries languished on half-pay, having not seen active service for years. Though baffling by modern standards, his youth and experience actually counted against him at Horse Guards, the headquarters of the British army. Powerful elements in the establishment were biased against men whose reputations had been won in colonial wars, were obsessed with following army protocol and distrusted young officers with political connections like Wellesley's. Therefore he was fortunate to gain this important post and yet, with the incredible political pressure to succeed that came with it, his appointment might prove to be a poisoned chalice.

Born in 1769 as Arthur Wesley, he was the fourth son of Garret Wesley the First Earl Mornington, an Anglo-Irish aristocrat whose musical ambitions at

Trinity College Dublin occasionally came before the needs of family and estate. The formidable Lady Mornington thought very little of her son but ensured that he gained a good education at Eton followed by tutoring in Brussels and Angers. Though noted for his ability at playing the violin, his family believed his talents were limited and certainly below the standard of his siblings. For example, his eldest brother rose swiftly within the establishment, becoming Governor General of India in 1797 and gaining a Marquessate in 1799. Lady Mornington bought Arthur a commission in 1787 but despaired of him achieving any notable success in the military.

Yet army life agreed with young Arthur and he not only progressed through the ranks but managed simultaneously to make a good beginning in politics, being elected as a Member of Parliament for Trim (1790–1795). His family connections and financial support allowed him to transfer through several different regiments until he became Lieutenant Colonel in the 33rd Foot in 1793, fighting in the ill-fated Netherlands Campaign and seeing action at Boxtel 1794. The Netherlands proved a disaster for the Duke of York's military career and few officers emerged from the campaign with enhanced reputations, yet Wesley refused to become disillusioned by the ineptitude he witnessed there and resolved to master his vocation.

From 1795 he devoted himself to military matters, introducing great improvements in his regiment and making a serious study of the profession of arms. When he sailed for India in 1798, his luggage included many books concerning military theory and great commanders, to which he applied himself with vigour. Wesley's talents as a commander became obvious in India and after the fall of the Tippoo Sultan at the siege of Seringapatam 1799, he was appointed Governor General of the city, despite General Sir David Baird's seniority. Although many recognized his achievements, his family's political influence was believed to have been a decisive factor in many quarters.

At his brother's behest he adopted the name Wellesley in 1799, the more aristocratic surname reflecting their family's rise in fortune. Over the next few years he proved himself an able civil administrator and a skilled commander, being promoted major general in 1801 at the early age of 33. Unlike many officers, he was prepared to study the less glamorous side of warfare, realizing that logistics was often the key to success. At Madras in 1804 he wrote 'rapid movement cannot be made without good cattle, well driven and well taken care of'.[7] In India vast numbers of baggage animals were necessary to carry an army's equipment, food and water, vital in such an arid climate. Wellesley realized that good troops alone were insufficient to secure victory if they lacked ammunition or were poorly fed, so India proved the ideal training ground for reinforcing this concept.

Wellesley's careful attention to detail in this area was reflected in his successful campaign against the Mahratta Princes in 1803, where he achieved two major victories at Argaum and Assaye during that year. He demonstrated an aptitude for judging the lie of the land at Assaye in particular, where he skilfully manoeuvred his army in a hazardous move across the enemy's front. He displayed remarkable coolness while under fire and beset with the myriad of difficult tasks that all commanders face in battle.

He learned an even more important military lesson off the battlefield. The enormous quantities of food and water that his army needed meant that the friendship, or at least the neutrality, of the local population had to be maintained. Likewise gaining intelligence about enemy movements required either the co-operation or non-interference of the people, so he made great efforts to ensure that property was respected and goods were paid for by his forces. Following these principles greatly improved his army's mobility, cohesion, supply and prospects for victory. Such lessons later served him well in the Peninsula.

His Indian experiences made Sir Arthur a formidable commander and he developed personality traits which would one day become famous. A keen horseman and abstemious by the standards of the day, he kept himself physically fit and was always highly mobile during the chaos of battle, riding from one crisis to another to ensure that his orders were carried out. His willingness to intervene personally and refusal to delegate was both a strength and a weakness. Although his personal presence often reassured subordinates and helped ensure that tasks were followed through, it sometimes undermined their confidence. Certainly the physical demands of Sir Arthur's mobility would have taxed a lesser man.

Yet he was also mentally agile, being a meticulous planner who paid great attention to detail. Ever mindful of the need to amass intelligence, he diligently analyzed reconnaissance reports, making careful assessments of enemy strengths, capabilities and likely strategies. On the battlefield he tried to anticipate enemy moves and often made contingency plans in the event of his initial strategy failing. Essentially he was a commander who took the extra time to make plans within plans, refused to take unnecessary risks and left very little to chance.

The fact that his detailed planning was evident off the battlefield was remarkable for the period and a precursor of the way in which future wars would be fought. Though many recognized the value of a good commissariat to ensure an army was well supplied, Wellesley was unusual in taking a direct personal interest, calculating the time his forces needed to march to objectives, ensuring that sufficient campsites were found and making baggage trains mobile and secure against attack.

On his return to England in 1806, Sir Arthur was given a Knighthood of the Bath and other awards were bestowed upon him, and yet he found gaining a suitable appointment elusive. Many were jealous of his success and either attributed his swift rise to the political influence of his brothers and associates or derided victories won against Indian rather than European enemies. Considering the high calibre of the Tippoo Sultan's and Mahratta troops, this prejudice now seems absurd but it was a widely-held belief during the early nineteenth century.

He was given the command of a brigade in Hastings when the fear of French invasion was no longer serious and this appointment was therefore unlikely to win him much renown. Being underemployed by the army, he resumed his political career becoming an MP for Rye, Mitchell and Newport in quick succession. Although they had made many political enemies, the Wellesleys were still a power in Parliament and Sir Arthur made many influential new contacts. Crucially, he won a ringing endorsement from William Pitt, shortly before the great statesman's death:

> Sir Arthur Wellesley is unlike all other military men with whom I have conversed. He never makes a difficulty or hides his ignorance in vague generalities. If I put a question to him, he answers it distinctly; if I want an explanation he gives it clearly; if I desire an opinion, I get from him one supported by reasons that are always sound. He is a very remarkable man.[8]

Sir Arthur impressed many acquaintances with the breadth of his knowledge and his ability to come swiftly to the point. Being a reserved and private man he was never popular and was sometimes noted for abruptness, but he commanded respect nonetheless. This was reflected in his written orders that were almost always concise, well-phrased and left little room for misinterpretation. In a profession where ambiguous orders could lead to disaster, this was a vital asset.

His friendship with Lord Castlereagh, whom he knew from his time in Ireland, was undoubtedly influential in gaining Sir Arthur a place in the Cabinet of Portland's administration with the position of Chief Secretary for Ireland (1807–1809). This appointment made him enormously powerful in the Irish government but administering Ireland was a difficult and unenviable task, particularly in the wake of the Great Rebellion of 1798, an event marred by atrocities on both sides. As a Protestant Anglo-Irishman, Sir Arthur despaired of resolving grievances between the opposed religious and nationalist factions in his homeland but devoted himself to the role, overseeing an unremarkable and relatively peaceful term of office. Although he disliked party politics, Wellesley was a natural conservative who believed in maintaining the established order, consequently becoming a firm opponent of the revolutionary reforms that Napoleon now represented.

In 1807 Wellesley saw action again during the expedition to Copenhagen, commanding a division in Lord Cathcart's army. He was sometimes considered aloof and uncaring but Sir Arthur resolved to avoid the bombardment of cities after seeing the terrible civilian casualties the Danes suffered during the siege of Copenhagen. His division saw action at Kiöge when the Danes tried to raise the siege but the well-trained British troops easily defeated the largely militia-based Danish force. The foray was technically brilliant in military terms but the seizure of a neutral fleet was politically ill-advised and little glory was won during this brief campaign.

Wellesley received his first official instructions on 14 June as commander-in-chief of the Spanish expedition being massed at Cork in Ireland and also other forces stationed at Gibraltar. The destination of the expedition was still officially unspecified and, for the rest of the month, Wellesley busied himself preparing the Irish-based section of his army for service abroad. Unfortunately the complex British system for assembling troops, equipment and supplies fell under the remit of a number of different government departments, making this a difficult task.

Though Lord Castlereagh was Secretary for War, responsibility for concentrating the army fell partly under the auspices of other ministries, which confused matters. Even worse was the fact that negotiations with the Spaniards were being handled by Lord Canning who pursued a long-standing feud with Castlereagh. Aware of Wellesley's close association with his rival, Canning was often slow to reveal intelligence about Spain, which would be helpful in assessing the best composition of the expeditionary force. The enmity between these two eminent men eventually ended in a duel that brought political disgrace for them both.

Wellesley believed that effective campaigning demanded an efficient commissariat but he immediately ran into difficulties in forming one as it was the responsibility of the Board of Ordnance and the Treasury rather than Horse Guards. Although the expedition had been under preparation for months, the artillery lacked horses and provision for the commissariat was totally inadequate. A small wagon train existed but Horse Guards had confined their use to Ireland, fearing another serious rebellion. Wellesley was obliged to petition both the Duke of York and Castlereagh to overcome bureaucratic opposition to use part of this force.

Lack of stowage space was a major problem in the twenty-one vessels allotted to the Irish part of the expedition, while still allowing room for thousands of soldiers. Stowage for horses and wagons was limited and ships had to be specially adapted to convey horses. A few weeks at sea invariably rendered animals sick and disorientated for days or weeks after landing in addition to a high mortality rate incurred during the voyage. Nonetheless, the awesome size of the expeditionary force should be considered, bearing in mind that the Royal Navy was already conveying substantial numbers of troops around Europe, such as the force at Gibraltar and Moore's mission to Sweden. Managing these tasks simultaneously, in addition to protecting the colonies and enforcing the blockade of Europe, was well beyond the capacity of most navies during the period. In many ways securing even this limited provision was a tribute to British ingenuity, willpower and efficiency in a service that was already overstretched.

Ultimately Wellesley was only able to find room for 564 horses, thirty-four for his staff, 306 for the artillery and 224 for the cavalry. The only vehicles he could take were eighteen gun carriages, eighteen ammunition wagons, four camp equipment wagons and three forge carts.[9] Only Sir Arthur's direct intervention secured the services of two companies of the Royal Irish Corps of Wagoners and he had to transfer two assistant commissaries from the Irish establishment, which was highly irregular. Yet there was insufficient space for their wagons, meaning the army would be hugely reliant on hiring or buying baggage animals and carts immediately after reaching their destination. Such arrangements left much to be desired and Wellesley wrote scathingly to Castlereagh that

> I declare that I do not understand the principles on which our military establishments are formed if, when large corps of troops are sent out to perform important and difficult services, they are not to have with them those means of equipment which they require and which the establishment can afford ...[10]

The eventual force of 9,738 men of all ranks in Wellesley's army varied in quality. The infantry contingent was excellent with the majority of line infantry drawn from first battalions that were mostly at full strength. Fourteen companies of riflemen accompanied the expedition, which was an unusually high proportion of these elite light infantrymen. As the mainstay of any army of the period, Wellesley was well satisfied with the infantry regiments allotted to his force.

However, though two batteries of artillery accompanied the expedition, their horses provided by the Irish Commissariat were largely second-rate, most being rejected cavalry remounts. Only the 20th Light Dragoons represented the mounted arm for this mission and, while an able and experienced regiment, the 381 cavalrymen of all ranks had only 224 horses between them. Good horses were difficult to obtain in the Peninsula and Wellesley's tiny cavalry force was likely to be massively outnumbered by an enemy known to field some of the finest cavalry in Europe.

The British army was not short of cavalry regiments but, with recent internal upheaval and industrial disputes, the establishment felt they were needed to put down potential unrest, horsemen being effective for quelling riots. Despite the recent surge of patriotic feeling over Spain's plight, Britain was war-weary and restive about the restrictions the conflict had placed upon civilian life. Furthermore, the lacklustre performance of the army from 1792 to 1806 had produced few victories to inspire the nation. The government was in a quandary since, although they desperately needed a victory, success abroad would do them little good if major unrest broke out at home.

There were problems but Wellesley had a reasonably cohesive and formidable fighting force to take to Iberia. Unlike the largely conscript-based French forces, this was a professional army and morale was high at the prospect of going to war. Captain William Warre wrote that by early June rumours were rife that their destination had been altered to Spain:

> The Army are in the highest spirits; indeed the cause we are engaged in is the noblest a soldier could wish, and to support the liberties and independence of a country so lately our enemy. To forget all animosity and cordially join against the common enemy of Europe, the would-be Tyrant of the world, is worthy of the British name ...[11]

Yet the exact destination of the expedition had still to be decided. Though the government preferred landing in Spain, Britain's new-found allies were reluctant to permit their old enemy a strong foothold in their nation. News of the insurrection in Portugal was therefore well received as it presented other options. As a maritime power, the British naturally wanted a deep water harbour as a base for operations. If the Spaniards were determined to deny them this, Gibraltar and Lisbon were the only viable alternatives.

Gibraltar had been British since 1704 and could be used without difficulty, yet the Spaniards resented the fact that it remained a British possession so its use might be politically damaging. Though Lisbon was ideal in many ways, the Portuguese army was considered ineffective even before 1807 and Portuguese lack of resistance to Junot's invasion, regardless of its cause, meant that the British cabinet placed little reliance on their military capability. The French were also believed to be occupying Portugal in some strength so landing there might be fraught with difficulties. However, the main advocates for using Lisbon were the Royal Navy who, being familiar with the port, rightly favoured its strategic position, ease of access and naval facilities. The long-term friendship between the British and Portuguese was also a positive factor.

Yet the government were not prepared to commit themselves, especially as intelligence reports from the Peninsula were often contradictory and unreliable. Therefore Castlereagh allowed Wellesley a considerable degree of latitude, leaving the choice of where to land at his discretion. Conveying his majesty's wishes, he wrote '... in the rapid succession in which events must be expected to follow each other, situated as Spain and Portugal now are, much must be left to your judgement and decision on the spot'.[12]

Castlereagh advised Wellesley to go ahead of the fleet in a swift sailing frigate, land at Corunna in northern Spain and assess the situation from there. Here he would negotiate with the Spaniards and decide how to proceed based upon their advice and his own estimation of the situation. He also recommended that he send a confidential officer to carry out these liaison duties but, typically, Sir Arthur declined to accept this advice. Wellesley trusted only his own counsel and judgement in such matters, considering the hazards to his personal safety as commander-in-chief a justifiable risk under the circumstances.

Wellesley was one of Britain's foremost generals but many were envious of his success and resented his appointment over officers of greater age and seniority. Castlereagh's patronage was not enough to make his position secure. One contender for the role was Lieutenant General Sir John Moore. An officer of great experience, he had begun his career fighting in the American Revolution and had fought in European campaigns such as Corsica, the Netherlands and Egypt. Like Wellesley, he was a career soldier and was renowned for instituting reforms such as intensive light infantry training. Though an able officer, his weakness was an overly forthright manner with a barely-concealed contempt for politicians. Though Castlereagh recognized his ability, his abrupt and arrogant attitude alienated many influential politicians and Canning, in particular, loathed him.

His recent expedition to Sweden with 11,000 men ended in near farce when King Gustavas placed him under house arrest in Stockholm. His troops were denied permission to disembark and never left the ships moored in Gothenburg harbour. Many in the army believed that Moore had been given this role in order to get him out of the way and, realizing that the Swedes were not going to co-operate, he sensibly aborted the mission. Although the cabinet privately agreed with his decision, the fact that he had done this on his own authority was held against him. His lack of diplomatic skill had made him political enemies in high places and ensured that many were determined to deny him another important command.

However, the Duke of York was not prepared to discard Moore so easily, especially at the behest of politicians whom he realized were motivated by personal animosity. He was also dismissive of Sir Arthur's qualities:

> The Duke knew the worth of Sir John ... he was convinced that the
> General had been unfairly treated. He was therefore not disposed to
> allow a senior officer of tried ability and merit ... to be set aside in

favour of one whose reputation had been won against native levies in India, who was not yet forty years old, and was low on the list of Lieutenant-generals.[13]

Therefore he used his influence to ensure that Moore would be sent out to the Peninsula and assume command as soon as he returned from Sweden. This decision did not meet with the cabinet's approval and they began to scan the army lists for men of greater seniority to Moore who could take over the expedition.

Meanwhile Wellesley's military preparations were nearing completion and, since he was still officially a member of the government, he made arrangements for others to act on his behalf during his absence. One of these was an old friend, John Croker MP for County Downpatrick. After dining with the Crokers, the two men retired to the drawing room and his host noticed that the General was in a state of deep contemplation. Upon inquiry, Sir Arthur revealed that he was mulling over the problems of fighting the French:

> I have not seen them since the campaign in Flanders, when they were capital soldiers, and a dozen years of victory under Buonaparte must have made them better still. They have ... a new system of strategy, which has out-manoeuvred and overwhelmed all the armies of Europe. 'Tis enough to make one thoughtful; but no matter: my die is cast, they may overwhelm me, but I don't think they will out-manoeuvre me. First, because I am not afraid of them, as everybody else seems to be; and secondly, because if what I hear of their system of manoeuvres be true, I think it a false one against steady troops. I suspect all the continental armies were more than half-beaten before the battle was begun. I, at least, will not be frightened beforehand.[14]

Wellesley arrived in Cork on 6 July hoping to put to sea almost immediately but loading operations were incomplete and it was not until 10 July that all troops were aboard. Even then harsh weather conditions meant that the Royal Navy declined to put to sea until 12 July.[15] Once the fleet set sail, Sir Arthur swiftly transferred to the frigate HMS *Crocodile*, which soon made good progress ahead of the main force. Anxious to make a success of his appointment, Wellesley must nevertheless have paused for thought when he read the wide-ranging objectives that the government hoped he could achieve:

> The entire and absolute evacuation of the Peninsula, by the troops of France, being, after what has lately passed, the only security for Spanish independence, and the only basis upon which the Spanish nation should be prevailed upon to treat or to lay down their arms.[16]

With a force of just under 10,000 men, this was a considerable task. However, the government planned for the 4,000 men at Gibraltar under General Spencer to rendezvous with him. Within days Castlereagh was writing to inform him that a further 5,000 troops were being sent out from England under Generals Acland and Anstruther. The 11,000 men under Moore's command, recently returned from Sweden, would also be dispatched as soon as possible. It seemed that Portland's administration had finally decided to make a firm commitment to a land war in Europe. Nevertheless, it should be remembered that these troop numbers were trivial compared to the forces Napoleon could send to Iberia.

Following an eight days' journey, Sir Arthur made port at Corunna on 20 July and received a warm welcome from the Galician Junta. Though they received the news that an army was on its way as a demonstration of British resolve, they were unwilling to see it disembark on Spanish soil and advised Wellesley to sail down the coast and land in Portugal. Currently they were content with the large quantities of gunpowder, muskets and military stores the British had landed at Ferrol and Gihon but they declined to accept the offer of troops, proclaiming grandly that they had over 40,000 men under arms.

Members of the junta and officers of the Spanish army also gave him an optimistic account of how the war was progressing. They had been forced into a strategic withdrawal after the Battle of Medina del Rio Seco but claimed that Marshal Bessières' forces had lost 7,000 men and six guns. In fact, the French had managed to pry the Spanish forces out of a strong defensive position, despite being outnumbered two to one, and routed them. Blaming each other for the reverse, Generals Blake and Cuesta divided their armies and left the road to Madrid unguarded.[17] They also claimed that the siege of Zaragoza had been lifted and that Dupont's corps had met with disaster in the south (days before this actually happened). The only reliable information they gave Sir Arthur was that the Portuguese uprising in Porto was serious and worthy of support.

Sir Arthur was greatly impressed by the reception he received from the Galicians and heartened to hear that sympathy for the French was virtually non-existent in Spain. As yet unfamiliar with the subtleties of Spanish diplomacy and the unreliable nature of regional intelligence, he took most of their news at face value and agreed that the Portuguese stood in greater need of assistance.[18] The Spanish were in fact living in a fool's paradise concerning the course of the war and would soon regret spurning the offer of British troops.

After a brief rendezvous with the fleet, HMS *Crocodile* again sailed ahead and landed at the city of Porto on 24 July. Although warmly received, Sir Arthur swiftly realized that the Supreme Junta were despondent about recent events. The intelligence he gained from the Bishop of Porto was dispiriting but honest and accurate. The Portuguese had learned of the recent battle and were under no illusions that Medina del Rio Seco had been a clear Spanish defeat. So far they had assembled only 5,000 infantry and 300 cavalry under General Bernardino Freire at Coimbra, a sizable proportion of which was militia. They maintained a garrison of 1,500 at Porto and had raised 12,000 volunteers but these were largely equipped with pikes and makeshift weapons. Even the regular troops lacked sufficient muskets and the Bishop admitted: 'The people are ready and desirous to take arms, but unfortunately there are none in the country.'[19]

Nonetheless, they were keen to see the British land to help them against the French and would gratefully accept any arms they could provide. Wellesley promised to equip regular troops but qualified this with the proviso that he needed to review them first and decide if they were worthy before distributing muskets. He inquired earnestly about baggage animals and transport in the locality and was pleased when the Bishop agreed to provide 500 mules and 150 horses for the expedition along with as many wagons as could be found.[20]

During the following campaign, in spite of the immense logistical difficulties Wellesley encountered, the British still managed to field more men than the French at the forthcoming battles of Roliça and Vimeiro. In addition, they amassed a near parity in numbers with the entire French deployment in Portugal by the end of hostilities. The British military system may have been confusing and occasionally inefficient but this was achieved despite the added problem of transporting all the forces concerned by sea to be landed in the kind of combined arms operation which even modern strategists find intimidating. The fact that they overcame these problems in 1808 is a tribute to the persistence and determination of both the British army and the Royal Navy.

All that remained now was to select suitable landing sites. Admiral Cotton and Wellesley agreed that the beaches further south were covered by the French-held fortress of Peniche and were close enough to Lisbon to risk serious interference from the French while the army was vulnerable during landing operations. Consulting with the Portuguese, they decided to disembark at Figueiras-da-Foz in Mondego Bay.

Artillery officer Captain Eliot was well-qualified to assess the coastal defences here, commenting '. . . the bay appears strongly fortified and is in the possession of the Portuguese who have lately risen on the French and driven them out'.[21] Therefore the fact that the Santa Catarina fort had fallen into Portuguese hands and was garrisoned by marines was indeed fortunate. Near the Mondego estuary were long beaches where troops could be set ashore. However, the Atlantic Ocean beats with exceptional ferocity on this exposed stretch of coastline and the task of landing horses and artillery would be a trial.

Disembarkation began on 1 August 1808 and local conditions hampered the operation, Warre recording: 'It took three days to land the whole army, and had we been opposed from the land I am positive we could never have effected it, so great is the surf both on the coast and the bar.'[22] Without the services of a large harbour, the warships and transports had to anchor offshore and munitions, horses and guns were rowed ashore in flat-bottomed boats. Morale was raised by the news that General Dupont had suffered a catastrophic defeat at Spanish hands at Bailén on 20 July. After an almost unbroken tally of French victories, this was welcome news and the allies set to work enthusiastically.

Just as operations were finishing, another fleet bringing General Spencer's 4,000 men from Gibraltar arrived. The force had been delayed through fears of antagonizing the Junta of Seville but eventually Spencer set sail, acting on his own authority, guessing correctly that his arrival would be welcomed. Captain Harry Ross-Lewin of the 32nd sailed with this force and recorded the struggle they had in landing: 'Some boats that made the attempt were swamped, and about twenty men and a few horses were drowned.'[23]

Yet help was at hand and local fishermen assisted with the landings, swimming out to rescue soldiers swept out of the boats and carrying many half-drowned men ashore upon their shoulders. These efforts were much appreciated, Ross-Lewin writing:

> No people could have behaved better ... they were full of enthusiasm; they regarded us as their future deliverers from the insolence and oppression of the French, and they certainly adopted a handsome method of giving us a welcome to their land.[24]

Wellesley now commanded an army of 13,000 men to lead against Lisbon and he expected even more reinforcements from England that would eventually bring British numbers in Portugal to over 25,000 men. Yet the dispatches contained ominous news. Castlereagh's letter dated 15 July informed him that he was about to be replaced, several officers being en route to Portugal who held seniority over him. Any officer would be dismayed to hear such news but Sir Arthur dutifully wrote back that:

> All I can say ... is, that whether I am to command this army or not, or am to quit it, I shall do my best to ensure its success; and ... shall not hurry the operations ... in order that I may acquire the credit for the business.[25]

Wellesley had always been aware that his position was likely to be short-lived but now he would be outranked by other officers in addition to Sir John Moore. Members of the cabinet, resenting Moore's appointment, had ensured that generals enjoying seniority over Moore were also dispatched. Horse Guards had instructed General Dalrymple to take over the expeditionary force with General Burrard as his second-in-command. Not only would Wellesley lose control of the army but he might be allotted a junior role and be lucky to command a brigade due to this political interference.

Many men would have resigned upon receiving such an unmerited slight but Wellesley was determined to see his part through in honourable fashion. Nonetheless, it was only natural that he was deeply upset and he wrote of his anger at the government's decision to Richmond (then Lord Lieutenant of Ireland) in a private letter. Contradicting what he had previously written, he admitted that: 'I hope I shall have beaten Junot before any of them arrive, and then they may do as they please with me.'[26]

Chapter 6

'One of our most important affairs'

One advantage of landing so far from Lisbon was that the British would have time for their soldiers and horses to acclimatize, having spent weeks in cramped conditions aboard ship. Had the expeditionary force landed closer to the capital, intending to mount a swift assault on the city, these limitations would have delayed them in any case. Sir Arthur also had time to liaise with the Portuguese, arrange for suitable transportation and get the army in a state of readiness to meet the enemy.

Having been born and raised in Portugal, Captain Warre spoke fluent Portuguese and was eager to see the country of his birth again. His linguistic skills meant his services were sought after, being the only Portuguese language-speaker in his entire brigade. As an ADC for General Ferguson, he was constantly riding from place to place, liaising between the British and locals to resolve problems during the landings. The whole operation was impeded by the need to campaign during the hottest season of the year: 'The severest part of the business is in these infamous roads and scorching sun, which with the large train of Artillery and Baggage will oblige us to move very slow.'[1]

Everything slows down in Portugal during August as attempting any taxing physical task in the oppressive heat is arduous. Warre's experience was shared by a number of diarists during the campaign, one of whom commented:

> We marched for twelve miles, up to the knees in sand, which caused us to suffer much from thirst, for the marching made it rise and cover us. We lost four men of our regiment, who died of thirst. We buried them where they fell.[2]

Marching in this intense heat presented a serious problem to all the armies involved in the 1808 campaign.

Writing to Captain Lord Burghersh, an aide on his staff, Wellesley thought he might add 2,000–5,000 Portuguese soldiers to his army. He was reluctant to take any more as combined allied operations were always difficult where command and language issues were concerned and accepting too many might be counter-productive.[3] He was eager to press on, writing: 'Spencer has arrived, and his corps will probably be here to-morrow. You had better return, therefore, as I shall march as soon as they will be on shore.'[4]

He inspected General Freire's infantry at Montemor Velho on 7 August, just north of the Mondego, and issued 5,000 muskets, along with bayonets and cartouches, to the best regiments. Freire wanted more arms and ammunition but Wellesley was reluctant to give munitions to inexperienced militia and volunteer levies. Relations between the two men got off to a bad start but Freire agreed to rendezvous with Wellesley's army when it reached Leiria.

What the allies really needed was more cavalry to form an effective army. Fortunately for the allies, French rule was so unpopular that even members of the deeply conservative Lisbon Police Legion questioned their allegiance to Junot's regime. Hearing that the insurgents were forming a regular army, Commander Elesiario de Carvalho of the Legion decided to join his country-men though some fellow officers 'did not approve of our projects, from want of resolution, fear, or urgent considerations of private interest'.[5] Nevertheless, upon parading his company he

> ... invited them to aid in the glorious enterprise of restoring the independence of Portugal, which had been so basely wrested from its lawful Sovereign ... energetically impressed them with the critical situation to which they would be reduced, should the Portuguese army come into contact with the corps ... that they would be forced into an action with their fellow countrymen, and involved in the guilt of mutual destruction – in the most dreadful and horrible of all contests ...[6]

The prospect of being forced to fight their own countrymen in a civil war proved decisive, his whole company agreeing to abscond. Joining with the 4th Company under Commander Andrada, they formed a combined squadron of fifty-six files and rode north.

Lisbon's Police Legion was the largest armed body of Portuguese fighting men left in the country under the French, being roughly 1,200 strong. The Legion was considered vital to maintain peace in the capital and, hearing about this defection its commandant, French expatriate Count de Novion, sent a dispatch to the Governor of Santarém requesting assistance. The French governor subsequently ordered Sergeant Gambus to take a detachment of Portuguese infantry and waylay them:

> A party of the cavalry of my legion had just deserted, with their arms and baggage ... I request in the name of his Excellency the Duke of Abrantes, that you will place in ambush some picquets of infantry, in sufficient force to intercept this party, who are proceeding to reinforce the insurgents, and to apprehend some of them for the purpose of making an example.[7]

Gambus did indeed lie in wait for the cavalry but, upon their approach, declared his hatred for the French and joined them with his entire command. Upon their arrival at Coimbra, they were welcomed into the ranks by the governor and General Andrada. Carvalho gave an impassioned speech claiming that they had abandoned their posts only through the patriotic desire to ensure the Regent's return: 'The effort to restore him is heroic; our fidelity is unalterable, and under your command, we shall without dread encounter every danger, the enemy, or even death itself.'[8]

The following day, Lieutenant Antonio Pereira led a column of men drafted from the former 6th and 9th Portuguese cavalry regiments into Coimbra. He had been serving under Baron de Viomenil at Salvaterra-de-Magos but now commanded sixty-six cavalrymen with seventy horses, having travelled 60 leagues to get there. Although the sergeants and men had been enthusiastic to desert, he wrote of the need for secrecy as at least four senior Portuguese officers would have reported or arrested him had they been aware of his intentions.[9]

Having set off on 3 July he joined with a party under Sergeant Teixeira. The sergeant was under the orders of a French officer and Pereira had ordered him 'to kill or carry off the Lieutenant should he offer any resistance'.[10] With many guard posts along the river to avoid, crossing the Tejo was difficult but they encountered increasing signs of disaffection towards the French as they rode northwards. Passing near Thomar, they learned that the town was in open revolt and Governor Antonio de Val asked for their help fearing attack by forces under General Laborde, though their assistance subsequently proved unnecessary. The peasantry were flocking to join the rebellion and their way north was blocked several times:

> All the towns and villages under arms, conceiving we were a French corps coming to attack them, were perpetually planting ambuscades on my route. I was obliged to appease them by gentle means, and had no little difficulty in convincing them, that I, as well as themselves, wished to join the army, in order to defend our most just cause.[11]

Arriving at Coimbra on 5 August, Pereira's men were reviewed by General Andrada and allowed to enlist. The scarcity of horses and trained cavalry in the Peninsula meant that their services would be invaluable to the allies.

Wellesley had around 13,000 British soldiers under his command, which he hoped to combine with approximately 5,000 Portuguese under Freire when they met at Leiria. Conferring with Admiral Cotton, he agreed to provide a veteran battalion of older soldiers who might not withstand the hard marching he anticipated. These would assist the Royal Navy in making a show of force near the mouth of the Tejo, which might persuade the French that landings were imminent and induce them to commit troops there who might otherwise oppose Wellesley's advance.

He hoped to receive 5,000 men under Acland shortly and was aware that even more would arrive over the next few weeks. In order to rendezvous with these reinforcements and receive provisions from the Royal Navy, Sir Arthur meant to hug the coastline as much as possible during his march south. By 8 August he had not decided whether to take Peniche but, if he received substantial reinforcements, he might have enough men to besiege this coastal fort in addition to detaching forces to send to Santarém. These would cut off one French escape route should they decide to abandon Lisbon. He reasoned that a French withdrawal on Elvas would be difficult to prevent but their need to cross the Tejo would slow such a move.[12]

Once Junot heard of the British landings, the prospects for the French during the developing campaign looked increasingly bleak. Though news of Bessières' recent victory had restored French morale somewhat, Dupont's surrender at Bailén was a shattering blow. In addition, King Joseph's retreat from Madrid to the line of the River Ebro placed thousands of miles of hostile territory between Junot and the main French forces in Iberia. With little prospect of reinforcement, his best chance was to concentrate a big enough army to defeat Wellesley before the allies gained a secure foothold. Failure to do this would see the insurgency grow in strength and, backed by a regular army, it would be extremely difficult to defeat.

French forces were spread over a wide area of Portugal when the British landed and Junot immediately sent out dispatches to recall those that he could. Loison was engaged in operations around Badajoz when he received orders to return. He felt obliged to garrison Elvas but marched back with around 6,000 men. The garrison of Almeida (1,200 strong) was deemed out of reach as it was ringed by insurgents and before those troops could be called upon, the fortress must be relieved.

Junot repeatedly sought Siniavin's aid, arguing that the campaign would undoubtedly decide the fate of his fleet. Now that their British enemy had intervened directly, the Russians no longer had the excuse of remaining neutral and yet: 'Siniavin obstinately turned a deaf ear to all the propositions that were made to him, declaring that he would not fight, unless the English vessels endeavoured to force the entrance of the river.'[13] Citing the overwhelming naval superiority of the enemy, the Admiral declared that his fleet would be annihilated within days if it left the protection of the estuary. Junot had hoped that the Russians could at least distract the Royal Navy by initiating an action close to the river mouth, allowing him to take men from the river forts' garrisons. Russian intransigence meant that men who he needed desperately to oppose the British must remain and protect the capital.

Aware of the allies' approach, Junot

> charged Delaborde, the senior general-of-division in the army,
> to advance against the enemy, to watch his movements, and to
> manoeuvre in such a manner as to retard his march, so that time
> might be gained for General Loison and the reserves to place
> themselves in line.[14]

General Henri Delaborde had joined the army as a private and, after becoming an officer, had risen from lieutenant to general in only two years (1791–1793). A highly-experienced soldier, he was also a capable commander and extremely popular with his men. Junot hoped that Delaborde could buy time for Loison to march up from the south, sending him north with an under-strength division of roughly 5,700 men on 6 August.[15]

Wellesley marched three days later; having made great progress in forming his artillery and baggage train, buying or hiring large numbers of mules and wagons. Yet a force of between 13,000–14,000 men required vast amounts of provisions and equipment and he issued a general order in consequence: 'The practice of pressing carts and mules is positively forbid. If carts are wanted for any service, application must be made for them to the Commissary-General ...'[16] The Bishop of Porto had been helpful in providing transport and Wellesley wrote to him, asking to retain the services of Mr Fernandez, who had already provided great assistance: '... his knowledge of the country and its inhabitants will give great facility to our endeavours to procure supplies and means of conveyance.'[17] Despite Sir Arthur's efforts, the logistical demands of the expedition were daunting and he still required further means of transportation.

Portuguese and British forces met at Leiria on 11 August but their commanders immediately began to argue. Freire had already stated that they should march on Lisbon by an internal route where they would find more supplies. Marching near the coast was likely to lead to a clash on open ground and he believed the allies stood a greater chance of success if they travelled through the hills towards Santarém, taking advantage of the high ground for defensive purposes. However, Wellesley did not want to sever connections with the fleet and, anticipating difficulties in dragging artillery through rough country, believed such a course would slow their progress.[18]

Supplies had been gathered at Leiria after prior arrangement with the junta but 'General Freire's people appropriated the provisions for their own use ...'[19] which provoked further disagreements, culminating in Freire's refusal to combine with Wellesley's army. Oman believed that a desire to retain an independent command lay at the heart of his objections[20] but, after some negotiation, Freire agreed to leave 1,600 light infantry and some cavalry with Wellesley under

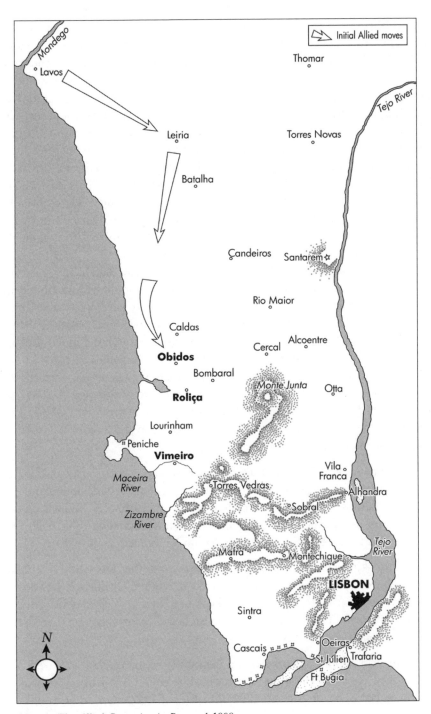

Map 4: The Allied Campaign in Portugal 1808

Colonel Nicholas Trant, an Irishman in Portuguese service. Leslie of the 29th Regiment wrote that: 'They were in a very indifferent state, and it could hardly have been otherwise, it having been the French policy to disorganise the whole army.'[21] General Hill later referred to these infantry as 'ragamuffins' but the cavalry that joined them at Caveiro and Caldas over the next few days were well-equipped and welcome additions to an army seriously deficient in that arm.

Wellesley suspected that he would soon encounter the enemy and left most tents and unnecessary baggage behind at Leiria, along with some guns due to the shortage of mule teams to drag them. Reaching Alcobaça, he was informed that General Thomières had abandoned the town the previous day and his cavalry brought news that the enemy were in the vicinity. Here the allies benefited from the support of the locals who freely told them all they knew about enemy activity, whereas the French had to rely on their patrols alone due to the hostility of the population.

Delaborde initially planned to stop the allies at nearby Batalha but, receiving reports of their superior strength, now judged that he would be surrounded and overwhelmed if he did so. Pulling back to a better defensive position at Roliça, he left a rearguard at Obidos.[22] It was here that the first British shots of the war were fired when light infantry in the vanguard encountered French picquets at a windmill on the outskirts of the town. Four companies of the 95th and 60th Foot attacked this outpost and immediately pressed on towards the town driving the enemy before them. However, they pursued too far and, being opposed by large numbers of tirailleurs, a vicious fire-fight ensued. They suffered some losses and the arrival of French cavalry compelled them to retreat, Rifleman Harris recalling:

> I had never heard such a tremendous noise as the firing made on this occasion, and I occasionally observed that the men on both sides of me were falling fast. Being overmatched, we retired to a ... hillock, in our rear and formed there all round its summit, standing three deep, the front rank kneeling. In this position we remained all night ...[23]

After this skirmish, the French withdrew from the town and the allied army followed in their wake. The initial clash, while inconclusive, had at least demonstrated that British troops were keen to fight and Wellesley recorded his satisfaction with their progress. He had also heard reports that another French force (Loison's) was nearby:

> The army is in high spirits, and beginning to march tolerably well, and I have every prospect of success. The enemy are retiring before us in two divisions, one of 4,000, the other of 5,000 men; and I would try to cut off one of them, only they outmarch us.[24]

The French had justifiably gained a great reputation for swift marching but, when Wellesley learned that Delaborde had halted and showed signs of opposing his march, it raised the potential threat of two French forces combining against him. Nevertheless, when reports came in that the French were in some strength at Roliça, he resolved to attack the next day. Wellesley habitually had the army stand to just before dawn and, when all was ready, they marched from Obidos at 7:00 am on 17 August.

Delaborde had selected good defensive ground. The town of Roliça lies on a sandy plain, roughly 3 miles south-west of Obidos. The plain is contained in a three-sided basin of hills with those to the south forming a cross ridge connecting the ranges on either flank and marked by a large eminence, which dominates the flatlands. Delaborde had drawn up his men on Roliça Hill, just before the village, but did not intend seriously to contest this area, planning to fall back to a secondary position behind the village of Columbeira. He meant to withdraw and defend the heights whose main approach from the plain was via four large ravines seaming the ridge. The hillsides were steep and marked with occasional woods and tough undergrowth providing concealment for light infantry, and the reverse slopes behind the hill crests would give some protection from artillery fire.

Wellesley divided his army into three main columns. Commanding the main force in the centre of 9,000 infantry in three and a half brigades with twelve guns, he decided to engage and pin the enemy while two forces moved up on either flank to envelop them. On the right flank Trant's brigade of 1,200 Portuguese infantry and fifty cavalry would work their way through the hills and fall upon the French left. Meanwhile, General Ferguson's force comprising two infantry brigades, forty Anglo/Portuguese cavalry and six guns would mirror this manoeuvre and attempt to turn the French right. If all went well, the French would be surrounded by a force four times their own strength and thus be compelled to surrender.

As Wellesley advanced, his artillery batteries unlimbered and deployed, opening fire at long range. The French were impressed by the precise and well-disciplined manoeuvring of the British infantry on the plain. Major Ross-Lewin with the 32nd recalled: 'As we approached the enemy, the utmost order was preserved, and the columns were increased and diminished with as much regularity as if we were at a review.'[25] French artillery fired upon the advancing British and their skirmishers clashed with the light infantry preceding the attack as they neared Roliça Hill.

The flank attacks initially made poor progress but Ferguson was now beginning to get into position and had engaged with his skirmishers. Yet Delaborde now gave the order to fall back just before the main body was seriously threatened.[26] The rear of his position was marked with low trees and

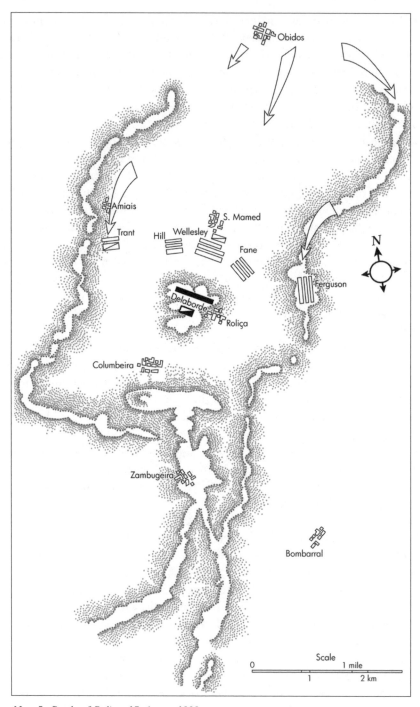

Map 5: Battle of Roliça, 17 August 1808

undergrowth, which the French made good use of during their well-timed with-drawal, Ross-Lewin conceding that they 'retired under cover as we advanced; this we had reason to expect from old soldiers, who knew how to take advantage of their ground'.[27]

The French levelled an accurate and telling fire on the allies as they advanced, to which they had little chance to respond due to the slowness of their flanking forces getting into position. The 29th pressed forward to pursue the enemy through Columbeira but were forced to redirect their march to the left of the village because of heavy fire from sharpshooters on the hillside and artillery covering the French withdrawal. Leslie commented:

> Their right was filing to the rear, masked by a cloud of skirmishers, posted on some rising ground covered with brushwood at the foot of the mountains, and warmly engaged with General Fane's rifle-men. Their left had retired through the village of Columbeira, and occupied the heights.[28]

Seeing many of his men fall as the attack faltered around Columbeira, Colonel Lake of the 29th felt the need to inspire his regiment, calling out: 'Gentlemen, display the colours,' the colours flew, and shortly afterwards he again turned . . . 'Soldiers, I shall remain in front of you, and remember that the bayonet is the only weapon for a British soldier.'[29] Lake had won a considerable reputation in India fighting under Wellesley and was extremely popular with his men as a fearless and experienced soldier who led from the front. Several sources attest to him having dressed in his finest uniform for the battle and remarking: 'Egad, sir, if I am killed to-day, I mean to die like a gentleman.'[30]

Wellesley now deployed his artillery on Roliça Hill and they began bombarding the heights. Undeterred by his failure to envelop the enemy, he repeated his strategy, sending Trant and Ferguson up the hillsides on either flank aiming to turn the second French position in the same manner. Since they outnumbered the French by so much, there was little the enemy could do about this, though it might take some time. One weakness in this plan was the possibility of Loison's division appearing on the eastern side of the battlefield but, should this occur, they were likely to encounter Ferguson's force first and Wellesley had purposely made this the stronger of the two flanking columns to compensate for the risk.

Trant's column was ordered to swing out far to the right, hoping to not only turn the French left flank but to enter the hills in Delaborde's rear and potentially cut him off.[31] Sir Arthur had chosen the Portuguese for this task partly because he may have distrusted their fighting ability, as this was their first battle, but also due to their knowledge of the local topography since manoeuvring around the deep gorge behind Columbeira would be a difficult task.

Though Delaborde had managed to withdraw successfully with only slight losses, all Wellesley needed to do was to engage and apply pressure on the French centre, then wait for Delaborde's flanks to be assailed. The British were now deployed before the heights and sent skirmishers up the four ravines before them as their artillery began to fire upon the hill crests. Delaborde had used the advantage of this ground to the full, positioning his main formations behind the crests where the lethal bouncing effect of roundshot would be lessened. The artillerymen were also handicapped by the need to fire upwards at a steep angle and some French officers ordered their men to lie down, which in itself limited the efficiency of roundshot, already reduced by the protection of thickets and bushes along the heights.

All the allies had to do was be patient and advance slowly but the impetuous Colonel Lake now led four companies of his battalion directly up one gully to assault the French position, one officer recording:

> We now entered the pass, which was extremely steep, narrow, and craggy, being the dried-up bed of a mountain torrent, so that at some places only two or three men could get up at a time. The enemy kept up a tremendous fire at point blank upon us ...[32]

Nevertheless, they climbed upward as fast as the ground would allow, wanting to come to grips with the enemy.

As soon as they reached more level ground near the top of the ravine, Lake deployed his men into line, using a thicket on his flank for protection. They had already suffered losses and Lake's horse was killed under him. Taking a horse offered to him by Major Way, Lake rode along the line exhorting his men to prepare for a charge as soon as they were reinforced by the rest of the battalion. At this point

> ... the enemy, who appeared to have been lying down behind a broken earthen fence ... suddenly rose up and opened fire, their officers seemed to endeavour to restrain them, and apparently urged them on to the charge, as we observed them knocking down the men's firelocks with their swords, but they did not advance.[33]

The action became confused, the 29th being shot at not only from the front but from both flanks and their rear, having advanced to a point above one French battalion. Some soldiers from the 4th Swiss Regiment even tried to surrender to them, many being discontented in French service. Way later commented that some French units declined to fire upon them, thinking that they must be their Swiss allies as both wore red uniform jackets, which must have added to the chaos on both sides.[34]

Men were now falling rapidly and Lake was wounded in the back of the neck by a skirmisher and then fatally shot through his left side at close range. With their Colonel down, the men wavered and Way remembered the intensity of the musketry fire, his sword blade being shattered in his hand leaving him holding only the hilt. Realizing that the enemy was behind them, and fearing to be cut off, a French battalion now rushed the harried companies from the rear:

> ... the French in considerable force charged us and myself and two more officers may thank the French General of Brigade – Brennier – for our lives who rescued us from the Bayonets and fury of the soldiers. At the moment we were captured I had the point of one entering my Sash at the time the French General averted the blow ...[35]

Wellesley felt obliged to order an advance to try to extricate the 29th without waiting for his flanking units to engage.

A series of French counter-attacks drove the remnants of the four companies back down into the ravine but they were now reinforced by elements of their own battalion and that of the 9th under Colonel Stuart, who fought their way upwards. Struggling back up to the brow of the hill, they began to deploy into line and engage in a more equal fire-fight with the French. As the 5th Regiment, who encountered considerably less opposition, came up on their flank the British began to gain a foothold.[36]

Observing that Ferguson's force had made contact with his right wing, Delaborde detached three companies of the 70th Ligne to skirmish with the approaching light infantry. The tirailleurs used the crest of the hill skilfully to shield their movements and, each time the British light infantry began to make progress, they mounted bayonet charges. Yet they were gradually pushed back by Ferguson's riflemen while the fighting in the centre intensified. For a while the French contested the ridge, advancing to the hill crests to trade musketry volleys and mount bayonet charges to try to dislodge the three battalions just above the ravines. At least three assaults were made against them, which were repulsed with difficulty until the allies brought up more troops. The ground before the ridgeline was difficult to fight over and Harris, skirmishing before Ferguson's advance, admitted: 'We had ourselves caught it pretty handsomely; for there was no cover for us, and were rather too near.'[37] As the three battalions were reinforced, the allies began to press the French back into the open farmland that gently sloped down behind the brow of the ridge.

By this time, Delaborde realized that Loison was unlikely to arrive on the battlefield and, seeing that his right flank was about to be turned by Ferguson,

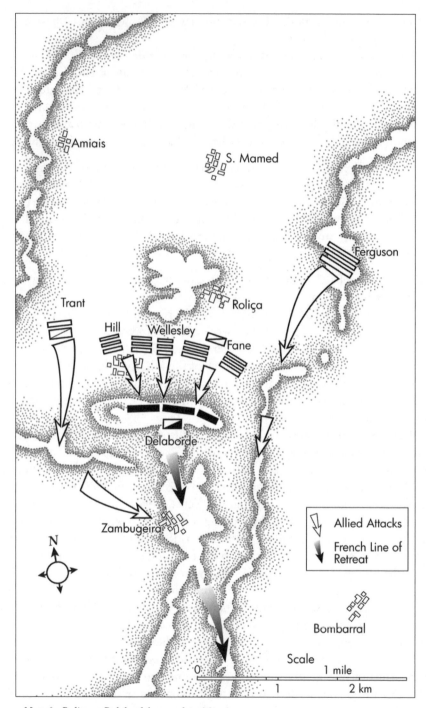

Map 6: Roliça – Delaborde's second position

he ordered a general withdrawal, bringing up the 26th Chasseurs à Cheval (his only cavalry) to cover the retreat. He had his division retire two battalions at a time, while the other two stood to repel pursuit. Delaborde skilfully alternated this pattern and gradually fell back while the Chasseurs made several short, controlled charges to discourage the British skirmishers pursuing them.

The small number of cavalry available now restricted allied ability to press the French retreat. The steepness of the ridge prevented Wellesley from advancing with cavalry in the centre and the slowness of the flank attacks meant the French had a considerable start on pursuers arriving from those directions. However, once they reached a defile beyond Zambugeira, the retreat became disordered due to the narrowness of the road and they were forced to abandon three guns and some prisoners, revealing that the pursuit was at least partly effective.

Harris recalled that French skirmishers covering the French withdrawal were established in a group of small farm buildings, from which they laid down a heavy fire of musketry at their pursuers. Maddened by this sustained fire and the losses they had taken, one of his comrades

> ... jumping up, rushed forward crying, 'Over, boys! – over! – over!' When instantly the whole line responded to the cry ... They ran along the grass like wildfire, and dashed at the rise, fixing their sword bayonets as they ran. The French ... could not stand the sight, but turned about, and fled ...[38]

After Roliça, alterations in British army uniforms came into effect, which went down well with the rank and file. Many pieces of equipment were now discarded as old-fashioned or, more importantly, too expensive: 'It is recorded that the men of the regiment fought in queues, and powdered hair, and carrying hairy packs of a pattern long forgotten; and the officers in cocked hats, worn athwartships, in the fashion of the preceding decade.'[39] Officers now wore their bicorne hats 'fore to aft' and the black, knee-length gaiters worn by most of the infantry were also dispensed with. Though many of these articles were tiresome to maintain and better suited to peacetime soldiering, Napoleon's Continental System was partly to blame, especially concerning the importation of hair powder and wigs. In any case, the majority of the army were pleased and did not mourn the passing of these adornments.

The French suffered 600 casualties at Roliça but, significantly, very few prisoners were taken. This appears to endorse Wellesley's oft-repeated complaint that he was poorly supplied with cavalry in the Peninsula, who were invaluable for pursuit, during which the majority of captives were usually taken. Nevertheless, the allies pressed the French withdrawal enough to take three guns; the capture of cannon often being taken as an indication of victory. The British suffered 441 killed, wounded or taken prisoner. The majority of the Portuguese soldiers present marched under Trant who, never having engaged the enemy seriously, either suffered no casualties or failed to record them. Yet Trant had a longer route to travel than Ferguson and needed to circumnavigate the deep gorge on the French left. Unsurprisingly, the first battalion of the 29th sustained the worst losses, with 190 casualties and prisoners. Warre commented on the high proportion of officers in the casualties suffered at Roliça, including his friend Colonel Stuart of the 9th Regiment who died of his wounds on 20 August, along with two other officers killed in his brigade alone.[40]

As is often the case regarding inconclusive clashes, both sides claimed a victory. Though the French made much of the disparity in numbers, the amount of troops who actually engaged had been nearly equal and the French enjoyed strong defensive ground at their secondary position. Nevertheless, as Oman conceded: 'Delaborde had fought a most admirable rearguard action, holding on to the last moment, and escaping by his prompt manoeuvres ...'[41] However, he went on to say that Delaborde could have avoided fighting at all since he had already delayed Wellesley and the likelihood of joining with Loison was remote, Loison being so many miles away that he barely heard cannon fire in the distance. In addition, Loison's force was tired and probably ineffective having marched for days and he would not have wished to fight a serious action. Therefore he concluded that Delaborde had risked his division for little gain.[42]

Wellesley was pleased with the way his army had performed. Admittedly, the flanking actions executed by his subordinates developed rather slowly but this was their first action in the Peninsula and Trant's force comprised largely untested men. Had it not been for Lake's impetuous actions, the British would not have suffered so many casualties and the fact that Delaborde withdrew only when Ferguson's two brigades came up on his right reveals that Sir Arthur's strategy was sound. In subsequent years, Wellesley became famous for his skill in defensive deployment, which led to unfair criticism over a perceived reluctance to attack. Although well-known for deploying his men on the reverse slopes of ridges to minimize casualties and for responding to enemy moves rather than taking the initiative, the impression that Wellesley was a purely defensive general is misleading as Hadaway argues

> ... at Vimeiro and Talavera he uses the 'reverse slope' tactic that has, quite wrongly, become the image of Wellesley in the Peninsula. It was not a tactic he used widely and certainly not one he invented. The first person to use this tactic in an Anglo-French battle, was Delaborde.[43]

Though Roliça revealed Wellesley's offensive capability, his campaigns in India gave ample evidence of this well beforehand. Hadaway remarks on Wellesley's surprising caution at Roliça, so much at odds with his fighting in India, though this may have been due to the potential for Loison to link with Delaborde.[44] His careful manoeuvring on the plain took up most of the morning of 17 August and his failure to outflank the French swiftly enough permitted them to retire to a better position and ultimately allowed them to evade pursuit without sustaining major losses. Certainly Thiébault's claim that Delaborde won valuable time for Junot to concentrate his forces is not unjustified.[45]

Long after the war, when Earl Stanhope, a close friend of Wellesley's, implied that Roliça was insignificant compared with his other Peninsula triumphs, the Duke objected:

> ... I called Roliça a skirmish. 'No,' said the Duke, who overheard me, 'Roliça was one of our most important affairs; it was terrible hard work to drive off the French. When we had got possession of the heights, they attacked us, and I had only three battalions to stand firm against them. Our men fought monstrous well.'[46]

It was indeed a hard-fought action. Aware of the fearsome reputation the French army had gained on the Continent, he advanced cautiously and refused to take risks in his first major encounter with them. The subsequent battle demonstrated his wisdom in adopting this strategy. Delaborde's skilful use of terrain and delaying tactics showed how formidable the French could be in defence, warranting this methodical approach. Anticipating a major battle within days, Wellesley must therefore have wondered what kind of opposition he would encounter when faced with a much larger enemy force.

Chapter 7

The Lion and the Eagle

News that a squadron conveying reinforcements from England lay off the coast persuaded Wellesley to alter his line of march to rendezvous with the Royal Navy. He received this information on the morning of 17 August and, following the clash at Roliça, dispatched messengers to the fleet to say that he would meet them at the mouth of the River Maceira and cover the disembarkation with his army.

The allied army reached Maceira Bay on 19 August, occupying positions in and around Vimeiro and along the ridges on either side of this village. Wellesley placed his main strength on the Valongo Ridge to the west of Vimeiro, where he believed any French attacks would be likely to concentrate since they could potentially cut his army off from the sea. At first, the weather was unusually calm, meaning that troop transports were unable to stand in towards the shore until late afternoon but the bulk of Acland's brigade landed that evening and Anstruther's brigade began to disembark the next day, though the high surf hampered these operations significantly.[1]

Enemy cavalry were now active in the area to the detriment of allied reconnaissance, their inferior numbers of cavalry preventing them from countering French movements effectively. Yet information still arrived through Portuguese sources, to the extent that Sir Arthur and his staff had difficulty sifting through it and judging its reliability. Most reports spoke of a large enemy force massing around Torres Vedras, confirming Wellesley's prediction that the French meant to give battle north of Lisbon. He gave orders that the army would march early on the morning of 21 August towards Mafra, which might allow him to make a move against the French left flank. He issued a general order: 'The men to sleep accoutred to-night, in readiness to turn out, and to be under arms at three o'clock in the morning.'[2] At 4:00 am the majority of the troops would be issued rations for a long march.

However, Wellesley's plans were disrupted by the arrival of General Sir Harry Burrard aboard HMS *Brazen*, which put into Maceira Bay that evening. Burrard initially intended to come ashore that night to assume command, but Sir Arthur pre-empted this by having himself rowed out to the frigate and the pair held a council of war concerning allied progress in the campaign so far.

At 53 Lieutenant General Burrard was a soldier of some experience but had seen little active campaigning in recent years. Under Generals Howe and Cornwallis, he saw extensive service in North America during the colonists' rebellion against British rule 1775–1783. He also served in Flanders 1793–1795 and had been captured by the French. During the Copenhagen Expedition 1807 he commanded a division and had briefly been second-in-command to Lord Cathcart. Dispatched at short notice to take over a campaign which was already under way, he was uncertain of his ground and wished to learn as much as he could from Wellesley. Naturally this state of affairs made him reluctant to act hastily in the knowledge that taking over shortly after a successful battle would undoubtedly cause resentment with his predecessor and within the army who had become used to his leadership. He was well aware that it was unlikely to be an easy transition of power.

Sir Arthur did his best to bring his successor up to date about affairs in Portugal but gave a poor impression of the campaign's prospects. Though progress had been made, allied cavalry was at a disadvantage and French superiority in that arm meant that Junot was likely to be well appraised of their numbers and positions and could prevent them from gaining similar intelligence about his own position. The enemy were already familiar with the territory and Burrard correctly guessed that Wellesley underestimated the number of French troops in the country (Sir Arthur believed the French fielded little more than 18,000 at this point). In addition, the artillery lacked transport whereas French artillery was renowned for its manoeuvrability.

Although Wellesley's efforts with the commissariat had assembled an adequate wagon train, it was only just sufficient for the troops he already possessed and the arrival of two new brigades meant that further provision was necessary. Burrard pointed out that the army was still largely reliant on supply by sea and, if the fleet were dispersed by the gales which were commonplace during this season, this tenuous link would be broken. Finally he argued that the recently-landed brigades needed time to recover from their voyage before they could be expected to march great distances. Therefore he ordered Sir Arthur to remain at Vimeiro while these problems were addressed and await the arrival of the fleet conveying Sir John Moore's troops, expected within days. The Anglo-Portuguese army now comprised around 18,000 men.[3]

Despite Burrard's reservations, Wellesley believed that the time had come to act decisively. It was probable that Junot's main army lay merely 20 miles away and it was dangerous to yield the initiative to an enemy who was so close. He considered Burrard overcautious but obeyed his orders and instructed the army to maintain its positions. Sir Harry decided to sleep aboard that night and disembark in the morning.

Yet these difficulties seem trivial in comparison to Junot's dilemma. Foy wrote that he feared to leave the capital, believing that if Lisbon fell to the allies, the French were doomed. Reports of dissent and rebellion were received on a daily basis and isolated forts and garrisons were threatened by insurgents. Loison's brutal repression of the south had bought the French time but Almeida was surrounded and use of its garrison was denied them. Junot thought that his personal presence in Lisbon reassured French and Portuguese officials there and considered a large military presence vital to retain the city.[4] He also feared that the Royal Navy could send a squadron up the Tejo to wreak havoc if the city was only lightly held, and yet, if he failed to meet and defeat the British, they would be reinforced and the insurgency would grow.

Junot finally left the city on the night of 15 August to march north. Though he realized the British were sending further reinforcements, he underestimated their current strength, thinking their numbers to be in the region of 13,000–14,000 men. He left at least 6,500 men in Lisbon and its region protecting the city, guarding the prison hulks and manning the forts along the Tejo. Oman believed that he should have stripped these garrisons, leaving no more than 3,000 men behind, as defeating the British was the only way to restore the situation and he needed every man. He thought that Junot's decision owed something to a contemptuous view of British arms, a widely-held opinion on the Continent at the time.[5] Junot's familiarity with the British as a former prisoner and during liaison duties as Governor of Paris casts some doubt upon this theory but he marched against a foe that he believed numerically equal to his own army, and likely to be reinforced, regardless.

By 17 August Junot had reached Villafranca, where he was briefly distracted by a false report that the British had landed at Cascais. Some troops were dispatched towards the town but recalled when the intelligence proved to be unfounded. However, they marched some distance and considerable time and effort was wasted.[6] On the same day, Junot and his staff rode to Cercal where he met with Loison.

Junot began concentrating his forces at Torres Vedras on 18 August and ordered Delaborde, then at Montechique, to join him there. He also wrote to his chief-of-staff that: 'I am collecting my army at Torres Vedras. We shall give battle to the English: make haste, if you wish to be of the party.'[7] Loison's vanguard reached the town that day but, during their long march, the column had become dangerously strung out and elements of the artillery and baggage were still arriving two days later. Foy believed that a sizeable enemy army could have easily overcome this force had it intercepted them at this time,[8] implying that Delaborde's Fabian strategy at Roliça had possibly saved Loison from disaster. It was also fortunate for Loison that Wellesley had turned towards the coast instead of marching further inland.

Junot amassed between 13,000–14,000 men at Torres Vedras but, realizing that this was probably insufficient, sent orders back to Lisbon for another battalion and a half to join him. His force possessed twenty-three cannon and he divided the infantry into two divisions under Delaborde and Loison. He kept four battalions of grenadiers as a reserve and placed all the cavalry in a division under General Margaron. Junot's army was particularly strong in cavalry with three dragoon regiments, the 26th Chasseurs and one squadron of volunteer cavalry amounting to around 2,100 men.[9] Over the next few days, French cavalry was present in sufficient force to scout the land up to the British beachhead and make it extremely difficult for their counterparts to operate.

Knowing that time was of the essence, Junot marched on Vimeiro as swiftly as possible. When within striking distance, he pressed his men on through the night of 20–21 August, hoping to catch Wellesley's army unprepared. Yet Wellesley had taken considerable precautions against being surprised, placing picquets of riflemen on the ridge before Vimeiro Hill and pushing cavalry vedettes forward 3 to 4 miles to watch the road towards Torres Vedras. A vedette of the 20th Light Dragoons detected the French advance in the night, hearing the rumbling of gun wheels as they crossed the wooden bridge at Villa Facaia around midnight. Riders were rapidly dispatched to inform Sir Arthur of large enemy movements to the south; he immediately ordered the army to be under arms before daybreak.[10]

The land to the south of Vimeiro comprised hilly country. The ground was sandy and covered in patches of heather or grass. Here and there it was dotted with small pine coverts and occasional vineyards. In 1808 it was mostly uncultivated and unenclosed. The village of Vimeiro lies before a gorge that divided a long, steep ridge running eastward from the coast and dominating the area. The western ridge was where Wellesley had placed most of his infantry. Extending down to the ocean, it is very steep in places with a narrow summit compared to its eastern counterpart. Behind it lay the river Maceira that widened as it flowed into the Atlantic and was contained in a rocky, steep-sided gorge, providing a formidable obstacle virtually impassable for the swift crossing of horses and artillery.

The eastern ridge is also steep in places but gradually subsides as it progresses inland and its top is broad enough to be considered a small plateau in places. Due to the lack of water on this ridge, Wellesley had placed only the 40th Regiment here but their presence amounted to little more than a strong picquet as he did not expect to be attacked on this side of his position. Both ridges dominate the land before them and Vimeiro Hill, lying to the south of the village, is also a prominent feature. The road running between Vimeiro and the village of Lourinha was particularly important as it was the allies' main line of retreat other than the road to Porto Novo, the village near Maceira Bay where the fleet lay at anchor.

Vimeiro Hill rises above the land to the south, which is essentially a long shallow valley with the opposing hills of lesser height to this eminence. Its forward slope is long and fairly steep and the summit is broad and flat. Wellesley had placed the 6th Brigade under General Fane and the 7th Brigade under General Anstruther here, guarding the main approach to the village. The bulk of the cavalry, artillery and commissariat lay in or around Vimeiro itself. Around 400 bullock carts, their teams and 400–500 mules were encamped on ground to the north and west of the village, causing Fortescue to comment:

> With his victualling train thus in the van rather than the rear of his army, and three-fourths of his infantry in a position from whence, if assailed, they could not retreat, it should seem that Wellesley did not look for an attack.[11]

Sir Arthur had selected this area mainly as a camping ground and to cover the beaches since he had intended to march south as soon as possible. He had not planned to defend this area to the extent that he would now be obliged to but, nonetheless, the bulk of the army was well posted and would be difficult to dislodge from their current positions, at least from the direction from which the enemy now approached.

As soon as he saw the French advancing, Wellesley sent additional artillery to Vimeiro Hill in the form of three 9-pounders and three 6-pounders. He rode with his staff to a position on the eastern ridge where they scanned the road to Torres Vedras intensely with their spyglasses. Though they took care to shield their advance using woods and folds in the land, French cavalry was spotted at about 7:00 am. Expecting to see the French infantry that followed in their usual blue uniforms, the British were surprised to observe that many regiments had rolled their tunics on their packs and wore long off-white linen smocks (similar to greatcoats but lighter and thinner) to protect them from the August heat and dust. Far from making them more visible, their dust-coloured appearance helped obscure them at a distance.

Junot deployed his army facing Vimeiro Hill. Not only did this hill before the village rise above the ridge where he now positioned his staff but he could see very little beyond the two ridgelines on either side of Vimeiro, where troops might be positioned. Wellesley had also taken care to place his battalions behind the crests of all these features, obscuring the French view of his deployment even further. Junot sent cavalry forward to reconnoitre and decided that the Valongo Ridge on his left was too steep for a successful assault and that the eastern ridge was virtually unoccupied. Foy and others later criticized this

Lieutenant General Sir Arthur Wellesley, a commander of proven ability but resented by some contemporaries due to his political influence.

General Jean Andoche Junot, a *beau sabreur* in the French army who gained the title of Duc d'Abrantes in Portugal. (*Mauduison*)

Emperor Napoleon I of France. In 1807 his armies dominated Europe.

Prince Regent Dom João VI, of the house of Bragança. Caught between Britain and France in 1807, he faced a terrible political dilemma. (*Nicolas-Louis Albert Delerive*)

unot's flamboyant style was legendary, along with his prowess in battle. (*Philippoteaux*)

Lord Byron – the lines that he penned concerning the Convention of Sintra ensured that controversy about the settlement continued long after 1808.

Napoleon was astounded when he received the news of Junot's defeat in Portugal.
(*W.B. Wollen*)

Lieutenant General Sir Hew Dalrymple, whose Armistice and later Convention with the French led to his disgrace.

British troops abandon Toulon 1793. During this siege, Junot first met Napoleon and became his protégé. (*Martinet*)

A view of Lisbon and the surrounding area showing the enormous width of the River Tejo at this point. (*Grünewald*)

A caricature of Tsar Alexander I and Napoleon dividing the world between them at the Treaty of Tilsit 1807. (*James Gillray*)

A caricature depicting Napoleon's plight during the Peninsular War as events in Portugal and Spain spiralled out of his control. (*James Gillray*)

Fort São Julien, one of the more formidable river forts along the Tejo. (Illustrated London News, 19 June 1847)

The Battle of Roliça, the first major clash between the British and the French in the Peninsula. (*T. Withy*)

Delaborde's skilful use of terrain at Roliça presented a formidable challenge for Wellesley, despite the allies' numerical superiority. (*Philippoteaux*)

General Brenier is captured on the eastern ridge during the final stages of the Battle of Vimeiro. (*Westall and Fielding*)

The Battle of Vimeiro witnessed ferocious fighting with hand-to-hand combat occurring at several stages during the struggle. (*T. Withy*)

Wellesley's headquarters in Vimeiro. (*G. Landmann*)

Sir Arthur Wellesley stayed in this house near the church before and after the Battle of Vimeiro.

The 43rd Foot defend the area around Vimeiro's church as the French fight their way into the village. (*Caton Woodville*)

A view of the city of Évora some years after the notorious events that occurred there during the insurgency. (Illustrated London News, *2 January 1847*)

General Junot and the first elements of his army depart from Lisbon 1808. (*H.L. Eveque and F. Bartollozi*)

A modern photo of the Rossio in Lisbon. Riots took place here when Junot had the tricolour flown from the castle battlements overlooking the city.

Fortifications at Cascais built to protect Lisbon and the Tejo estuary.

The Torres de Belém fort. This sixteenth-century structure was outdated but still formidable enough to merit a garrison in 1808 to protect the approach to Lisbon.

The gorge behind Columbeira village, which demonstrates how difficult it was to assail Delaborde's left flank, his main force being deployed on the hills to the left of the eminence on the left here.

Colonel Lake's grave, said to be positioned very close to where he actually fell.

The beach at Porto Novo where the Royal Navy landed reinforcements for Wellesley's army.

A view of Vimeiro Battlefield from the approximate position of Junot's command point. The houses on the ridge are on the top of Vimeiro Hill where Fane and Anstruther's brigades stood.

The church in the centre of Vimeiro village where the 43rd made a stand to repel Kellerman's grenadiers.

A remarkable modern statue in Vimeiro of an NCO in the Portuguese army of 1808.

Vimeiro's monument to the slain erected in 1908 for the battle's centenary.

A view of the stunning Palace of Queluz near Lisbon, one of the locations where the Convention of Sintra may have been signed.

The Monastery of dos Jerónimos which guards the Holy Bible of Belém, misappropriated by General Junot.

The impressive Monument to the Heroes of the Peninsular War in Lisbon.

reconnaissance as inadequate and Thiébault remarked that a good commander would have personally verified it.[12]

In fairness, the lie of the land and extensive lines of skirmishers that Wellesley had sent out to prevent scouts from approaching made an accurate assessment of the allied position very difficult for the cavalry. Yet Junot was also anxious to come to grips with the enemy, defeat them, and return to Lisbon as soon as possible. Impatient and overconfident of success, he felt compelled to attack the allies immediately, still hoping to catch them off guard.

Junot ignored the western ridge and concentrated on seizing Vimeiro itself, where he believed the bulk of allied troops were positioned. He decided to attack at three points, with two brigades approaching Vimeiro Hill from the south and one assaulting the allied flank by advancing along the eastern ridge. To this end, he dispatched General Brenier with four battalions of infantry and two regiments of dragoons in a wide flanking movement to his right. Unfortunately Brenier was obliged

> ... to make an independent turning movement round the English left – a disposition which was all the cruder that it required Brenier to go three times as far as it was necessary, thus in broad daylight giving the English thrice as much time in which to get ready for him.[13]

He compounded this error by dividing Delaborde's division (Brenier's brigade forming one half of it) and then combining Delaborde's 2nd Brigade with Loison's 2nd Brigade for the assault on Vimeiro Hill. These deployments baffled his subordinates as conventional military wisdom dictated that troops fought far better alongside brigades they were familiar with. Thiébault later remarked that it would also have been better to have sent Delaborde's 2nd Brigade after Brenier, rather than to split Loison's force, thereby maintaining the cohesion of both divisions.

Watching from the ridge above, Wellesley was bemused by the enemy manoeuvres he saw unfolding below him. Foy thought that the movement of the 3rd Provisional Dragoons under Major Contans gave Wellesley the first indication of a move to turn his left flank, passing near Toledo village and pausing near the hamlet of Fontanell west of Ventosa.[14] He had anticipated a move against his right flank but now it seemed that the French would not even make a demonstration there. Ironically, he had been considering shoring up his right but, responding to Brenier's movement, he now did the opposite.

He brought Ferguson's brigade onto the eastern ridge, sending them along the summit to intercept Brenier. Meanwhile he dispatched General Catlin Craufurd's brigade and Trant's Portuguese brigade, to take the longer route along the heights running behind and parallel to the eastern ridge towards

Lourinha. These forces, he surmised, were more than enough to deal with Junot's flanking movement using a single brigade. He also brought more troops down from the western ridge, moving three brigades behind the village with the possibility of reinforcing Vimeiro Hill or the eastern ridge, leaving only General Hill's 1st Brigade on the Valongo ridge.

It is likely that, at least in the initial stages of Wellesley's redeployment, Junot was unable to observe these moves as Ferguson's march was partly obscured by Vimeiro Hill and the sight of Craufurd and Trant's march was completely obscured by the eastern ridge from his position. Junot formed his infantry into attack columns and now prepared to assault the allied centre. Once again he used troops from both divisions, attacking with Thomières' brigade under Delaborde, who was still recovering from a wound sustained at Roliça, and committing Charlot's brigade under Loison on their left.

The French now prepared to advance. As part of an army that had stunned Europe with an almost continuous record of victory over more than a decade, they were confident of seizing the positions before them and driving the British back into the sea. Their regimental standards, the famed French Eagles, were brought to the fore and musicians struck up a martial air to inspire the troops and drive them onward. The artillery began a cannonade of the hill before them and skirmishers were sent ahead. By the time the columns reached the summit, they hoped the British lines would be ragged and disordered from cannon fire and the harassment of their sharpshooters.

The French marched forward in two columns approximately 400 yards apart. There were various types of attack column but these comprised two battalions each, both having a frontage of about seventy-six men. They were twelve ranks deep, each platoon being three files deep with an interval between following platoons to lessen the effects of cannon fire. Each column was between 1,500–2,000 men strong.[15] Anstruther's and Fane's brigades were drawn up in line on the summit of Vimeiro Hill with artillery placed between them and on their flanks. Fane sent forward a particularly strong chain of skirmishers who began a heavy engagement with the French voltigeurs preceding Delaborde's attack. A series of small fights broke out in the brushwood and vineyards on the lower slopes as British light infantrymen, operating in pairs, fired downwards. One man would fire, and then the other would cover him in turn as they slowly retired, trying to delay the voltigeurs and prevent them firing at the men standing in lines above them. This attack was partly obscured from the hill by woods and scrubland to their front but Wellesley had a good view from his vantage point and sent a message to Anstruther urging him to redeploy his nearest battalion to the left to meet Charlot's column head-on. However, this dispatch arrived too late.

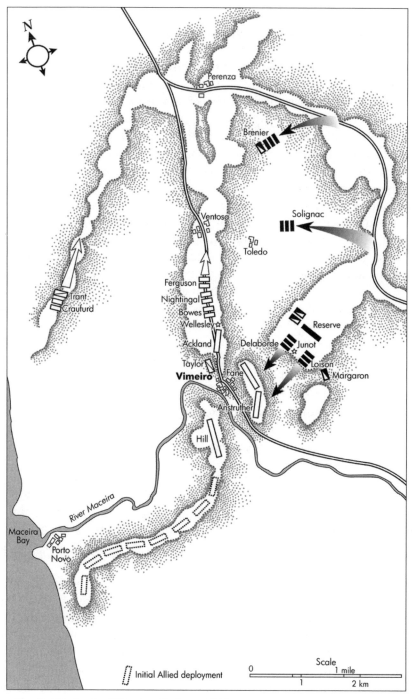

Map 7: The Battle of Vimeiro, 21 August 1808

The fight between the skirmishers continued for some time. Although Fane's riflemen possessed an advantage in accurate range, it is worth bearing in mind that a fit man can run 150 yards in twenty seconds and the aggressive rushes the French tirailleurs made would have been difficult to counter with the slower loading rate of the rifle.[16] Many of the British light infantry were also armed with muskets rather than rifles and French tirailleurs and voltigeurs were well trained and confident after years of success in battle. They hoped to draw fire from the British main formations so that the following columns would be exposed to massed musketry fire for as short a time as possible. However, the resistance they were met with prevented them from doing this and slowed the attack's progress.

Thomières' column came under heavy artillery fire as they advanced, Colonel Robe's battery setting twelve cannon against them as they marched forward. When it struck true to the gunner's aim, roundshot would impact just before the column's frontage, ricocheting off the ground over the heads of the first few ranks and tearing into the lines of men behind them, often striking down several men. Cutting through flesh and blood as though it were paper, the heavy cannonball would then bounce off the ground again and again, plunging through the column and knocking down all those in its path until its momentum was spent.

As they marched into the valley before Vimeiro Hill, the French were exposed on the forward slope of their own ridge to the British cannon, whose gunners could see their entire formation from this angle. The two brigades marching down simultaneously in densely packed columns would have made an easy target. Seven French guns had been brought up to cover them but they encountered difficulty in responding effectively to the numbers of British cannon set against them.

The skirmishers of the 95th lingered so long before retiring that the 97th Foot could not fire on the French for fear of hitting them, having altered their alignment to meet the French column on their own initiative and being within range. Observing the column's progress, Colonel Robe briefly thought his guns would be overrun with the 50th Foot bearing the brunt of the attack as the French approached the crest.

The frontage of the column was overlapped by the long formation of the 50th Foot. The British battalions on the summit were deployed in long lines, only two men deep, except for the colour party in the centre of each battalion, whose standards stirring gently in the hot August breeze proclaimed their presence. Colonel Walker of the 50th ordered his right wing to pivot to their left and fire into the flank of the column as it approached. Likewise, the three companies on his left had deployed slightly too far over on their side and were able to achieve the same manoeuvre with ease.

The front ranks of Thomières' column had no hope of matching the number of muskets the British could fire at them and struggled in the ensuing fire-fight.[17] It was too late to deploy into line as they were too close to the enemy and disorder set in as they were fired upon from both sides as well as in front. The French had brought up three guns in support but, coming under heavy fire, the drivers cut the traces of their limbers and rode back with their teams. They veered into the column, knocking men down and causing chaos. After firing several musket volleys, Walker prepared to mount a bayonet charge but, as they advanced to do so, the French broke and fled back down the hillside in a rout.

Meanwhile Loison led Charlot's column, comprising the 32nd and 82nd Ligne battalions, up on the left of Delaborde's attack. While the drummers pounded out the *pas de charge*, the men shouted '*Vive l'Empereur*' at intervals to bolster their courage and frighten the enemy. This roared challenge, coming from the throats of hundreds of men, had terrified opponents on many previous battlefields before French columns had even marched within range. Meanwhile the officers capered in front or alongside their companies, brandishing their swords and shouting revolutionary slogans to inspire their men. The size of this formation and the noise and steadiness of its advance must have been intimidating. British cannon fired into the advancing mass, their roundshot ploughing into the ranks and striking down dozens of men but sergeants yelled orders to close ranks and they pressed on.

Anstruther had deployed his battalions further behind the crest than Fane and they suffered comparatively little damage from enemy artillery fire as the French gunners could only guess at their position, hidden as they were behind the brow of the hill. The 97th Foot was concealed by a slight fold in the land and, as the column approached, advanced to the crest and opened fire. Placed in echelon to them, the 9th and 52nd also moved forward. The 97th fired three shattering volleys, bringing down many men in the front ranks of the column. After each volley, the redcoats grounded their muskets and rammed down their cartridges almost simultaneously, the result of months of laborious practice. The famed 'Brown Bess' (India pattern) was faster to load than the French Charleville musket and British infantry were justly renowned for their quick reloading.

The front of the column staggered as dozens of men fell and their advance faltered. Without waiting for orders, the 97th lowered their bayonets and slowly marched down towards the enemy, keeping a menacing silence. Realizing the futility of trying to stop them, Anstruther ordered the 52nd to move around their rear and attack the column's left flank. Beset on two sides, and blanching at the grim sight of the levelled bayonets, Charlot's brigade fell back in disorder. Delaborde and Charlot had both been wounded during the attack on

Vimeiro Hill and all the guns brought forward in support were taken as the British infantry finally gave a great cheer and charged down the hill. Few stood to cross bayonets with the redcoats and those groups that did were rapidly overwhelmed as the British tore downwards and set about them. They pursued them no further than the foot of the hill and then withdrew back to their original positions.

The first attack had been repulsed with serious loss and the two brigades were incapable of any more offensive action that day. Junot had sent these assaults forward without waiting for Brenier to appear on the right and now detected signs of large-scale troop movement on the ridge heading in Brenier's direction. Guessing that he would be outnumbered, he dispatched General Solignac from Loison's division to march after and support Brenier but, incredibly, failed to send any message ahead to inform Brenier of this. It was virtually impossible to conceal this move from the ridge above and, consequently, Wellesley sent Nightingall's and Bowes' brigades after Ferguson and brought Acland's brigade onto the eastern ridge.

The attack in the centre had failed but Junot hoped that the allied battalions had also suffered serious casualties and decided to commit his reserve. These were the elite of his army, the 1st and 2nd Regiments of Reserve Grenadiers. Most were large moustachioed men, renowned for their capability with the bayonet and often used as shock troops, to exploit a recent success in battle. Junot hoped that the British troops were sufficiently weakened for them to punch through their positions and take the village.

The four grenadier battalions advanced in two columns: the first under Colonel St Clair began to climb Vimeiro Hill while Kellerman led the second to the right, heading directly for the village. Once again they were exposed on the forward slope of the hill before Junot's command position as they marched downwards. British howitzers had been brought up onto Vimeiro Hill and began to fire the new spherical-case shrapnel shells, the first time they had been used in a major battle. With the enemy marching down the long wide slope, the gunners had an excellent opportunity to observe the fall of shot as they bombarded the columns, starkly visible against the hillside. Timing the fuse length of these shells was difficult but most worked well, exploding above the formations and showering men below with a hail of musket-balls and casing. They tended to cause more wounds than deaths but as many as ten men at a time were struck and the columns left a painful trail of dead or writhing injured men behind as they came on.

Under heavy fire, St Clair's column began to march upward in the wake of Delaborde's previous attack. They advanced to within 100 yards of the summit when the 9th Foot marched to the crest and received them in front with enfilading fire. The 50th Foot also marched forward, pivoting to their right in order to fire into the column's flank while the 97th did likewise on the other side. With the narrow frontage of their column engaged in an unequal musketry contest with the line above them, its centre staggered and heaved as French officers shouted a bewildering set of orders. Blinded by smoke, the French reeled under artillery fire as the British gunners switched to firing canister at this close range, blasting gaping holes in the front of their formation. The men in its midst were naturally reluctant to tread upon the dead and wounded that lay among them as they tried to reform their ranks. As the column halted, it proved next to impossible to extend the formation into a firing line to match the long British formations above them as, with volley fire biting into their flanks, men were loath to step out into the fusillade.

The French had brought up guns to support the attack but the converging fire of three battalions was devastating: 'Almost all the horses of the artillery and the ammunition-wagons were killed. The Colonels-of-artillery, Prost and Foy, were wounded. The first two platoons of grenadiers disappeared, as if they had been annihilated ...'[18] Although officers shouted orders and encouragement, the French could not hope to match the enemy's firepower and the column first inclined to the right and then rushed back down the hillside in disorder, taking refuge in a ravine at the foot of the ridge to avoid the hail of musketry directed against them.

Two artillery batteries followed the grenadiers and took up positions on either side of their advance. Captain Hulot of the 16th Artillery commanded the right-hand battery but found his guns were too low to be aimed effectively against the British positions above him as they could not fire at such a steep angle. He resorted to indirect shellfire with howitzers and was looking for a better position for his guns when he realized that things were going badly from the agitated manner of one of Junot's aides bringing up new orders. His fears were confirmed when grenadiers began to rush past his guns:

> Just at this moment a column of English troops hove into view and made as if to rush my battery. I had my gunners load canister, but just at that moment a crowd of fugitives streamed past and masked the enemy from sight.[19]

Seeing more and more men falling back, he ordered his battery to limber up and withdraw.

Meanwhile, Kellerman led his two battalions onto the road leading into the village. The artillery on the ridge fired down at Kellerman's column and roundshot tore into it as they advanced. Rifleman Harris was among those skirmishing with the French sharpshooters to the fore of the attack and occasionally fired into the column itself:

I myself was very soon so hotly engaged, loading and firing away, enveloped in the smoke I created, and the cloud which hung about me from the continued fire of my comrades, that I could see nothing for a few minutes but the red flash of my own piece among the white vapour clinging to my very clothes.[20]

Though the battalions on Vimeiro Hill were occupied in repelling St Clair's column, riflemen from Acland's brigade, now positioned on the ridge, began to fire down at Kellerman's attack. Yet these were the elite of Junot's army and, accustomed to victory, they pressed grimly forward, driving the skirmishers before them. Harris recalled '. . . we pelted away upon them like a shower of leaden hail. Under any cover we could find we lay; firing one moment, jumping up and running for it the next.'[21]

Anstruther had sent the 43rd Foot into Vimeiro to meet this new attack while Acland dispatched four companies of light infantry down from the ridge to block its progress. On the ridge, Major Leslie of the 29th had a magnificent view of the fighting and saw light infantry hotly engaged with French skirmishers. His position allowed him to see the action on the hillside and Kellerman redeploying as he followed the skirmishers into Vimeiro: 'They moved with great rapidity and admirable regularity, pushing on in the most gallant and daring manner, apparently making a dash to force our centre.'[22] As the French neared Vimeiro

. . . we observed a party of the 43rd Light Infantry stealing out of the village and moving behind a wall to gain the right flank of the enemy's lines . . . then our gallant fellows, suddenly springing up, rapidly poured on them two or three volleys with great precision, and rushing on, charged with the bayonet.[23]

The 43rd met the attack just before the village, taking position among vineyards, but the enemy continued to advance. After a brief exchange of musketry, the French charged, pushing them back. Retiring stubbornly through the narrow streets, they turned to fire volleys at the French or stood to receive them at close quarters in brutal hand–to–hand fighting with bayonets, swords and musket butts. The grenadiers fought their way up the street towards the church of São Miguel, their foremost companies stretching across the road between the houses and presenting a row of levelled bayonets. Many of the 43rd were shot down or overtaken and bayoneted as they withdrew. They made a determined stand at the church, firing down from behind the churchyard wall as the grenadiers advanced up the shallow slope of the road before it. A heavy engagement ensued and thick smoke swirled above Vimeiro.

Yet, in the wake of St Clair's retreat, the grenadiers were beginning to receive fire from Vimeiro Hill and British reinforcements were entering the village. The din of the fighting echoed through the streets as the savage, confused struggle continued but Kellerman realized that if he remained, having only penetrated the southern edge of Vimeiro, he would be cut off or overwhelmed. Disengaging his men with difficulty, he pulled the grenadiers back the way they had come, pressed by rifle and artillery fire on his flanks.

The cavalry under Lieutenant Colonel Taylor held a position on the lower slopes of the eastern ridge, slightly behind the village. Observing the French withdrawal, Taylor led them forward to press the allied advantage. He had 240 men of the 20th Light Dragoons and as many as 260 Portuguese cavalry from mixed units. Once they had passed the village, he formed his dragoons in line with a squadron of Portuguese cavalry on each flank, hoping the more experienced dragoons would steady his combined force during the action. Once he had done this, he began to advance at a walk. As they neared the fleeing grenadiers, he ordered the pace increased to a trot and as soon as they came to close range he ordered his trumpeter to sound the charge.

Though some units of the grenadiers withdrew in relatively good order, turning periodically to fire ragged volleys at the infantry pressing their retreat from the village, the chaotic nature of the street-fighting had dispersed many platoons and officers struggled to rally their men back into formation. Nevertheless, the land before Vimeiro was covered with scattered individuals hastening to the rear.

French dragoons had been sent forward to cover the retreat but the 20th swept into and through them, benefiting from the momentum that the slope added to their charge. Harris was involved in pursuing the grenadiers from the village and remembered being almost ridden down by his own cavalry. After getting out of their way with some difficulty, he witnessed Taylor leading the charge: 'He was a brave fellow, and bore himself like a hero; with his sword waving in the air, he cheered the men on, as he went dashing upon the enemy, and hewing and slashing at them in tremendous style.'[24]

Still struggling to reform, some grenadier platoons and companies managed to fire at the oncoming cavalry, bringing down horses and emptying a few saddles. Sergeant Landsheit of the 20th alleged that this fire was enough to check the Portuguese squadrons charging with them and many brought their mounts up sharply when they received it. As the 20th rode on, he recalled that the majority of their allies milled about in confusion, eventually retiring and riding to the rear, taunted by the jeers of Anstruther's brigade, watching from the hill.[25] Yet the bulk of the cavalry continued to follow Taylor and rode straight into the French dragoons '... cutting and hacking, and upsetting men and horses in the most extraordinary manner possible until they broke and fled in every direction ...'[26] The French cavalry could not withstand the charge and, after briefly crossing swords in a fierce mêlée, dispersed and fled.

The cavalry now turned upon the grenadiers, riding into their midst and striking down at those around them. It was too late to form square and most infantrymen panicked and ran. Landsheit recalled the savagery of the fighting:

> Though scattered, as always happens by the shock of a charge, we still kept laying about us, till our white leather breeches, our hands, arms and swords were all besmeared with blood. Moreover, as the enemy gave way we continued to advance, amid a cloud of dust so thick, that to see beyond the distances of those immediately about yourself was impossible.[27]

Colonel Taylor charged straight into one of the groups of infantrymen, desperately trying to assume formation and present their bayonets at the frenzied cavalry. As he slashed down at them with his sabre, a corporal raised his musket and shot him through the heart, killing him instantly.[28] Yet their efforts to reform as the yelling dragoons bore down upon them were futile as every group that stood was beset on all sides. Though some turned to fire their muskets or lunge upwards with their bayonets at the dragoons, the withdrawal swiftly degenerated into a rout as the grenadiers scattered and ran back into the valley.

Maddened with bloodlust, the dragoons chased them up the opposing ridge, almost as far as Junot's command post, where their progress was checked by a low stone wall. The Duke d'Abrantes now ordered elements of the 26th Chasseurs forward, who were acting as his guard, to counter-charge them. Other cavalry were also in the area, one regiment being partly concealed by a small copse on the hillside, and the 4th and 5th Dragoons formed line and swept down upon the allied cavalry, dispersed over the slope after their charge.[29] They retreated but many were caught and cut down by the French onslaught. A series of small running fights now developed as the French cavalry drove them as far as the foot of Vimeiro Hill. It had been a brilliant charge that had decimated the grenadiers' withdrawal, but the cavalry had advanced too far and paid the price for their recklessness.

Sir Harry Burrard had arrived at 9:00 am but graciously allowed Wellesley to retain his position for the present, knowing better than to interfere with the command system in the middle of a battle. At around 10:30 am the action in the centre was drawing to a close and it was only at this time that the French began their attack on the eastern ridge.

Brenier had marched too far to the east, perhaps wishing to circumvent the steepest section of the ridge but, hearing the din of battle and seeing smoke rising over Vimeiro Hill, probably altered his course hoping to arrive there sooner. The assault had clearly taken place before he could get into position but he meant to arrive in time to support it. Solignac also modified his route to try to intercept the 1st Brigade's march and quickened his pace. Turning west, he took the track towards Toledo and then turned northwards, marching up the ridge just below the village of Ventosa. Solignac's brigade actually began to climb the slopes before Brenier's.

The ridge gave a distinct view of the developments below him and Ferguson estimated that seven battalions, in the three brigades now under his command, outnumbered Solignac's force by almost two to one. Wellesley had personally checked their dispositions and the force lay in three lines now aligned with the area where the French were expected to emerge after their climb.

They first encountered seven companies of light infantry who skirmished with French tirailleurs as they climbed the ridge. The contest was uneven as the British skirmishers were firing down at the men toiling up the slope and could use outcrops of rock and rough ground to good effect. Solignac deployed his force into a line of three battalion-sized columns. As the skirmishing line faltered and the columns caught up with them, they came under fire from British skirmishers and officers were obliged to send men forward from the leading companies to support the tirailleurs and force them back.

The British main body was in two lines and had been ordered to lie prone to conceal their numbers from the French below. As the light infantry retired, the men in the first line were ordered to stand and knew they were about to engage. The tension was mounting and one soldier looked anxiously at his comrades: 'I looked alongst the line. It was enough to assure me. The steady, determined scowl of my companions assured my heart and gave me determination. How unlike the noisy advance of the French!'[30] All Solignac could see as they ascended the ridge was the scattered line of red-coated skirmishers before him. He had hoped that his force was roughly equal in strength to whatever opposition lay ahead but, when the British battalions stood, he realized he was outnumbered.

Shocked at the repulse of his grenadier reserve, Junot must have taken heart when he heard firing and observed clouds of smoke to his right, revealing that a serious engagement was taking place. If they gained a foothold and he saw his eagles advance along the ridge towards Vimeiro, perhaps something could still be achieved. Yet all three of the infantry brigades in his centre had suffered heavy casualties and, with most of their men dispersed and having trouble regrouping, it would be difficult even to hold his centre if the allies advanced. Unless Brenier and Solignac inflicted great damage on the allied left, the battle was lost.

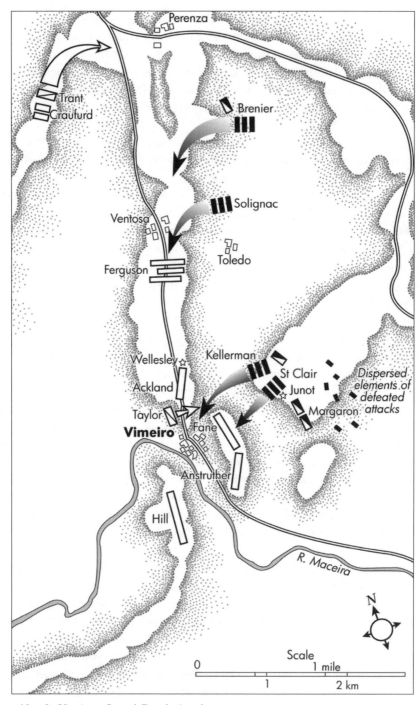

Map 8: Vimeiro – Second French Assault

Solignac's skirmishers had barely held their own against the British light infantry and the main British line had taken very few casualties so far. Ferguson ordered his first four battalions to march forward as the French cleared the crest of the ridge and, at roughly 100 yards range, they started to fire 'rolling volleys'. This was the timed firing of volleys by half company along the line, with a short pause in between each discharge, producing an almost continuous volume of fire as the British infantry stood and reloaded calmly and rapidly, around 3,000 muskets being set against the French columns.

With a combined frontage of about ninety men, the three columns were outmatched as only the men in the first two or three ranks could fire their muskets. Once again, the British line was long enough to overlap the French force, allowing the two battalions at either end to pivot and fire into the French flanks, causing further confusion. At first the French pushed forward into the face of this withering fire, intending to charge. One soldier in the 71st recalled:

> We gave them one volley and three cheers – three distinct cheers. Then all was as still as death. They came upon us crying and shouting, to the very point of our bayonets. Our awful silence and determined advance they could not stand.[31]

The ominous quiet which they maintained, as they marched forward with levelled bayonets, was a chilling sight and a deliberate psychological tactic.

Solignac tried to deploy his columns into lines but it proved hopeless under such intensive fire, which had all but swept away the first few ranks. The artillery he had brought up had barely unlimbered, having time to fire only a few salvoes before the infantry began to break. The 40th Foot was one of the regiments that now charged the French and Sergeant Lawrence recalled '. . . we fired and charged them. The fighting was severe and kept up for some time, but we drove them from the position they occupied, capturing about seven pieces of cannon, and some ammunition wagons.'[32] The French fled down the ridge, abandoning their artillery behind them.

Ferguson let the battalions of the 36th and 40th continue their advance, pursuing the French down the slopes but checked their progress before they reached the foot of the ridge. Nonetheless, they managed to force the main body of the retreating French into a gully where there was little chance of further retreat if pressed. Meanwhile the 82nd and 71st remained to guard the cannon they had just overrun.

Brenier had been further delayed in his long march by ravines and broken ground but now advanced along the ridge, hearing the sound of the firing before him. Heading towards the smoke swirling over the site of Solignac's defeat, he observed two battalions standing at ease around the captured guns and immediately deployed for an assault. Attacking with four battalion columns in a line abreast he also sent his cavalry out to threaten the enemy flank. The French approached from the flank and rear, surprising the British, who perhaps thought the force they had just defeated was the only one in this sector or that Brenier's and Solignac's brigades had already combined. The 71st and 82nd Foot were alarmed to observe this force bearing down upon them but Brenier's need to surmount a slope before him slowed his progress and they were able to realign and confront this threat.

The 29th Foot had been present in the first fight against Solignac but, positioned in the second line of Ferguson's deployment, had not engaged the enemy, to the men's frustration:

> Our men were ordered to lie flat down on the ground, yet we lost a considerable number. We found it rather difficult to keep the men still, as they were impatient to get forward, particularly as they were under a galling fire, and were not allowed to return a shot.[33]

Yet now the 29th would have their chance. With the threat to his centre over, Wellesley had ridden to this part of the field and ordered the 29th to advance and support the battalions around the captured guns. Nevertheless, the 71st and 82nd fell back and were forced to relinquish the captured artillery. As the 29th advanced they adopted an unusual formation, seeing cavalry on their right: 'We were instantly ordered to form four deep, which formation afforded the advantage of showing a front to meet the enemy in line, and at the same time of sufficient strength to resist cavalry.'[34]

The two threatened battalions withdrew in some disorder but the pursuing French were surprised to come under unexpected skirmish fire from light companies of the 8th and 29th Foot who lay concealed in bushes and willow trees before them. The arrival of the 29th allowed the 71st and 82nd to rally and they stood to exchange fire with the French who now halted. The French enjoyed a slight superiority having around 3,200 men to the British 2,400 and had probably redeployed into firing lines by this time. Yet they could see Bowes's brigade behind their opponents advancing towards them and knew they would soon be outnumbered.

The French began to withdraw but the British were gaining the upper hand in the fire-fight. Brenier was wounded and unhorsed at this point, falling into British hands, as the French fell back up the slope into Ventosa. The French guns had been recaptured and British artillery was brought up to press the retreat, setting well-directed fire against the village.[35] The French then retired in confusion, covered by the dragoons who had hardly engaged, just as Craufurd and Trant's brigades arrived towards the end of the action. The cavalry prevented the retreat turning into a rout, firing carbines from the saddle and threatening to charge the oncoming British infantry, but they suffered some loss in doing so.

By noon the fighting was over. General Burrard then took command of the army and Wellesley rode up to him, proclaiming: 'Sir Harry, now is your time to advance, the enemy are completely beaten, and we shall be in Lisbon in three days.'[36] The allied army was indeed in a fortunate position, the brigades of Generals Hill, Bowes, Craufurd and Trant had not seen any serious action and their fresh troops would be able to march against an enemy whose own men were weakened and disheartened. Many allied officers eagerly anticipated the order for a general advance.

However, Burrard had a different view of the situation. After the mauling that the 20th Dragoons had received, the allies were even more deficient in cavalry, an arm vital in the pursuit, particularly as the French still possessed large numbers of cavalry to cover their withdrawal. In addition, the inadequate provision of horses for the artillery meant that they would encounter difficulties in following up the retreat. Burrard also felt that they had other pressing matters to address. He had not seen the aftermath of a battle for some time and the number of wounded and dead lying stricken on the field was horrific. He argued that it would take time to tend to them and the unfortunate condition of the baggage train would also handicap an allied advance.

The French attack on Vimeiro had panicked the civilian carters manning the wagons who, in all fairness, were not paid to fight. Indeed, one man had been killed and three injured when Kellerman's grenadiers penetrated the village. Unsurprisingly many had fled, taking their carts and teams with them. At least fifty carts had rushed from the village during the battle along with many mules and other baggage animals. The Commissariat would need some time to reassemble the baggage train, vital not only for supplying the troops but also for conveying the wounded off the battlefield.[37]

Burrard also believed that Junot still possessed uncommitted troops and that the enemy were not as helpless as Wellesley believed. Sir Arthur contradicted this by revealing that General Brenier, brought before him shortly after his capture, had asked if the grenadier reserve had been committed, unintentionally revealing that Junot had used all his troops during the clash as indeed he had.[38] Yet Burrard was unconvinced and argued that they were still in unknown territory and should proceed carefully.

Seething with frustration, Sir Arthur pleaded that they might at least move troops down on the left wing against Solignac's brigade, still trapped in a ravine near the foot of the eastern ridge. Yet Burrard was totally intractable, insisting that all offensive movement now cease and the army must maintain its positions. Sir Arthur was appalled. Having witnessed the chaotic turmoil below them, as the enemy struggled to get their army back into order, he felt that they were missing a chance to turn a major victory into a crushing defeat for France. Careless over whether Burrard or his staff overheard, he '. . . turned his horse's head, and with a cold contemptuous bitterness, said aloud to his aide–de–camp, "You may think about dinner, for there is nothing more for soldiers to do this day." '[39]

Chapter 8

A Tainted Victory

While the British generals argued on the ridge, French officers tried frantically to disengage their army, extricate it from the field and organize an orderly retreat. Foy recorded that his comrades fully expected to see the allies descend from the heights above in overwhelming force to press their retreat, which could easily become a rout. All over the battlefield their assaults had been repulsed with loss and only Margaron's cavalry was relatively unscathed. All the infantry brigades were finding it difficult to reform, their men being bewildered and demoralized after their defeat.

Terrified French infantry were still hastening to the rear, expecting the arrival of allied cavalry any minute. The prospect of cavalry attacking broken infantry and cutting men down with their sabres was an horrific one and it was some time before officers managed to assemble enough men around them to rally their units. Riding back through the chaotic mass of fugitives, Hulot did his best to slow the retreat:

> We tried in vain to stem the panic by falling back a short distance and occupying a small village that stood behind us. Barricading the main streets, I set my guns up to cover the few ways in, but such was the press that they were in several places overturned, while I myself was almost knocked down despite being on horseback.[1]

French artillery kept up a sporadic cannonade against Vimeiro Hill. With the majority of enemy troops concealed, they were firing blind, hoping mainly to discourage pursuit and restore French morale by their actions. The weight and unwieldiness of cannon meant that they were always difficult to handle in a retreat. Captured guns were often used to illustrate the scale of a victory, so gunners knew a pursuing force would target them above all but, as the retreat slowed, they began to hope that they would elude their enemies. Hulot expressed his amazement at the lack of allied action, remarking: 'I was surprised not to see the enemy fall on my pieces.'[2]

While disordered French infantry streamed to the rear, Junot realized that he had suffered a crushing defeat. Thiébault claimed that, without issuing orders or trying to organize the withdrawal, he left for Lisbon:

... no sooner was the battle over than Junot got into a carriage with Mme Foy, whose husband had recently been wounded, and in this way went right through our whole column; conduct which would have been offensive after a victory, and after a disaster could not but cause indignation.[3]

Junot had quarrelled with his chief-of-staff many times and, while this may have been an exaggeration, his departure was rushed to the extent that he left important letters on the battlefield to be captured. Junot fell back on Torres Vedras with the main body of his army but left the rallying of isolated units to subordinates.

General Margaron swiftly brought up his cavalry to screen and cover the withdrawal and Delaborde managed to rally the troops on the left wing remarkably quickly. The belated arrival of reinforcements also allowed the French to deploy some infantry to discourage pursuit. These consisted of one battalion of the 66th Ligne and four companies from various regiments stripped from garrisons around Lisbon. Numbering between 1,000–1,200 men, these alone would have been insufficient to withstand a determined assault considering the number of allied units that had not been engaged and could be sent against them.[4]

Meanwhile Thiébault and his staff rode to the right to help organize the retreat of Solignac's and Brenier's brigades, both commanders having been wounded or captured. With some difficulty he rescued Solignac's brigade from the ravine where they had taken refuge. British light infantry stood above their position, firing at them occasionally, but could do little but harass their retreat without orders to advance. They fell back by echelon to the rear of Toledo and subsequently marched to rejoin the army.[5]

The allies were counting the cost of their triumph. Returning to the village, Ross-Lewin witnessed the grim aftermath of the fighting in Vimeiro. French dead lay in heaps along the approach to the village where shells had burst above them. The path of Colonel Taylor's charge was marked by stricken forms of men and horses and many wounded sat clutching horrific sabre wounds or staggered about seeking assistance. The village's defenders had also suffered heavy casualties:

A great number of the 43rd lay dead in the vineyards ... they had landed only the day before, and they looked so clean, and had their appointments in such bright and shining order, that, at first view, they seemed to be men resting after a recent parade, rather than the corpses of the fallen in a fiercely-contested engagement.[6]

The narrow streets were choked with bodies and scattered equipment but the wounded were gradually being picked up and taken to the church for treatment.

Entering the churchyard, Ross-Lewin was aghast to see piles of amputated limbs as overwhelmed surgeons struggled to treat as many wounded as they could.

Warre met M'Kayes, a bagpiper from the 71st in one of the aid stations established behind the lines. His courage during the action later became one of the most famous incidents of the battle. When marching forward he

> ... was playing to the men while advancing to charge, when he was wounded badly in the lower part of the belly and fell. He recovered himself almost immediately and continued to play on the ground till quite exhausted ... I shook him by the hand and told him I was very sorry to see so fine a fellow so badly hurt; he answered, 'Indeed, Captain, I fear I am done for, but there are some of these poor fellows,' pointing to the French, 'who are very bad indeed.'[7]

The 71st were involved in serious fighting on the eastern ridge and, when one private captured Brenier, he had the decency to decline the General's offer of his watch and money in return for his life, saying that he would need them in captivity.

Yet many of the wounded remained in the fields overnight and well into the next day, lying fully exposed in the sun's heat. Some soldiers wandered over the battlefield searching for loot on the slain but local villagers also participated. Yet the peasantry had other reasons for prowling the scene, one soldier of the 71st recording how they killed all the French wounded that they came across and even mutilated some of the dead in their fury. Warre was involved in operations to recover the wounded some hours after the battle and was horrified at the excesses his countrymen committed before his eyes. Weeks afterwards he wrote a letter conceding that the Portuguese had cause to hate their oppressors:

> The Natives have murdered every straggler or unfortunate French-man they met behind the column and, but for very strong English guards and patrols, would destroy every person who supported them, and their houses. It is cowardly in them now, but when we hear of the ferocious cruelties and insolence, of the system of robbery and plunder and murder, almost incredible if we had not seen such proofs of it, we cannot wonder at the fury of this naturally passionate and revengeful people.[8]

In addition to reprisals against the Portuguese, the French system of allowing armies to live off the land was partially to blame for this. One Portuguese newspaper commented:

> Junot pays for nothing in the villages he passes through. The
> Portuguese army is abundantly provided with every-thing, and the
> English carry along with them 500 wagons, loaded with provisions
> of all kinds. They punctually pay for every-thing they want, even for
> the water brought to them. What a noble contrast![9]

The countryside had never been prosperous and, with recent blockades and
Napoleon's extraordinary tax, storehouses were empty and there was nothing
to spare. When their goods and possessions were seized by soldiers who were
prone to brutality, due to fear of guerrillas, the peasantry were bound to react
badly. Napoleon's tyrannical policies and methods of waging war resulted in
great hardship for Portugal. Many brave men who had fought for him and lay
wounded in the fields now paid the price for their Emperor's indifference to
Portuguese suffering.

The French had suffered a severe defeat at Vimeiro. Some sources claim that
they had sustained as many as 3,000 casualties and lost fourteen guns, but more
modern studies put the figures closer to 1,500 killed and wounded, 300 taken
prisoner and twelve guns captured. The British lost 134 killed, 534 wounded
and fifty-one missing. Trant's Portuguese brigade had not engaged but historian
Luz Soriano claimed that the Portuguese squadrons in Taylor's charge lost two
men killed, seven wounded and eight horses killed or injured. Joaquim Paes
de Sa, an officer who rode in the charge, also wrote that one officer of the
Lisbon Police Legion was killed outright and at least three or four men were
wounded.[10]

Wellesley had good reason to be pleased. He was bitter about his replacement
but Burrard's delayed takeover had allowed him a crucial period of respite.
Outwardly he maintained his usual composure but he exulted in a private
letter:

> Sir H. Burrard came here on the night of the 20th, but did not land,
> and, as I am the most fortunate of men, Junot attacked us yesterday
> morning with his whole force, and we completely defeated him. You
> will see the account of the action. The French have lost not less than
> 3,000 men.[11]

Wellesley displayed formidable strategic and tactical skill at Vimeiro. Crucially
he did not panic when Junot declined to attack the Valongo Ridge as predicted
and assailed his left flank instead. Observing this, he simply transferred troops
across the rear of the allied position to counter the assault, remaining calm under
pressure and revealing the good quality of the troops under his command.
While not the complete victory he had sought, for a brief time this had been

possible but the decision of whether to pursue or not had been taken out of his hands. Critics at Horse Guards would now be forced to concede that Wellesley could add a considerable European victory to his triumphs.

In contrast, Junot's performance as a commander-in-chief had been lack-lustre to say the least. His contemporaries were exasperated by his command decisions:

> Loison and Solignac were foaming at the mouth; Kellerman, who was entrusted with negotiating after that disastrous scuffle, thought only of bringing them to a successful issue, so convinced was he that under similar leadership we should have no hope save in them. Delaborde was heart-broken, and I was no less so. How often has that worthy soldier talked over that deplorable day with me to try and find some explanation of it![12]

Thiébault blamed Junot's mistakes for the defeat, believing the entire affair had been needlessly rushed and poorly planned. With some justification, he thought reconnaissance and deployment should have been carried out with greater care and that the main attack should have been sent along the eastern ridge rather than straight at the allied centre.[13] He criticized Junot for dividing his forces and most particularly for weakening the attack on Vimeiro Hill by detaching Solignac's brigade, arguing that even three brigades would have encountered difficulty in taking such a strong position. He was further dismayed by Junot's decision to combine the brigades of different divisions, contrary to usual practice, and reducing their cohesion.

Struggling to find an explanation, he advanced the theory that Junot had been slightly drunk on the eve of battle, saying that at breakfast that morning '... the general had drunk various wines and liqueurs, he had taken too much, or, at any rate, too much considering the heat of the day, if not in actual quantity'.[14] Others believed that Junot had become wildly overexcited at the prospect of action, though this theory lacks credibility in the light of his extensive fighting experience.

Ultimately Thiébault believed that his chief was a brave man but lacked any conception of strategy and tactics beyond the wild, impetuous assaults of his beloved cavalry. He continued that the role of commander-in-chief was beyond his abilities and even believed that the situation '... must have been com-plicated by the beginnings of mental derangement'.[15] A few years later, the consequences of Junot's many wounds and licentious social life did indeed affect his mind but whether this was the case in 1808 is debatable. Certainly his adroit handling of the political situation in the aftermath of Vimeiro implies that he retained his mental capacity at this time.

Judging by numbers alone, many historians believe that the French were doomed to failure before the battle had even begun. Both Napier and Oman thought that they should have concentrated more force and ruthlessly depleted Lisbon's garrisons before marching north. Napier remarked: 'Junot seems to have reigned long enough in Portugal to forget that he was merely the chief of an advanced corps whose safety depended upon activity and concentration.'[16]

In Fortescue's opinion, the fact that 18,000 allied soldiers in a good defensive position repelled 13,000 French was unsurprising but he deplored Junot's recklessness, shamefully wasting good troops in a series of ill-timed and poorly co-ordinated assaults. Yet what the clash revealed about French army tactics was far more relevant than their commander's ineptitude. The French soldiers' performance and courage at Vimeiro had been notable but the tenacious defence of the British infantry brought them to a standstill. Even during the direct assault on Vimeiro by grenadiers renowned for their effectiveness in close-quarter combat, the well-disciplined and obstinate British infantry repulsed them.[17]

Weller agrees with this and goes as far as to say that the French were defeated by superior tactics rather than Junot's strategic decisions. He argued that if Junot's first assault had succeeded, it was part of a co-ordinated plan that might have produced better results.[18] Yet this disregards some of Junot's more questionable decisions concerning the splitting of his army, accepting a perfunctory reconnaissance, fatally weakening his first assault and sending Brenier over 2 miles away to climb the eastern ridge. Indeed, he was so impatient that he allowed the attack to proceed without even waiting for signs of Brenier's progress, which should have supported the attack on Vimeiro Hill. Dividing his forces created a situation where the battle was split into two separate clashes and his decision to reinforce failure by attacking with his reserves in the centre could have led to total defeat, had the allies pursued his shattered army. Had they done so, it is likely that they would have taken many prisoners and perhaps all of his artillery. Junot's arrogance and overconfident strategy certainly contributed towards the French defeat and he was fortunate that the allies failed to follow up their success after his attacks had been repulsed.

Nevertheless, Weller was correct to emphasize the importance of superior British tactical doctrine. Vimeiro demonstrated the column to be inferior to the line in terms of firepower and there is some evidence to support the theory that the French had previously used columns to batter right into an enemy formation, attempting to settle the issue at close quarters with the bayonet and using the legendary élan of the French infantryman with this weapon. Even so, at Vimeiro, after weakening the French with musketry, the combat was ultimately decided by a British advance or bayonet charge. Their psychological tactic of keeping the men's emotions in check until just before a charge was also highly effective and it must be remembered that most French attacks were only fully repulsed in this manner rather than by firepower alone. Essentially British tactical thought had produced a far more sophisticated and flexible system than the French approach when they were attacked in this manner.[19]

Yet, when the French did try to redeploy into line, they were usually denied the opportunity, the exception being with Brenier's force after driving the British away from Solignac's guns. In most examples, with the British largely concealed, the French usually approached too close and were consequently surprised when their enemies advanced to meet them at hill crests and fired devastating volleys of musketry into their columns. Being too close to redeploy and match allied firepower, the result of ensuing fire-fights was usually a foregone conclusion.

Such tactics also relied on an enemy line being weakened prior to assault columns marching within range. Wellesley's deployment of his forces on the reverse slopes of hills and ridges greatly reduced the chances of French artillery inflicting enough damage on the British to achieve this. French artillerymen could barely discern where British formations were placed and the angle at which roundshot struck the reverse slope often meant that they overshot their targets. The British practice of ordering the men to sit or lie down also limited the chances of roundshot knocking down numerous men standing in formation and the combination of these factors contributed to make the French cannonade far less effective than they hoped.

The harassment that the French skirmishers hoped to achieve was effectively countered by the British use of light infantry. Wellesley's deployment of large numbers of skirmishers usually protected his men but, in some cases, was so successful that they were able to inflict losses on the advancing columns themselves. The French were sometimes forced to disrupt their formation by detaching men from the first ranks to support their skirmishers, which slowed the attack. Since columns relied upon speed to reduce the time they were exposed to concentrated artillery fire and musketry, such delays could have a marked effect on the outcome of the assault.

The fact that Wellesley had secured the high ground, which allowed a good view of the battlefield, is also highly relevant. Attacks using columns relied upon targeting weak points in an enemy line and emerging at unexpected points. Placed on the high ground, Wellesley was able to observe their approach, predict where attacks were likely to take place and reinforce threatened areas. His use of natural features, such as woods or outcrops of rock, to anchor the flanks of some units, also reduced French chances of outflanking his positions. All these factors made Wellesley's defence extremely difficult to overwhelm in this manner without vastly superior numbers.

Finally, though the French employed several kinds of attack column, they appear to have used the most closely restricted version at Vimeiro. This was vulnerable to artillery, particularly when they marched down into the valley where allied batteries enjoyed an uninterrupted view of their advance and therefore inflicted considerable losses. The weakness of columns against lines demonstrated a crucial flaw in the French military system that they never fully overcame during the wars of the First Empire. Over the next seven years, the French continued to use these tactics despite the fact that, in the Peninsular theatre at least, they recognized that they were increasingly ineffective.

At around 11:00 am on 22 August, Sir Arthur was overseeing the embarkation of wounded when General Sir Hew Dalrymple's ship put into Maceira Bay. Aged 58, Dalrymple had enjoyed a long military career but had not seen much campaigning. As a Guards officer, his selection gained the approval of both the king and Horse Guards and it was felt that Moore would feel the sting of being ousted less keenly by an officer with this kind of seniority. Yet Castlereagh still wanted Wellesley to command and informed him that his tenure as commander-in-chief was probably temporary, while singing Sir Arthur's praises. The implication of this was not lost on Dalrymple who may have resented Wellesley's influence before he even set foot on Portuguese soil.[20]

Much of Dalrymple's military career had involved diplomatic missions such as his Lieutenant Governorship of Guernsey 1796–1801. He was Governor of Gibraltar, an important posting involving considerable diplomatic skill, British occupation of the rock being a sensitive issue with the Spaniards. Since 1806 he had held this office and, since the invasion of Portugal, had pursued secret communications with the Spanish via General Xavier Castaños. When the southern provinces turned against France, he even began tentative negotiations over granting asylum to the Spanish monarchy in Gibraltar, though nothing was ever agreed.[21] He had done well liaising with the Spaniards during a period of British indecision over foreign policy in Iberia, despite receiving little support from London. His fighting experience was limited but his knowledge of Spanish diplomacy could prove useful if the British eventually marched into Spain as planned.

Dalrymple sailed on the *Phoebe* from Gibraltar on 13 August but possessed little information or guidance over the government's plans regarding the war. Wellesley sent dispatches informing him about the army's progress but the majority failed to reach Dalrymple before his arrival. He received limited intelligence from Admiral Collingwood shortly after embarkation but only gained reliable information when his ship reached the mouth of the Tejo on 19 August. Boarding Admiral Cotton's flagship, he was informed that the army's progress had been slow. Cotton had reservations over maintaining the supply link with the military on such an exposed coastline and predicted that the weather would soon deteriorate. He also suspected that the entire French army in Portugal was about to descend on the expeditionary force, though he was dismissive of their likely numbers and capability.

Sailing onward, Dalrymple received further intelligence from the captain of a ship lying off the coast on 21 August. The welcome news that the brigades of Acland and Anstruther had now landed was somewhat tempered by a gloomy and rather inaccurate report of the action at Roliça. All this persuaded him that allied prospects were bleak with crippling supply difficulties and the certainty of a major battle occurring within days.[22]

When Dalrymple met Sir Arthur for the first time, he was wary of the young general's political influence, recalling Castlereagh's advice that he should take him '... into his particular confidence'.[23] The scale of his recent success may also have provoked some jealousy in the older man, who was entering into a situation for which his superiors had failed to prepare him. Wellesley now made the unfortunate mistake of immediately requesting permission for the army to advance after the victory at Vimeiro, giving his new commander the impression that he was trying to undermine Burrard's authority at the first opportunity.

Dalrymple made an effort to judge things for himself but was probably dismayed at the extent of the carnage and the number of wounded being brought in. After discussing the supply situation and the state of the army with Colonel Murray, the Quarter Master General, he held a council of war and clearly favoured Burrard's advice that they await the arrival of Moore's forces before resuming the offensive. Wellesley argued that they should march on Mafra to outflank the French position at Torres Vedras, while Moore should move against Santarém to prevent enemy movement to the north. Yet the strategic situation had changed now that Junot's army had had time to recover and Dalrymple wished to assemble a large force when Moore arrived, anticipating another battle or an assault on Lisbon.

Meanwhile Junot had also convened a council of war. After the reverse at Vimeiro, he felt that the army was incapable of fighting another battle immediately. The losses sustained had drastically lowered French morale and they had lost the bulk of their field artillery. Though Torres Vedras was defensible, they had received news of massive allied reinforcement and a defensive campaign was likely to be hampered by widespread Portuguese insurrection. Junot believed that they could become trapped in the capital but was reluctant to march for the border, fearing the worst as so little information had reached him about events in Spain. Although the French still retained important fortresses, they were ill-provisioned and could not expect help from France for many months. At the end of the conference:

> Opinions were unanimous ... Enough had been done for the honour
> of the army. The troops were now no longer able to keep the field.
> To give battle to such numerous enemies, would be only leading the
> soldiers to the slaughter.[24]

Junot decided to send Kellerman as an emissary to negotiate with the allies. As
he rode to meet them, Kellerman was overheard saying that his mission was
essentially '... to see if he could get the army out of the mousetrap'[25] in which
it was caught.

Cavalry picquets brought news of a French advance on 22 August and
initially the allies beat to arms in preparation for further hostilities. It was soon
determined that this force only comprised General Kellerman, accompanied
by two aides and a small escort of cavalry, so Wellesley proposed that he meet
him at the outposts. However, Dalrymple declined this offer and snubbed Sir
Arthur by not inviting him to attend the talks that commenced at his own
headquarters once Kellerman entered the lines under a flag of truce.

The French proposed an immediate cease-fire, which would be followed by
a formal treaty in due course. They offered to evacuate Portugal completely
but demanded concessions in return. Kellerman had been selected by Junot for
his diplomatic skill yet, much to his surprise, Dalrymple was so enthusiastic
over the prospect of liberating Portugal that he seemed prepared to accept their
initial proposals almost without reservation. The terms the French offered were
the best they could hope to gain under the circumstances for they had been
prepared for lengthy disputes and to accept a less favourable settlement.

Sir Arthur was summoned at the last stage of the talks and Dalrymple asked
his opinion of the terms the French were requesting. In brief, the nine articles
of the Armistice agreed that hostilities would be suspended for forty-eight
hours and that all French forces, civilian officials and Portuguese collaborators
would be allowed to sail back to France, conveyed by the Royal Navy. The
French would not be deemed prisoners of war and would be allowed to retain
their arms, horses, artillery, baggage and standards. Fortresses in French hands
would be surrendered but Siniavin's squadron in the Tejo was to be treated as
if they were in a neutral port and allowed to depart.[26]

Dalrymple was ecstatic that the French had agreed to relinquish the entire
nation and was prepared to offer generous concessions in order to achieve this.
Kellerman pointed out that it was improper for the commander-in-chief to
sign the agreement with him as he held an inferior rank, being present only as
Junot's representative. Therefore Dalrymple requested that Wellesley endorse
the document, realizing that his status as a member of his majesty's government
carried some weight.

Dismayed by some clauses, Wellesley raised several objections. Allowing the French forty-eight hours' grace was too long, he argued, permitting them time to secure their positions should they decide to resume hostilities. Personally he believed that no cease-fire should have been agreed until the terms had been finalized. He entertained grave reservations about allowing the French to keep all their property without adding restrictions concerning its origins. Otherwise, he argued, large amounts of plunder seized from their Portuguese allies might be included. Furthermore, he disagreed with granting the Russian fleet neutral status. Surely this was a naval matter for which Admiral Cotton would claim jurisdiction? Was the army entitled to negotiate in this area? Ever a master of understatement he commented that it was '. . . a very extraordinary paper',[27] but, at his commander's insistence, he felt obliged to sign it.

Although Dalrymple had diplomatic experience, he had allowed himself to be blinded by the prospect of liberating Portugal, regardless of the cost. Glover considered almost every one of the nine articles in the agreement objectionable on either military or political grounds and the French were amazed that they had won so much from an enemy in such a strong position. Dalrymple made decisions limiting the movement of allied forces without consulting the Portuguese and, while allowing the French to retire gracefully, failed to demand financial reparations for their actions in Portugal. He had even referred to Napoleon as *sa Majesté Impériale et Royale*, a title that the Portuguese objected to and which the Court of St James had refused to recognize. Glover later wrote that the result of Dalrymple's negotiations was no less than 'a masterpiece of ineptitude'.[28]

Chapter 9

An Infamous Act

Some hours after signing the Armistice, Sir Arthur became deeply troubled over possible complaints about the agreement, which now bore his name. Although he had protested vociferously over the terms, he worried that his signature alone might be sufficient to damn him should there be repercussions back in Britain. The more he considered the matter, the more it seemed likely that this would be the case. That night he wrote to Castlereagh insisting that the Armistice had been negotiated by Dalrymple and drawn up by Kellerman. He particularly objected to the way in which it was phrased, the suspension of hostilities and the fact that the army had acted on behalf of the Royal Navy. He acknowledged certain advantages such as gaining enemy-held strongholds without a fight, thereby relieving the army of campaigning in the worst season of the year, but pleaded: 'Although my name is affixed to this instrument, I beg that you will not believe that I negotiated it, that I approve of it, or that I had any hand in wording it.'[1] He had felt compelled to sign under protest and

> I will not conceal from you, however, my dear Lord, that my situation in this army is a very delicate one. I never saw Sir Hew Dalrymple till yesterday; and it is not an easy task to advise any man on the first day one meets with him. He must at least be prepared to receive advice.[2]

Wellesley believed that, now that the campaign was almost over, his uncertain status meant that his services were no longer required. Though he assured Castlereagh that he was prepared to stay, he announced that he would prefer to return home.

Meanwhile Dalrymple also began to wonder if he had acted wisely. Feelings of alarm were raised when General Freire visited him the day after the Armistice had been signed. The Portuguese general was outraged that he had not been consulted, though the time it would have taken him to travel there would have delayed the talks considerably. He was briefly prevailed upon by being presented with a copy of the terms but soon returned with Major Ayres Pinto de Sousa (the son of Viscount de Balsemão), as his liaison officer. He raised many objections to various clauses but found article 6, regarding the treatment of Portuguese collaborators, particularly offensive as its jurisdiction fell under civil rather than military responsibility.

Dalrymple defended this by indicating that the present civil authorities contained many French appointees and the government should be reconstituted before it would be acceptable to the allies. The junta established in Porto also lacked the Regent's official backing so he felt justified in taking this responsibility upon himself. He requested that Freire put his objections in writing and promised him a place at the negotiating table along with representatives of the junta as the final terms were not yet agreed. Freire never took advantage of this offer and relayed his complaints to Porto where the junta then wrote to Dalrymple's superiors in London.

When Kellerman returned to Lisbon on 23 August he found the capital in a state of uproar. French officials and Portuguese collaborators feared the people's likely reaction to recent events and desperately sought refuge in French garrisons or on ships in the port. Though Junot's re-entry into the city had restored order to an extent, the Police Legion had to be reinforced by French soldiers and ships were moored close to the quaysides in order to sweep them with grapeshot should there be serious unrest. Unruly crowds gathered in the Rossio, Commercial Square and the lower part of the city and riots were only prevented with difficulty by General Travot. Fortunately this officer had gained a good reputation by distributing alms to the needy while commanding the garrison at Oeiras and had no association with the brutal suppression of revolt in the south. Backed by only a few guards, he bravely addressed the angry crowds and managed to placate them.[3]

Murray was sent to begin talks with Kellerman in Lisbon but difficulties soon arose over the matter of the Russian fleet. Admiral Cotton refused to accept what the army had negotiated and insisted on conducting separate talks with the Russians. Eventually Siniavin accepted that his stores would be impounded and his ships would sail to Britain, where they would be held for at least six months, and that his officers and men would be repatriated to Russia. The Russians gained some concessions such as the Russian flag being flown while the Admiral was aboard ship, even in English harbours, but this agreement pleased all concerned due to Russia's ambivalent position.[4] The Portuguese saw no need to become involved and French attempts to intervene were politely but firmly rebuffed.

After halting his landing operations on Dalrymple's orders, Sir John Moore re-embarked his force at Mondego Bay and sailed to Maceira Bay, arriving on 24 August. Troop transports began to disgorge men and supplies and soon the British had concentrated far more troops than Junot had available to him in Lisbon, which placed them at an advantage if talks broke down. Moore swiftly acquainted himself with the situation and reached the conclusion that

Wellesley had been right to argue for a pursuit at Vimeiro and that subsequent events had been mishandled:

> It is evident that if any operation is to be carried on it will be miserably conducted, and that seniority in the Army List is a bad guide in the choice of military commander ... the conduct of the government on this occasion has been absurd to a degree.[5]

Having been passed over himself, Moore was somewhat biased over the question of seniority but, after meeting his new commander on 25 August, soon formed the opinion that Dalrymple was overwhelmed by his new responsibilities.

Meanwhile he formed a good opinion of Wellesley, the pair agreeing that more concessions could and should have been won at the Armistice. However, they also concurred that, with the weather worsening as September approached, the army could no longer rely on supply by sea. Furthermore, autumnal rains would make providing shelter for troops in the field more difficult and the poor roads would soon become muddy and almost impassable for artillery and supply wagons. Now that the main campaigning season was over, a negotiated settlement was the only option without the war in Portugal dragging on into 1809.

Castlereagh replied to Wellesley in September congratulating him on his recent achievements and good fortune:

> There was something whimsically providential in the enemy forcing upon you, at the very moment the command was passing ... the glory of an achievement which your personal moderation and sense of duty had induced you not to invite by any extraordinary acceleration of your operations.[6]

Nonetheless, he cautiously declined to comment fully on the matters he had raised with him until he had reviewed their implications with the cabinet. Ending his letter with vague reassurances, he counselled his friend to remain in place for the time being.

By now Dalrymple had decided that his initial concessions had been overly generous and endeavoured to apply further restrictions to the final treaty. The British insisted that firm dates were imposed for the transference of fortresses; the Royal Navy would have the full use of Lisbon and navigation of the Tejo once the Convention was ratified; and the promise to transport horses with the French army was withdrawn owing to their scarcity in the region and the difficulty of conveying them by sea. Rochefort was named as their destination, being the furthest French port from the Spanish and Austrian frontiers – it being likely that Austria would re-enter the war. The question of a prisoner exchange was also raised. The fact that this had been left out initially was remarkable and some attempts were made to limit the possessions the French were allowed to take with them.[7]

Kellerman objected to nearly every issue raised and continually referred to the original Armistice terms, insisting that they be respected. Regarding prisoners, the French even refused to free Spanish soldiers held on the Tejo prison hulks until Seville agreed to release corresponding numbers taken in Spain. During the talks, Portuguese troops broke the limits imposed upon their movements and Freire marched on Mafra. This created sufficient concern among the French for Junot to declare angrily:

> Take back your treaty, I am not in need of it; I will defend the streets
> of Lisbon inch by inch; I will burn all that I am not obliged to leave
> to you, and you will see what it will cost you to win the rest.[8]

Though Foy believed this threat was sincere, many British officers considered it an empty gesture. With the campaigning season over, there was little prospect of reinforcements arriving, especially with the French army in Spain in disarray, and safely retiring over the Tejo was virtually impossible with the close proximity of the allied army poised to interfere with such a move. The likelihood was that the French would become trapped in the capital and any deliberate mass destruction of property would bring down the vengeance of the already angered population upon them. Even the impetuous Junot was unlikely to resume the campaign under these circumstances. Nevertheless, Dalrymple denounced Portuguese violations of the Armistice and, when measures were taken to halt their progress, talks resumed.

On 29 August, Dalrymple called a meeting of senior officers to discuss the first draft of the Convention, including Generals Burrard, Moore, Wellesley, Hope and Fraser. Murray had imposed some restrictions but the Convention remained close to the initial Armistice terms. One crucial point was that he had failed to persuade the French to share the cost of their evacuation, the entire operation being carried out at British expense. Though commissioners (such as General Beresford and Lieutenant Colonel Lord Proby) were assigned to check through French baggage, the definition of legitimate French property compared to what was deemed loot remained vague. Furthermore, no change had been made in granting Portuguese collaborators exile in France, despite vocal Portuguese protests, and Dalrymple even gave a vague promise to negotiate with the Spanish regarding further prisoner exchanges.[9]

Though Freire left Major de Sousa with Dalrymple as an intermediary, the Portuguese were largely unrepresented at any stage of the negotiations. High-ranking officials were invited but neither Freire nor the Bishop of Porto attended any of the discussions or responded to Dalrymple's invitations. Considering their strong objections to the Armistice and the final treaty, Napier believed this a calculated ploy to exaggerate their grievances and gain political leverage with London. Indeed, he considered the Bishop '. . . a meddling ambitious priest'.[10]

Just how far Dalrymple went to try to secure Portuguese participation is open to question and in any case, offence had already been taken with their exclusion from the initial talks. Nonetheless, upon receiving details of the final agreement, Freire sent a formal protest letter to Dalrymple objecting to articles 1, 4, 12, 16 and 17 in particular. On 9 September General Count de Castro Marim, commanding forces in the Algarve, wrote a similar missive to Admiral Cotton.[11]

After some discussion, during which only a few minor amendments were decided upon, Dalrymple ratified the Convention on 31 August. Historians cannot agree exactly where the Convention was negotiated and signed with sites in Lisbon, Torres Vedras and even the Royal Palace of Queluz being suggested. However, Dalrymple wrote the dispatch that accompanied it to London from Sintra on 3 September, which he had recently made his headquarters. For this reason the agreement was misnamed the Convention of Sintra.

Events now moved swiftly, the British army setting up camp closer to Lisbon and the transition of the sea forts passing smoothly from the French to marines landed by the Royal Navy. In his dispatch, Dalrymple informed London about the results of the negotiations, expounding upon the recent success at Vimeiro but understating Wellesley's role in bringing it about. He argued that a swiftly negotiated settlement had been imperative, being

> . . . principally founded on the great importance of time, which the
> season of the year rendered particularly valuable, and which the enemy
> could easily have consumed in the protracted defence of the strong
> places they occupied, had terms of convention been refused them.[12]

He also implied that Sir Arthur had played rather more part in the negotiations than may have been the case.

Details of the Convention terms soon spread throughout the army and many were aghast that the enemy had been treated so leniently. Yet the reaction of the Portuguese had the most immediate effect, Commissary Schaumann remarking: 'The Portuguese foamed with rage, and rightly too. The stupidest owl in the army saw how badly Sir Hugh (sic) Dalrymple had allowed himself to be diddled by the French generals.'[13] Hearing that peace had been declared but their enemies would shortly depart with their plunder, hundreds of angry insurgents flooded into the capital, many carrying arms.

Foy recalled that in Lisbon the French were encamped in the city squares or confined to barracks and their discipline, along with strategically placed artillery batteries, deterred major unrest. Nonetheless, the streets echoed with wild cheering and derisive jeers against the French, punctuated by exploding firecrackers and pistol shots. Some French soldiers and Portuguese sympathizers were murdered and small patrols were attacked.[14] Being associated with the treaty, even the British became unpopular for a time and one soldier of the 71st recalled having to travel in large groups to avoid being attacked and beaten by outraged locals. The fact that British soldiers were increasingly used to protect their recent enemies from Portuguese vengeance did not improve the situation: 'The French had given the Portuguese much cause to hate them; and the latter are not a people who can quickly forgive an injury, or let slip any means of revenge ...'[15]

There were angry scenes when Junot and his army left Lisbon's docks but the embarkation of the first two divisions went smoothly. The commissioners tasked with going through French baggage did their best to confiscate illicit goods but the sheer amount of material to be loaded, along with the urgent need to hurry the operation in the face of Portuguese anger, largely frustrated their efforts. General Beresford wrote to Wellesley that the Convention had drastically reduced British standing in Portuguese eyes and he had been appalled by the terms when he read them. He also dealt directly with the Duke d'Abrantes, commenting good humouredly: 'I breakfasted yesterday with Junot, but he does not appear to have taken any great liking to me, at which you will believe I am not breaking my heart.'[16]

Indeed, Junot's personal acquisition of property in Portugal was suspicious. One glaring example was the misappropriation of the Holy Bible of Belém. He had requested a three-day loan of this national treasure from the Mosteiro dos Jerónimos. Bound in seven jewel-studded volumes, this manuscript was beautifully inscribed and highly venerated by the Portuguese, having been presented to King Dom Manuel by Pope Julius II. The monks charged with its protection were not allowed to relinquish it without specific royal permission. Afraid to challenge Junot's authority, the Prior agreed to briefly lend him the bible, only to be horrified when the General failed to return it. Questioned over its whereabouts by the commissioners, Junot replied that it had been sent to the Emperor along with the documentation detailing the Convention and the matter was therefore out of his hands.[17]

By the time that the 3rd Division began to embark, angry crowds had gathered and stones and abuse were hurled at the French. Consequently large numbers of British troops had to be deployed to control the situation. Days later when transports conveying soldiers from the 2nd Division put into harbour at Porto due to a storm: 'The populace, as soon as they were apprised of what kind of *merchandise* they had on board, took possession of the vessels, and seized all the plunder and baggage which were landed.'[18] Although there were no reports of fatalities, this was a discreditable scene that portrayed no one in a good light.

The evacuation of the garrisons from Elvas and Almeida had to be conducted separately due to the distances involved. The Spanish had decided to intervene and General Galluzo called upon French Governor Girod de Novilars to surrender Elvas when he crossed the frontier and took up positions around the town. Although the demand was rejected, the arrival of 6,000 regular Spanish troops accompanied by siege artillery on 7 September persuaded the Governor to abandon most of Elvas and withdraw to the key forts of Saint Lucia and Fort La Lippe. Though no assaults were attempted, there were exchanges of fire and the Spanish were reluctant to let the French leave when British troops arrived to enforce the Convention terms. The garrison was marched under escort to Lisbon and embarked on 17 October.[19]

Similar problems were encountered by the garrison at Almeida who, though only beset by Portuguese militia, were obliged to conduct several sorties to maintain their defence. Although this modern fortress was never in serious danger of falling, the French were harried by many attempts to dislodge them including the efforts of local insurgents led by a monk, José de la Madre de Dios, who poisoned several wells in the vicinity used by the French to water their livestock.[20]

When the British arrived, they escorted Almeida's garrison to Porto but received a similar reception to the ships that had docked there the day before. Surrounded by hundreds of enraged townsfolk, the small British escort proved unable or unwilling to protect the French under their guard and only the direct intervention of the bishop and Sir Robert Wilson, who had arrived to form what became the Lusitanian Legion, prevented serious bloodshed. The French lost most of their arms and all their baggage but managed to scramble aboard the waiting ships with their lives if little else.

Wishing to get his troublesome subordinate out of the way, Dalrymple wrote to Wellesley on 9 September suggesting that, considering his military and political experience, he go to Spain to liaise with their allies and attempt to gain more reliable intelligence about events unfolding there. However, within days he had reconsidered and withdrew his request, realizing that formal government approval was required.[21]

Yet Wellesley was already eager to leave Portugal and wrote to Sir Hew on 17 September announcing that his deputy in Ireland had died and that his presence there was necessary. Dalrymple immediately granted him permission to leave but, before Wellesley did so, he met with and wrote to Moore on several occasions, stating: 'It appears to me to be quite impossible that we can go on as we are now constituted; the Commander-in-Chief must be changed, and the country and the army naturally turn their eyes to you as their commander.'[22] Moore received this compliment with mixed feelings as Sir Arthur was clearly being disloyal to his superior, whatever his motivations were. However, the two generals had formed an accord and parted as friends, Wellesley boarding HMS *Plover* bound for England on 21 September.

In Great Britain reactions to the campaign's progress had initially been favourable as news of two victories arrived. Vimeiro was the first decisive land victory for the British since the Battle of Alexandria seven years before (Maida 1806 notwithstanding) and the public celebrated with great enthusiasm. However, confused reports were coming from the Peninsula and by mid-September rumours abounded that something had gone awry in Portugal. Although the cabinet received Dalrymple's dispatch on 15 September, they had already been sent unofficial reports but concealed the news. Indeed, the Portuguese ambassador in London had complained about the treaty on 3 September after receiving letters from the junta in Porto. Even when the Armistice and Convention terms were printed on 17 September, they still tried to play down the affair and ordered the firing of salutes in London to celebrate Roliça and Vimeiro.

When the terms became known, the public were outraged. The Annual Register summed up views printed in opinion columns:

> The regret and the indignation of the British nation was raised by the convention of Cintra to a painful height. The throne was besieged, as it were, with petitions from all parts of the kingdom, calling loudly for an inquiry ...[23]

Dicey later wrote that, distracted by victories such as Trafalgar 1805 and Waterloo 1815, it is difficult for modern readers to appreciate the impact that the Convention had on the British population at this time. However, when one considers the recent threat of invasion, the seemingly unstoppable military might of Napoleon and the lack of successful British responses, it is easy to imagine their anger when the fruits of a dearly-bought victory seemed to have been thoughtlessly cast away.[24]

Since Wellesley was known to have commanded the army at Vimeiro, many assumed that he must have been responsible for the Armistice that followed and he was widely castigated in the press for what was branded a shame to British arms. When he disembarked at Plymouth, the reaction of the people of Devonshire was portentous:

> You will readily believe that I was much surprised when I arrived in England to hear the torrents of abuse with which I had been assailed; and that I had been accused of every crime of which a man can be guilty, excepting cowardice.[25]

Ross–Lewin also travelled aboard HMS *Plover* and witnessed some dis-
agreeable scenes, commenting that Sir Arthur's recent victories were entirely
forgotten in the people's eagerness to cast aspersions: '. . . hissings and hootings
greeted him at every town and village of that county . . .' Yet he had first-hand
knowledge of events in Portugal and gave Sir Arthur some credit:

> But the people of England should have considered that, had he been
> left to follow up his victories, there would have existed no necessity
> . . . for such a convention . . . than the fixing of the hour on which the
> troops of Junot should lay down their arms.[26]

Wellesley reached London on 6 October and immediately wrote to Castlereagh
repeating his denial that he had anything to do with negotiating the Armistice
and had signed it only to ensure the French were swiftly expelled from the
country. Two days later he met with Castlereagh and learned that Dalrymple
had been recalled and Burrard would also return to London in due course.
Public and official disquiet over the affair was so intense that there was to be an
official inquiry.

Over the following weeks, despite the opprobrium heaped upon him in the
newspapers and occasional catcalls from passers-by, Wellesley maintained a
dignified silence. Though he wrote to the Secretary of State refuting some of
the contents of Dalrymple's dispatch, he believed it improper to engage in
public mud-slinging in the press, despite the counsel of some friends that he
should respond. Indeed, the efforts of friends and political associates writing in
his favour merely drew more attention to the scandal and did little to help his
cause, one newspaper commenting:

> But what shall be said of the effrontery which can declare that the
> man who signed such a compact with his own name, and afterwards
> gave such an opinion of its propriety, had 'obviously no part whatever
> in its conclusion,' and that those who said he had 'were enemies of
> the Government and of the army?'[27]

Nevertheless, despite convening the inquiry, the establishment backed Sir
Arthur and, far from being ostracized, he was welcomed by the king and other
members of the royal family, at a levée held in St James's Palace. The king
even spoke out on behalf of all the generals concerned when the Lord Mayor of
London and a deputation presented him with a petition complaining about the
Convention.[28]

On 1 November the government announced that a Board of Inquiry into
recent events would be held in the Great Hall of Chelsea College (now Chelsea
Hospital). This body convened on 14 November with General Sir David
Dundas presiding over a panel of six generals. The 70-year-old Dundas was

highly respected in military circles, being of long service and having written the standard army drill book. Three were full generals holding seniority over Dalrymple, Wellesley and Burrard, while the remainder of the board were lieutenant generals.[29] The youngest was 49 and they had been selected in order to be free of political bias as much as any other qualification. Essentially their purpose was to examine the huge amount of documentation set before them (over 200 orders, dispatches and letters were presented), examine witnesses and assess whether any criminal or dishonourable acts had been committed before submitting their findings to the government.

Though Wellesley's family wealth and connections would probably shield him from really serious consequences, it was conceivable that his reputation could be tarnished and his military and political careers brought to an abrupt end. His relative fame, achievements and political connections handicapped him to an extent since Dalrymple's reputation was barely known and many political opponents would dearly love to see the influential Wellesleys humbled.

Dalrymple's strategy was to argue that he had been unceremoniously thrust into a difficult situation, for which he had been ill-prepared by his superiors, and had subsequently received poor counsel from Wellesley who resented losing his former command. As commander-in-chief, he technically bore responsibility for both documents but, as generals, the board would all appreciate that this was a situation that they themselves could have been placed in. Dalrymple was also a long-serving member of the establishment, whereas Wellesley was a young, upcoming star from relatively obscure origins, whose rapid success had caused some jealousy.

Dalrymple began his testimony by protesting about damaging and ill-informed newspaper coverage. Concerning the Armistice, he insisted:

> I must say, that during the whole of that discussion, Sir Arthur Wellesley took the most prominent part in the arrangement of that treaty, a part which he was most certainly entitled to take, from his previous command of the ... army, from the recent victory he had obtained, and from the incidental and local knowledge, which, from such circumstances, he must possess.[30]

As his stance became clear, the inquiry swiftly turned into an adversarial contest between Dalrymple and Wellesley with the latter nobly trying to defend his actions without accusing his former commander of impropriety.

The board questioned both men intensely but Wellesley maintained his claim that, though he had signed the Armistice, his views were only consulted after the terms had been drawn up by Kellerman and his opinions were therefore redundant:

> I certainly did differ in opinion with the Commander-in-Chief upon
> more than one point ... of what I was thus called upon to sign ...
> but as I concurred in and advised the adoption of the principle of
> the measure, viz. that the French should be allowed to evacuate
> Portugal ... I did not think it proper to refuse to sign the paper on
> account of my disagreement with the details.[31]

Proceedings continued into December with both men sturdily maintaining their
ground. Under questioning Wellesley refused to become flustered, responding
in a calm manner, sticking to the truth and refusing to resort to accusations
against his superior. On one occasion, when his objections to the length of the
cease-fire were repeatedly challenged, he gave a sharp retort claiming that
the process was tantamount to victimization, but generally remained steadfast.

Yet on one point he was very clear: 'in the first interview I had with Sir Hew
Dalrymple after his arrival ... I ... had reason to believe, that I did not possess
his confidence; nay, more, that he was prejudiced against the opinions which
I should give him.'[32] At first, journalists attending the inquiry found Sir
Arthur's claims discreditable:

> We are, however, gently amused at the incessant endeavours of Sir
> ARTHUR to shake this Armistice from his shoulders. He is like the
> good man in the Pilgrim's Progress, striving to get rid of the burthen
> of his sins; when up jumps the Giant Irresolution, in the shape of Sir
> HEW, and immediately re-affixes the odious load to his back ...[33]

Yet Dalrymple's obvious dislike of Wellesley and refusal to accept any
responsibility, regardless of his overall authority, gave them pause for thought.
It became increasingly clear that Wellesley had only been invited to attend at
the end of the negotiation process and the extent of his participation in actually
drawing up the terms was open to question. Furthermore, many had assumed
that he had played a greater part than had been the case due to his recent
former command. The fact that he had been replaced at such an awkward
moment came as a revelation to many observers. When several high-ranking
officers, who had served under him, appeared and gave testimony supporting
his version of events, it cast doubt on Dalrymple's claims.

On 13 December Burrard appeared before the board after a long voyage back
from Portugal. His main contribution was to explain his reasons for ordering
the army to halt at Vimeiro and forbidding a pursuit. As an honourable officer,
he conceded that he had been wrong to forbid Ferguson's brigade to advance
when at least one battalion of Solignac's force lay at their mercy and could
easily have been taken captive. However, he persisted that he was right to deny

permission for a general advance due to the army's lack of cavalry, inadequate transportation and his belief that Junot possessed more reserves.

Though he argued that a pursuit would have been effective, Wellesley engaged in correspondence with Burrard's family insisting his differences with the general were over military matters and had nothing to do with his conduct during the Armistice negotiations. Though he earnestly believed that 'great advantages would have resulted' if his advice had been heeded, he had the decency to admit that 'others besides Sir Harry were of a different opinion, and that there were not wanting military grounds to support the latter'.[34] The trouble was that decisions taken during a battle are always open to question. Indeed, there are no certainties in war; variable weather conditions, supply difficulties and unexpected events during combat making it unpredictable by nature. Yet Wellesley was a gentleman and, much to his credit, subsequently wrote:

> I acknowledge that I should be very sorry to have my own opinions and conduct taken up and scrupulously weighed and considered perhaps by prejudiced persons weeks and probably months after the occurrences which gave them birth have been forgotten.[35]

Final evidence was presented to the board on 14 December and they passed on their findings eight days afterwards. They praised Wellesley's performance at Vimeiro but, as a marked criticism of army custom and governmental decisions, judged that changing the army's command at such a time was ill-advised:

> ... considering the extraordinary circumstances under which two Commanding Generals arrived from the ocean and joined the army (the one during, and the other immediately after a battle ... within the space of twenty-four hours), it is not surprising that the army was not carried forward until the second day after the action, from the necessity of the Generals being acquainted with the actual state of things ...[36]

The decision to appoint anyone other than Moore, due to his unpopularity in government circles, was reprehensible and had great bearing on subsequent events.

Ultimately they refused to give a definite opinion over Burrard's refusal to carry out a pursuit, allowing that the best course to follow had been debatable and both generals had sound military reasons for their views on the matter. Though they concluded that erroneous decisions had been made, they decided that Dalrymple and Burrard had done their best under highly trying circumstances and that no criminal or dishonourable acts had been committed. The board was happy to let the matter rest without taking measures against individuals or proposing reform of the system. Under normal circumstances, most administrations would have been delighted with this excuse to dismiss a troublesome investigation, but the strength of public feeling was such that the establishment felt compelled to take further action. The widespread view of the military bungling a settlement after much bloodshed meant demands that someone be held accountable could not be ignored.

The Duke of York insisted that each member of the board issue an individual statement. Three members believed that the terms of the Convention were too easy on the French, while two qualified this position by indicating that this was a price worth paying with Moore's reinforcements still in transit at the time. Only Lord Moira demurred, believing that Junot's army was vulnerable and far more favourable concessions should have been won:

> I humbly conceive it to have been erroneous to regard the emancipa-
> tion of Portugal from the French, as the sole or principal object of the
> expedition. Upon whatever territory we contend with the French, it
> must be a prominent object in the struggle to destroy their resources,
> and to narrow their means of injuring us, or those whose cause we
> are supporting. This seems to have been so little considered in the
> convention, that the terms appear to have extricated Junot's army
> from a situation of infinite distress ...[37]

Moira believed that, if the French had held out for unreasonable terms, fighting should have continued and that his majesty's forces were strong enough to force them to an unconditional surrender.

Though no court martial was convened and no official repercussions resulted, King George III issued an official censure against Dalrymple, saying that he '... felt himself compelled at once to express his disapprobation of those articles, in which stipulations were made, directly affecting the interests or feelings of the Spanish and Portuguese nations'. He went on to voice the crown's general disapproval and particularly deplored Dalrymple's failure to inform London about the negotiations until 4 September which '... was calculated to produce great public inconvenience'.[38]

Dalrymple was dismayed by these statements but knew that protesting against his sovereign's remarks would be futile and would only result in further vilification. Shortly afterwards he was relieved of the governorship of Gibraltar and, though he and Burrard received home service appointments, neither was given an active posting abroad again. Dalrymple's main sin had been to offend the Crown's Portuguese allies and, though he was in many ways a victim of unfortunate circumstances, he had tried to shift the blame and deny responsibility for his actions. His reputation never truly recovered.

Meanwhile Wellesley returned to Ireland to attend to the demands of his office but petitioned the government for a chance to return to the Peninsula. Though some stigma had inevitably been attached to his name, he regretted that the army's business had been dragged into the public arena and even felt some sympathy for his erstwhile commander's fall from grace: 'I was obliged to go further into the subject than I intended, owing to the attacks which Sir Hew Dalrymple had made upon me ... The consequence is that he cannot escape censure.'[39] Nonetheless, he did believe that a gentleman would have taken his fair share of responsibility, which Dalrymple had conspicuously failed to do. Sir Arthur had acted with great dignity and forbearance throughout the affair and this attitude ultimately paid off and saved his reputation.

His political associates endeavoured to salvage what they could after the furore surrounding the Convention, Lord Liverpool proposing a Vote of Thanks in the House of Lords on 23 January 1809, which was carried. Castlereagh did the same in the Commons two days later. While acknowledging Vimeiro as a fine performance of British arms, there was some debate about attaching Burrard's name to the motion as he had been the senior officer present, Lord Moira demanding that he be officially recognized having been there for the majority of the engagement. Only Lord Folkestone raised a serious protest:

> ... as he did not think it of that brilliant description to demand a Vote of Thanks, and it fell short of those good consequences which ought to have resulted from it; but on the contrary, the whole of the expedition had ended in a manner that was disgraceful to the country.[40]

Yet the opinions of one member did not stop the motion from being carried, especially after Burrard was given due credit, and it was felt that events occurring in the aftermath of the victory did not detract from the army's achievement. A consequent Vote of Thanks was also proposed for Sir Arthur Wellesley on 27 January and was carried while he was present in the House.

Nevertheless, the Convention remained a highly contentious document that many felt had tarnished Britain's military reputation and marred what would otherwise have been a splendid victory. William Wordsworth wrote a passionate and lengthy tract alleging that the agreement was a shameful act and the result of British incompetence. He argued it gave hope to a tyrant who would otherwise have suffered a far more serious reverse and that many had suffered, fought and died for the allied cause only to be betrayed: 'There is a spiritual community binding together the living and the dead; the good, the brave and the wise, of all ages,'[41] he solemnly declared.

For many years the Convention was recalled as an example of shocking political ineptitude. Lord Byron visited Portugal in 1809 on his Grand Tour and ensured that memory of the debacle lived on, referring to it in his poetic epic 'Childe Harold'. 'Here Folly dash'd to earth the victor's plume, And Policy regain'd what arms had lost,' he penned. While common soldiers had fought valiantly, Britain had been cheated out of the reward of their sacrifice by fools at the negotiation table, duped by a cunning adversary:

> And ever since that martial synod met,
> Britannia sickens, Cintra! At thy name;
> And folks in office at mention fret,
> And fain would blush, if blush they could, for shame.[42]

Chapter 10

Europe in Flames

As many in London seethed with indignation, Napoleon had some cause for satisfaction. Although a French army had suffered a defeat, Junot had managed to leave Portugal without shaming French arms and could claim to have extracted far more from the victors than could reasonably have been expected. Never being one to dwell upon failure, Napoleon made little of the affair in public and instructed his newspapers to be careful in their coverage of the campaign. Yet his plans had suffered a setback and, when he granted Thiébault an audience, after the curtest greeting he subjected him to a torrent of criticism, shouting:

> 'So you capitulated to the English and evacuated Portugal!' 'Sir,'
> I replied, 'the Duke of Abrantès yielded only to necessity, and he
> extorted an honourable treaty from people who, if he had been in
> command of them, would not have granted us even a capitulation.'[1]

While Napoleon recognized the truth of this, he believed Junot should have used all the troops in Lisbon to defeat the British before they could establish a presence in Portugal, arguing that the city could easily have been retaken had it fallen in his absence. If Junot had succeeded at Vimeiro, there would have been no need for a treaty and he 'would have beaten him (the enemy) if great blunders had not been committed'.[2]

Though he defended his friend's actions to the Emperor, in private Thiébault believed that he had indeed committed many errors and: 'A thousand men like Junot could have marched through hell; but a thousand like him could not have planned, directed, and won a battle.'[3] In spite of this, the Emperor was still at fault for appointing Junot to this role in the first place. Junot was a man that you could set at anything on the battlefield but was no strategist or diplomat. Establishing him as both commander-in-chief and de facto ruler of Portugal is an example of poor judgement in the often far-sighted Napoleon. Although it is true that he made similar mistakes where his family was concerned, he was clearly influenced by the bonds of friendship in this case, the appointment of Junot revealing his contempt for the Portuguese and an underestimation of the difficulties involved in conquering their nation.

Much of the blame for the failure of the French occupation of Portugal can be attributed to Napoleon. He dispatched Junot with a small army that proved inadequate to occupy the nation securely and defend it against British incursions. Insisting on ruling with a firm hand, he prevented Junot from governing with any significant consideration for the Portuguese and his ruthless policies drove them into rebellion. Most of those who supported the French were alienated by Napoleon's disdain for their nation, displayed by inflicting commercial ruin upon Portugal with his Continental System and unreasonable taxation policies. When revolts were brutally repressed, those who still harboured French sympathies were silenced by their countrymen's hostility and the Portuguese turned against France.

A man as intelligent as Napoleon would hardly have imposed such measures without being aware of their likely impact. Therefore it is clear that he was determined to treat Portugal as a hostile state from the outset and, in the short term at least, would offer her people nothing but hardship unless they accepted his domination of Europe. Ultimately his actions forced Portugal into the arms of his greatest enemy when they would otherwise have remained neutral. With hindsight, his blockade of Great Britain was flawed and could never have been fully enforced. Many states who adopted it failed to abide by their agreements and it would have been better for Napoleon to have tolerated Portuguese trade infractions rather than create a new enemy.

Not only did he fail to send adequate forces to support Junot, beyond 4,000 men to replace those lost during the invasion, but he was so unconcerned about potential British intervention that he ordered Junot to support operations in Spain, which would have crippled his army had they been carried out. Perhaps in acknowledgment of this he reassured Junot that:

> You have done nothing that is dishonourable. You have brought me back my soldiers, my standards, and my guns. I had hoped, however, that you would do better. You secured the convention, not so much by your foresight as by your courage, and the English are right in blaming the general who signed it.[4]

However, following his defeat at Vimeiro, the Emperor had previously been considering a far harsher response, writing: 'I was going to send Junot before a council of war, when fortunately the English tried their generals and saved me the pain of punishing an old friend!'[5]

What really pardoned Junot in Napoleon's eyes was that he considered the loss of Portugal to be a temporary setback in his grand strategy. Having imposed his will upon the nation, he believed Portugal to be commercially ruined and her people humbled, having been deprived of their government, wealth and armed forces. He was dismissive of the capability of insurgents to defeat a regular army and intended to invade Portugal again once he had conquered Spain with a vast army, which he would lead in person. He told Junot that 'Before the end of the year, I intend myself to place you once more at Lisbon.'[6] This was a promise that Napoleon would find impossible to keep.

Napoleon was wrong in his assessment of the Portuguese and almost certainly underestimated the difficulties involved in invading that nation, which crucially had not been opposed militarily during the First Invasion. Junot's swift success was deceptive, especially when viewed from Paris, where the obstacles he overcame and losses his army endured were less apparent. Nevertheless, what Junot's capitulation really cost Napoleon was valuable time. Napier believed that, had Junot continued to fight after Vimeiro:

> ... it is certain that six months more would have been wasted before the country could have been entirely freed from the invaders; but long before that period Napoleon's eagles would have soared over Lisbon again! The conclusion is inevitable. The convention was a great and solid advantage for the allies, a blunder on the part of the French.[7]

Napier thought that Dalrymple's decision to bring Moore's reinforcements down to Maceira Bay, rather than marching to Santarém and isolating Lisbon, meant that Junot's position was far from untenable. At the very least, the French could have drawn out the campaign by adopting a defensive strategy utilizing their remaining fortresses. Had they been able to do this effectively, they might have prevented British forces from marching into Spain in 1809 and possibly altered the course of the Peninsular War. Although he would have encountered great supply difficulties and problems due to the hostility of the Portuguese, Junot could certainly have created difficulties for the allies had he held out to the bitter end.

Initially the Portuguese were furious about the Convention but, as the Board of Inquiry commented:

> It appears that pains were taken to misrepresent and raise a clamour in Portugal against this convention; but when it was generally known, and its effects felt, the people of Lisbon, and of the country, seemed to express their gratitude and thanks for the benefits attending it.[8]

There was some truth to this as Portuguese resentment quickly subsided with the realization that, while both nations had suffered a loss of face along with some property, it was a small price to pay considering the long-term implications for the war effort. It was also clear that the British intended to stay and remain true to their obligations. The fact that the Portuguese eventually forgave their diplomatic folly is perhaps attributable to the strength of the ongoing Anglo–Portuguese relationship.

What was certainly true was that the Portuguese continued to work well with the British, who rapidly recruited, trained and attached a substantial Portuguese element to their army that became increasingly effective as the war progressed. Rather than being cowed by the violence and destruction wrought during attempts to put down the insurgency, the Portuguese continued to oppose Napoleon and the Anglo–Portuguese alliance defeated two more French invasions in 1809 and 1810.

As far as the Portuguese view of Wellesley's campaign is concerned there is some division between historians, many emphasizing the relevance of the Portuguese revolt against the French but acknowledging that Vimeiro was the decisive factor. However, historian Raul Brandão went as far as to dismiss the battles of Roliça and Vimeiro as 'irrelevant trivia', arguing that the scale of popular resistance made French defeat inevitable, even without British interference.[9] Although the actions of Portuguese irregulars created serious problems for the French during the occupation, this theory exaggerates their influence. The French army proved their ability to overcome superior numbers of insurgents on several occasions, notably at the battle and subsequent massacre at Évora. They were only dissuaded from their purpose at conflicts such as Teixeira by vastly superior numbers and even then did not suffer a clear defeat. Had the British not landed in support of the Portuguese, it is likely that Junot would eventually have received enough support from Bonapartist Spain to crush the revolt. Similar arguments are made for the success enjoyed by Spanish guerrillas during the Peninsular War but the safest conclusion is that, though Wellesley's small army along with those of the Spanish could not outmatch the French without guerrilla aid, the same was true of irregulars who could only hope to harass the French but never to defeat them in the field. Ultimately it was the combination of conventional and irregular warfare that drove the French from Iberia.

Though the active resistance of the people could probably have been overcome by the French, Junot never had enough men to match both a regular army and suppress the rebellion simultaneously. The hostility of the people restricted French movements and made large garrisons and escorts for supply columns a necessity. Furthermore, in the face of antipathy or indifference, local intelligence was nearly impossible to gather and restricted the effectiveness of the French field army. Brutal and repressive French measures saw antipathy turn into outright hatred, making the task of subsequent commanders, during the second and third French invasions of Portugal, even harder.

Junot disembarked from an English ship in typically flamboyant style, stepping ashore in the company of the Countess d'Ega and Madam Foy, much to his wife's distress.[10] As he had secured far more favourable terms than expected, both his officers and men received some praise for the campaign. The Legion of Honour was awarded to several men while officers such as Solignac, Maransin, Thiébault and Foy all received promotions.

The Duke d'Abrantes was soon given another command but never received an appointment of the same prestige that he had enjoyed during the invasion and occupation of Portugal. After his repatriation, he returned to Spain and played an important role in the second siege of Zaragoza, briefly running the operation but eventually being superseded by Marshal Lannes. He then commanded III Corps alone until the end of the siege on 20 February 1809. Returning to central Europe in June, Junot served on the Rhine commanding the reserve army of Germany.

He served under Marshal Massena during the Third French Invasion of Portugal in 1810. While commanding the army's VIII Corps, his resentment of Massena's appointment became obvious as he believed he should have received the position himself due to his experience. He incurred his commander's wrath for allowing his men to run amok in Coimbra and for failing to inform him about the terrain which Wellington used with such skill when he constructed the fortified Lines of Torres Vedras to protect Lisbon. He was wounded during a cavalry skirmish at Rio Mayor on 19 January 1811 but was fit enough to ride when the French retreated back into Spain that year. Junot delivered a lacklustre performance at the battle of Fuentes de Oñoro 1811 and, though other officers also undermined Massena, his jealousy and occasional misconduct contributed to the frustration of this last French attempt to seize Portugal.[11]

Yet it was during Napoleon's Invasion of Russia 1812 that Junot's fortunes really fell into decline. He was given a series of appointments in the *Grande Armée*, commanding the II, IV and VIII Corps in turn but was criticized for allowing his troops to fall behind on several occasions during the march into Russia. He fought at Smolensk but, in the aftermath of the victory, failed to seize the initiative and cut off the retreating Russians at Valutina. Marshal Murat rode to his headquarters and did his best to persuade him to act, urging: 'You are annoyed at not being a marshal,' he said. 'Here is a fine chance! Take it! You are sure of winning your baton.'[12] Both Murat and General Girod de l'Ain stated that Junot behaved erratically, appeared intoxicated during the discussion and, by the time he took action, the Russians had evaded them.[13]

Napoleon was furious at this ineptitude, ordering his replacement by General Rapp, and was only dissuaded when Rapp refused to accept the appointment out of respect for Junot. Caulaincourt recalled the Emperor's reaction to Valutina: 'Junot has let the Russians escape,' he said bitterly. 'He is losing the campaign for me.'[14] In fact Napoleon had been occupied in Smolensk and had failed to organize a suitable pursuit himself. Furthermore, he had previously reprimanded him for disobeying orders and, consequently, Junot may have been reluctant to act on his own initiative. Nevertheless, the incident drove a rift between them and their friendship never truly recovered.

After the Battle of Borodino, Napoleon gave Junot's corps menial tasks, such as clearing the immense battlefield of its dead, possibly as a punishment for his infractions but eventually ordered him to guard his lines of communication to Smolensk and establish supply depots. During this time, further evidence of Junot's mental breakdown occurred when he wrote confusing and contradictory letters to several people, including his wife, lamenting his predicament. He even began to send letters to the Emperor questioning orders with improper language and sarcasm. Self-pity had never been one of Junot's character traits, so family and friends became concerned.

During the retreat from Russia, VIII Corps suffered great losses and eventually had to be combined with Prince Poniatowski's command. Junot's role in the retreat was a minor one and, after he crossed the Beresina into Poland, he requested leave due to ill health. Napoleon's letter to Prince Eugène revealed just how much their relationship had soured: 'You can dismiss the duc d'Abrantes. That will be one less encumbrance for the army, and indeed he is a man who would not be of the slightest use to you.'[15] Shortly after his return to France, he was relieved of the title 'Governor of Paris' and was no longer listed as Napoleon's 'First Aide-de-Camp'. Only his ducal title and military rank remained.

Laure Junot was horrified when she set eyes upon her husband, writing: 'He returned not only changed, but changed in an alarming manner. He was suffering from moral destruction. I saw it in his heart ... I could read all the sickness and pain he had suffered.'[16] Indeed, he began to complain about insomnia, regularly burst into tears and began drinking heavily. He was regularly observed wandering forlornly around his house and estate lamenting '... the Emperor does not love me anymore'.[17] Dr Jean Portal examined the Duke d'Abrantes and swiftly realized that he was mentally disturbed, prescribing the use of opiates to calm him.

In 1813 Napoleon appointed Junot Governor of Venice and subsequently commander of the Illyrian Provinces but during this period his behaviour deteriorated. Junot's already violent temper became increasingly volatile in both speech and action. On one occasion he seriously beat a Venetian lawyer with a wooden club and had him cast into gaol for refusing to support his wife.

Subordinates began to submit concerning reports, implying that Junot was losing his grip on sanity, citing events such as dismissing all of his servants but one and wild behaviour at civil functions. At a ball he held in Ragusa, Junot kept 400 people waiting for more than an hour and then appeared with a bicorne hat under his arm and naked except for gloves, shoes, sword belt and sabre. Ladies shrieked and ran at the sight while other guests and servants stumbled about in consternation as he strode unconcernedly into the ballroom. A similar reaction occurred with the local townspeople when Junot climbed and mounted an equestrian statue, dressed in similar attire.[18]

When the Emperor became aware of these matters he immediately ordered Junot's removal from office on 6 July 1813. Refusing to leave, Junot was forcibly restrained and bound before being carried back to France. He was taken to Montbard and placed under the care of his family. He was now increasingly delusional, suffering frequent paranoid hallucinations and regularly made wild involuntary outbursts. Yet for a brief period his surroundings appeared to calm him and he became more lucid, being able to recognize and converse with his father. However, while walking in the grounds together he suddenly declared: 'Do you think I am a bird and I can take to the air as I like?'[19] This statement probably meant that the event that followed only hours afterwards was perhaps the result of misadventure, caused by insanity, rather than a suicide attempt.

While Junot walked about his mansion on the first floor: 'With one bound he jumped through the window, which fortunately had been elevated above soil, rapidly crossed the garden, climbed the wall, ran down the road, fell and broke his leg.'[20] In great pain after trying to run on a broken leg, he was picked up by his anxious servants and carried back into the house. He had sustained a double fracture in his left leg, the most serious break being just above the ankle. Doctors were sent for but his injuries quickly became gangrenous and, while unattended, Junot grabbed a pair of scissors at his bedside and tried to amputate the limb himself. He died shortly afterwards on 29 July 1813.

Napoleon changed his mind about Junot after hearing the details of his decline into madness:

> It really pains me to read what you say about poor Junot. I lost my good opinion of him during the last campaign; but never my attach-ment to him. Now I respect him again, for I see that his timidity was a result of illness.[21]

Napoleon had been one of the few individuals that Junot respected and stayed loyal to throughout his life and his Emperor's rejection had been a hard blow to take when combined with his failing mental powers during his final months. After such devotion, it was fitting that Napoleon acknowledged his friend had not been himself towards the end of his life.

There are numerous theories concerning Junot's madness and subsequent death. His wife's belief that his insanity was caused by his many wounds, especially those taken to the head, seems logical. Certainly the fact that several injuries never fully healed and bled occasionally (particularly those sustained in 1796 and 1811) adds some credence to this. Yet Henri Jamme wrote a thesis in

1910 on the subject and believed that though gangrene and blood poisoning were the actual causes of death, mental paralysis contributed to his demise and was brought about by excessive drinking, drug-taking and bouts of syphilis contracted during his many sexual encounters. In 1972 Dr Jacques Poulet voiced similar opinions, citing that his wild lifestyle greatly influenced his mental collapse.[22]

Junot left debts amounting to 1,400,000 francs and his family was eventually obliged to sell his château and estates to meet the demands of his creditors. Consequently Laure Junot became virtually impoverished and received little help from Napoleon (who considered her a great annoyance) and even forbade her to live within 150 miles of Paris. Laure flouted her Emperor's wish and remained in the capital to witness many of the momentous events surrounding his fall, brief return to power and eventual exile. Her memoirs are one of the most credible sources concerning her husband's career but she died almost penniless on 7 June 1838.[23]

Junot was a man of many faults: brawler, spendthrift, gambler, womanizer and looter being some of the unsavoury titles attached to his name. Yet his ungovernable passions helped make him a consummate warrior and cavalry general of the old school, who served his country valiantly on many occasions. He was no great commander and Wellesley defeated him with little difficulty at Vimeiro though, in truth, his opponent had more experience of army command and went on to humble superior generals, such as Massena, in the Peninsula. Therefore Junot's failure against one of the foremost commanders of his age is unsurprising but the feat of winning a favourable settlement after this crushing defeat was an achievement in itself. Though this owed a great deal to Kellerman's manipulative diplomacy, Junot deserves some credit for the Convention as Kellerman was carrying out his instructions, though neither of them predicted the long-term consequences of the treaty.

With heavy sarcasm, the Portuguese refer to him as *El Rei Junot* (King Junot) and rightfully denigrate the evils of the French invasion and the cruel occupation of their country under his leadership. There is much to criticize about Junot, yet to a significant extent, his hands were tied by his Emperor, and he cannot be held solely accountable for the mistreatment of the Portuguese and their nation.

Had he been successful at Vimeiro, it is more than possible that Napoleon would have bestowed the title of Marshal of Empire upon him but many historians have simply assumed that he gained this status due to his close association with the Emperor, making him 'the marshal that never was'. After Portugal he never really regained the position in the French army he had enjoyed up to 1808 and his shocking mental decline and wretched death seem a poor reward for his unswerving loyalty and courage. He was buried with full military honours in Père Lachaise cemetery in Paris, where fourteen marshals are interred or commemorated nearby. Though denied a place among them in life, he joined them in death.

In contrast, the fortunes of Sir Arthur Wellesley went from strength to strength after the 1808 campaign. His character was as far removed from his adversary's nature as could be imagined. Reserved and even austere in public, he had none of the reckless, 'devil-may-care' spirit that typified Junot's persona. He was no angel and kept mistresses but was always discreet and took great care to conduct himself as he believed a true gentleman should. He kept a firm grip on his impulses and emotions, whereas Junot was always prepared to indulge his passions when an opportunity presented itself.

The attitude which Wellesley displayed in his private life was reflected in his military performance. He studied his profession with an intensity that Junot would never be prepared to match, despite his intellect. Meticulous in preparation, Wellesley took an active interest in nearly every aspect of his army's operations, an approach that clearly brought success on the battlefield. His constant, almost obsessive, intervention kept his subordinates focused and ensured that their functions were usually performed efficiently and, perhaps more even importantly, on time. In comparison, Junot was always willing to delegate even important tasks, as witnessed by his actions during the invasion of Portugal and the retreat from Vimeiro.

Wellesley's performance at Vimeiro had been exemplary, a fact that did more to save him than anything else during the inquiry that followed. His careful observation, considered reactions and refusal to panic allowed him to predict and match his opponent's moves as they were developing. His experience in India, denigrated though it was at Horse Guards, had prepared him well and he was already a master of his profession by this time. Junot's inexperience as a commander-in-chief meant that he never really stood much chance of overcoming such an opponent.

Though Wellesley's reputation suffered because of the inquiry, the damage proved far from being irreparable. After Moore's retreat from Spain and death at Corunna, he returned to command Britain's Peninsula army and frustrated two successive French invasions of Portugal, forging in the process an Anglo-Portuguese force that would prove to be one of the finest armies Britain ever sent into the field. With this army, he went on to gain an unbroken tally of victories that are unmatched in British military history.

Although the spectre of Sintra continued to be a source of humiliation for the British, they had cause to be thankful for the swift ejection of the French, the main benefit arising from the controversy. At least it had prevented Lisbon from sustaining serious damage, which would have created significant problems for the allied cause. As well as being the nation's foremost city, liberating this deep-water port was vital if Portugal was to be effectively supplied and supported by sea, a necessity for an island-based power like Britain.

Securing Lisbon without widespread destruction was a triumph in itself and, as men and munitions continued to pour into Iberia through this port, Napoleon began to curse his earlier optimism about retaking Portugal. Though Wellesley's first Portuguese campaign involved few troops in relation to other theatres of conflict, it was significant as it allowed Britain to commit and sustain an army on the Continent, allowing a dramatic escalation in her war effort against France.

As previously stated, Vimeiro revealed that a well-mounted British defence was difficult for the French tactical system to overcome. British methods frustrated the French by denying them the ability to disrupt enemy lines and prepare the way for their attack columns by protecting allied troops from artillery and skirmisher fire. Unshaken infantry deployed in line were clearly superior in terms of firepower to a column formation and, crucially, Wellesley anticipated the French approach with cunning deployment, negating the benefits usually enjoyed by this form of attack. His use of terrain not only denied the French the advantage of surprise but effectively turned the tables upon them, allowing his troops to counter-attack at unexpected points, which often broke the momentum of an assault, prevented columns from redeploying into line and usually resulted in a French retreat. Junot's poor handling of this battle may have handicapped his army but the flaws in their military system are just as relevant when it comes to explaining their defeat.

Vimeiro had been an unpleasant surprise for the French but, as the struggle continued, clashes at Talavera 1809 and Busaco 1810 confirmed the effectiveness of British tactical doctrine. Wellesley's initial suspicions about French tactical weakness had been proved correct but it all began in 1808 and he later confided that at Vimeiro the French had advanced '... with more confidence, and seemed to *feel their way* less than I always found them to do *afterwards*. I received them in line, which they were not accustomed to.'[24]

Indeed, as early as 1808, Wellesley was already referring to the French coming on in the 'old style'. Three years later, when they still used such tactics, he wrote caustically 'really these attacks in column against our line are very contemptible'.[25] Nonetheless, after 1811, the French became increasingly wary of the firepower and steadiness of British infantry. Eventually commanders declined to attack if they were well-deployed in defensive positions and attempts were made to outflank them rather than mount frontal assaults in battles such as Fuentes de Oñoro 1811.

Vimeiro allowed the allies to secure a tentative foothold on the edge of Napoleon's Empire, though its relevance has been somewhat overlooked due to the famous battles that followed. After Talavera, Wellesley gained the title of

Viscount Wellington and by 1811, with Portugal relatively secure, he took the war into Spain. Lesser men, and an intractable system, may have thrown away some of the fruits of his victory at Vimeiro but the lessons he learned during 1808 began the process of forging one of the best armies that Britain has ever had. The experience he and his army gained on the dusty slopes before Vimeiro helped them drive the French back over the Pyrenees and eventually contributed to the defeat of Napoleon himself.

Chapter 11

Touring the Peninsula

Although visiting Iberia can enhance a historian's understanding of the Peninsular War, in which topography had such a crucial influence, it can also be a great pleasure. Both Portugal and Spain are fascinating countries with a wealth of historic sites to see from many eras other than the Napoleonic period. The majority of sites described here are within reach of Lisbon and can be accessed using the capital as a base. However, this chapter does not cover the possibilities of visiting relevant sites in northern Portugal or tracing Junot's invasion route, both of which are worth pursuing but are beyond the writer's current personal experience. Enthusiasts who wish to go further north than Coimbra, further south of Évora, or further east than Castelo Branco, are advised to book accommodation along their routes as returning to Lisbon is beyond a day's easy travel. With any battlefield tour it is essential to remember that time will be a pressing factor, considering the constraints of mileage, map-reading problems and the sheer multitude of locations to see. One possibility is spotting unexpected but unrelated sites along your route, which you may wish to see, but will have to sacrifice some other location in your itinerary to do so. It is one of the delights of the Peninsula that there are so many points of interest to choose from.

Lisbon
Lisbon is a marvellous city and one visit is not enough to appreciate its charms. It has many fascinating old buildings and even the pavements are laid with small, mosaic-style stones whose patterns are sometimes worthy of closer scrutiny in themselves. The people of Lisbon are helpful and welcoming to tourists and the capital boasts a stunning range of bars and restaurants. Lisbon is renowned for its seafood and wine, and prices are extremely reasonable compared with most capital cities.

Although a hire car is advisable for visitors wishing to view locations outside Lisbon, driving within the capital is fraught with difficulty. Traffic congestion is rife in this busy metropolis and most locals rely on trains, buses, trams and taxis – it is wise to follow their example. Lisbon has an occasionally confusing one-way system along with frequent underpasses and large roundabouts so, though it is best to keep driving to a minimum within the city, a satnav is invaluable should you choose to do so. When driving to and from Lisbon, try to avoid rush hours, especially on a Friday when traffic increases as locals drive in to enjoy the nightlife and restaurants. Rush hours are roughly 8:00–10:00 am and 5:30–8:00 pm with traffic levels decreasing at weekends. It is advisable to choose a hotel that provides a car park as roadside parking spaces are rarely vacant.

One obvious site of interest is the São Jorge Castle that dominates the city, giving fine views of Lisbon and the river. By Napoleonic times it was almost obsolete against armies equipped with artillery but it is easy to appreciate the awesome breadth of the River Tejo from the castle, demonstrating how difficult the city would be to approach by an army on its southern bank. Indeed, one friend mistook the Tejo for the ocean from our hotel near the Avenida da Liberdade. When you see its vast expanse running by the capital for the first time, you will see that this was an understandable error.

Two vast modern bridges span the Tejo. The impressive Ponte 25 de Abril suspension bridge is clearly visible from the castle and most areas along the waterfront. The Vasco da Gama bridge, supposedly the largest of its kind in Europe, lies to the west on the outskirts of the city and is extremely impressive. For stunning views of the area, take the lift up the immense Cristo Rei Monument located just over the 25 de Abril bridge on the southern bank. This 28-metre (92 feet) tall monument, topped by a gigantic statue of Christ, affords spectacular views of Lisbon and gazing down at the river from this point, you realize that even a modern army would be daunted by the prospect of an opposed crossing here without substantial naval support.

In the city centre the Praça Dom Pedro IV, known as the Rossio, is regarded as a focal point in Lisbon with its cafés and bars. A statue of Dom Pedro IV stands in its centre and the swirling patterns of the mosaic pavement dazzle the eye and make it even more photogenic. For Napoleonic historians, the Rossio is of some interest as a major riot occurred here on 13 December 1807 when the French raised the tricolour from the castle, to the fury of the Portuguese.

The buildings around the Rossio are high enough to obscure the castle from street level, except on the square's western side, which was also the case in 1807. Consequently the author asked a Portuguese friend whether this really was the site of the event as the adjacent Praça da Figueira allows a much better view of the castle and would have been preferable for a military review. He replied that the people of Lisbon were, and always have been, highly inquisitive. With resentment against French rule simmering, he thought it likely that everyone would have known about the event well in advance and it would not have mattered if the flag-raising ceremony had been held in private – the people would have learned about it and acted accordingly.

Napoleonic enthusiasts will be impressed by the Monument to the Heroes of the Peninsular War, which stands upon the roundabout in the Praça de Entrecampos. Unlike many military monuments, this depicts guerrillas and civilians involved in the struggle in addition to soldiers. Yet photographers should be aware that this three-lane roundabout is usually busy and that there are no official crossing points enabling safe access. A bust of the Duke of Wellington can also be seen outside the British hospital on the Rua Saraiva de Carvalho. It is interesting as it gives the great Duke a more Hispanic appearance than most portrayals and, for that reason alone, it justifies a short taxi ride from the centre.

A visit to the Belém district to the south-west of the city is worthwhile for a number of reasons. The area boasts palaces, churches, gardens, statues, museums and galleries, all of which are spectacular. The Palace of Belém and the Monastery of dos Jerónimos are relevant to this period. Dom João frequently used the Belém Palace, and the monastery is a magnificent structure that houses the famous Bible of Belém, which Junot 'borrowed' to the under-standable indignation of the Portuguese. Along the waterfront, the former Royal Docks can be seen, though they are now pleasure-boat marinas. Lisbon is still a major port but the larger modern docks are located further upriver or on the southern banks.

A visit to the Torres de Belém castle is a must. Constructed to protect the Tejo in the sixteenth century, it was originally surrounded by the river but land around it has since been reclaimed and visitors can now reach it using a footbridge. The citadel's ornate, almost fairytale appearance makes the structure a firm favourite with Lisbon's postcard manufacturers but, though it was garrisoned during the nineteenth century, its ancient design made it vulnerable to artillery. Nonetheless, its good defensive positioning is revealed by the fact that the more modern Forte do Bom Sucesso was constructed adjacent to it.

The Museu Militar, Portugal's largest and most famous military museum, lies to the east of the centre near the waterfront. It contains one of the largest collections of artillery in Europe and, though the Napoleonic gallery is small, several exhibits are of interest including a wall painting of the Battle of Busaco 1810 and an electronic map of the Lines of Torres Vedras 1810–1811. There is an archive that can be used by the public containing Napoleonic sources. Visitors should be aware that, since the museum is still an active military installation, security passes must be obtained from the military police guarding the rear entrance. A passport or relevant identification papers will have to be shown to use the archive.

Queluz-Sintra

The Queluz Palace is situated in the district of Queluz-Sintra just outside Lisbon. This is one of the possible locations where the Convention of Sintra may have been negotiated. Debate still rages over where the treaty was actually signed but Queluz and Torres Vedras are among the main contenders for this controversial event. Nevertheless, both British and French delegates are said to have met at this magnificent palace to discuss terms, regardless of whether the final agreement was reached and signed here.

Even though Dom João stripped the interior of valuables when he left for Brazil, this splendid building would still have been spectacular in 1808. Stately ballrooms and galleries give an impression of decaying splendour, the condition of the many mirrors along the walls testifying to their great age. With many treasures restored, visitors can see an array of royal paraphernalia including rare portraits. There are many portraits and busts of Dom João along with paintings of his mother Queen Maria I, his wife and family. The palatial gardens and the palace's magnificent exterior are a visual treat.

Oeiras, Estoril and Cascais

These locations can be reached using the train from Cais Sodré station near the waterfront to the west of the centre. This service is easy to use, relatively cheap and stops at numerous stations along the coastline, including Belém, Estoril and Cascais. Alternatively, the road following the coast to Cascais is easily followed by car, and trams and buses are also available.

Many forts can be seen along this route including the São Lourenço do Bugio on the island of Bugio, which lies roughly 2 kilometres (just over 1 mile) off the coast. This circular fortress was constructed in the eighteenth century and would have to be captured by a naval force wishing to navigate the river with any safety. Today it also has a lighthouse but is extremely difficult to reach as there are no regular boat tours to the island and special permission from the authorities is required to land there.

Fort São Julien can be seen at Oeiras either from the road or by getting off at the station here and walking up to the structure. It is still an active military base and visitors should be cautious about taking photographs, though the Portuguese army are usually friendly and approachable. During the Third French Invasion, this was a key part of Wellington's contingency plan to defend his emergency embarkation beaches should the French overcome the Lines of Torres Vedras. It was part of the third line, though the earthworks supporting it have long since vanished.

Estoril and Cascais are two of the most famous beach resorts along this coastline. Although there are forts at Estoril, those protecting the beach date from long after the Napoleonic Wars but they are worth looking at nonetheless.

However, an older fortification exists at Cascais which can be reached after a short walk from the station and the beach. It lies next to the marina and is of huge construction with impressive walls. At the time of writing, it appears to be closed to the public.

Mafra

The town of Mafra is best reached by driving north along the A8 motorway out of Lisbon. Leave the motorway at junction 5 and take the A21 signposted towards Mafra, joining the N116 to drive directly into the town. The main location to see in Mafra is the massive Convent Palace, built by King João V, whose original intent was to construct a new monastery and basilica for the Franciscan friars. Yet the project expanded with wealth pouring in from Portuguese colonies during the eighteenth century and it became half-convent and half-palace, many kings using it as a vast hunting lodge for the nearby royal parks.

During its construction the monarchy ordered so many bells from Belgium that the suppliers wrote to the king querying the size of the order, assuming that there must have been a mistake. No expense was spared during the palace's construction with 52,000 workmen involved. The Prince Regent preferred Mafra to other palaces in the region, due to its religious connections. After his departure, General Junot spent some time here but eventually decided on a more convenient base in Lisbon.

Tours of the palace are available and the extent of the structure is truly staggering. It is famous for the beauty of the basilica, extensive libraries and the royal hunting trophies that adorn some areas. An interesting Portuguese war memorial stands on the right of the palace with three statues of Portuguese soldiers from the Medieval, Napoleonic and modern colonial periods depicted, making this an unusual and effective monument.

Évora and Elvas

Travelling from the capital, it is best to drive over the 25 de Abril bridge, straight onto the A2-IP7 motorway. Continuing past Setúbal, this highway changes its name several times before the border, becoming the A6-IP7 E90 by the time it reaches Elvas but it is essentially the same highway and it is difficult to get lost in this open region. The wide plains here are largely cultivated and cannot have changed that much since Loison led his forces against Évora in 1808, making it easy to imagine how the French must have suffered in the July heat in this arid and exposed region. The city is impressive from afar with its central cathedral visible from a considerable distance and large parts of the city walls and fortifications still exist. If you wish to travel further south, it is well worth booking accommodation here and there is much to see including a medieval castle, museum and a Roman temple dedicated to the goddess Diana.

Travelling further along the E90, the fortress town of Elvas is just as impressive, the old town being entirely walled with the fortifications mostly intact. Signs of outlying works can be detected on nearby hills and the entire town is charming and a pleasure for a historian to visit with eighteenth-century bastions and gatehouses built on an imposing scale. The opposing fortress town of Badajoz lies within easy reach of Elvas and, with border controls no longer enforced, it is easy to cross into Spain to view it.

Obidos and Roliça

From Lisbon, take the A8 north to Torres Vedras to visit the main battlefield sites relevant to this book. If you are interested in the Third French Invasion, it is worth stopping at Torres Vedras after which Wellington's famous fortifications were named. They ran from the coast all the way to the Tejo, entirely blocking the approach to Lisbon from the north-east. The town contains a monument to the lines, a museum and a medieval castle, utilized as one of the forts in the first line. The more modern fortress of São Vicente overlooking the town is well worth a look and gives an impression of just how difficult forcing the lines would have been for the French in 1810.

Driving north from Torres Vedras, it is best to view Obidos and Roliça in reverse order, leaving the A8 at junction 13 for Roliça. There is a small monument to the battle in the village itself and, driving towards the heights, it is easy to appreciate the nature of the horseshoe-like enclosure of surrounding hills about the plain into which Wellesley led his army. It is difficult to discern exactly where the first clash occurred and it is almost certainly built over now but there is no difficulty with the second location of Delaborde's cunning deployment.

An impressive range of heights dominates the area, culminating in an imposing eminence on the right as you drive towards the gorge. This is topped with a religious cross and is now an official viewpoint. The four gullies seaming the ridge can be made out but they are partly overgrown with bushes and trees. Though these can be approached from the plain, it is easier to drive through the gorge and approach the eminence from the rear, which is signposted as a viewpoint. Drive through the small village immediately behind the gorge and take the farm track through the vineyards towards the viewpoint. Delaborde conducted a fighting withdrawal over this sloping ground behind the ridgeline.

Walk up to the viewpoint for a panoramic view of the plain below and the slopes but then proceed to your right and search for the points where the gullies emerge. The top of the gully where the 29th fought upwards through a storm of musketry is now marked by a stone cross, enclosed by metal railings.

This is the grave of Colonel Lake who fell upon or near this spot when he led his ill-fated attack. The nature of the ground and steepness of the ridge clearly reveal how difficult it must have been for the British to attack these heights, making Roliça one of the most interesting battles that Wellesley fought in Portugal.

Rejoining the A8 and heading north, Obidos is clearly signposted and can be reached by leaving the motorway at junctions 14, 15 or 17. There is less to see here as the exact location of the skirmish is open to dispute and is probably built upon. However, it is worth a visit to the castle, which Wellesley almost certainly used as a viewpoint at some stage during his advance.

Peniche

If you have visited both Obidos and Roliça, it may be wise to return to Lisbon and retrace your route the next day depending upon how long you lingered at these locations. The fortress of Peniche is also reached by driving north up the A8 but this time leave the A8 at junction 14 and follow the IP6 towards the coast. Peniche is a small, low fort that would have presented great difficulties to any naval force trying to land troops on the beaches hereabouts. It is set upon a tiny peninsula and was consequently referred to as a 'mini Gibraltar'.

Vimeiro Battlefield

As the decisive battle of the campaign, Vimeiro is probably the most important and informative location to visit concerning events covered in this book. Once again, the best approach is via the A8, which this time you leave at junction 9. From here follow the N8-2, searching for a minor road on your left. This can be difficult to spot and you will know that you are on the right road when you drive through the small village of A dos Cunhados, though Vimeiro is well signposted.

Vimeiro is a small unspoilt village, though now expanding with new developments. Shortly after entering the village you will find the monument signposted to your right. There is a modern statue of a Portuguese infantryman on one of the small roundabouts in Vimeiro, which is almost worth the trip alone. This is a fine, imposing statue depicting a Portuguese NCO though, in reality, few present in 1808 would have been as well-equipped as the soldier depicted after the French had disbanded or removed the bulk of the regular army.

It is probably best to park your vehicle in the village and walk up to the monument, though it is possible to drive up and park nearby. Throughout the village you will notice that street signs often have pictures of Napoleonic soldiers next to them. The monument commemorating the battle was erected in 1908 and displays the lion image often associated with Britain and the allies, surmounted by a cannonball. It is well maintained and surrounded by many inclined tables with tiles painted to show maps and scenes from the battle.

Vimeiro has benefited from the addition of a recent battlefield centre near the monument, marking the bicentenary of 2008. As a modern museum, it is beginning to amass a good collection and it is worth studying its exhibits and signs relating to the battlefield. The staff are remarkably well-informed and can direct you to points of interest around the area. The monument and centre stand on Vimeiro Hill and Junot's command post and the slope before it can be clearly seen from the viewpoints here. It is easy to see how exposed the French columns attacking this position would have been to cannon fire as they marched down the slope of the opposite ridge.

The museum curators can tell you a great deal about the battle. A large amount of shot of various kinds has been discovered at Vimeiro by villagers and donated with much of it on display. In addition to shako plates and other items, the discovery of musket-balls and cannon projectiles can tell us a great deal about where engagements were fought. For example, an area of woodland before and to the right of Vimeiro Hill is where the majority of shell casings and shrapnel was discovered, strongly implying that a French column advanced upwards at this point and was fired upon by several batteries. Another intriguing area is a patch of marshy ground at the centre and roughly towards the base of the allied slope. Due to the number of artefacts discovered here, it is believed that many fugitives were killed in this area, pursued either by Fane's or Anstruther's infantry or cut down during Taylor's cavalry charge. This has led to local people giving it the ominous name of 'blood lagoon'. Villagers recall tales of their forefathers digging musket-balls out of nearby trees long after 1808 and it is definitely worth asking the curators about such intriguing local history.

Walking back into the village, the church of São Miguel, where some of the most vicious street-fighting took place, can be found easily by following the main road into the village. However, it should be borne in mind that the slope around it has been modified over the years and the walls heightened and improved. A large old corner house to the south of the church is also reputed to have been taken over by Wellesley prior to the battle and was probably used by him for some days afterwards. Currently it houses the village mortuary.

It is possible to drive up onto the eastern ridge, which affords a grandstand view of where the French deployed. It is easy to see how Wellesley could have fully observed and been able to counteract Junot's moves from points along the ridge. It is probably as steep as it was in 1808 as the area is relatively un-developed but even the museum staff are uncertain over exactly where the clashes occurred between Ferguson's brigades and those of Solignac and Brenier. Most authorities agree that these occurred in the region of Ventosa village but perhaps only battlefield archaeology, planned over the next few years, will reveal their exact location. Bear in mind that Portugal has strict laws about archaeology and that metal detectors can only be used by those with official permission.

Junot's main command point is thought to have been opposite the battle-field centre near an isolated modern building that stands out on the hillside. Travelling up to this area, use the position of the battlefield centre before you to judge where Junot would have stood, which would have been directly opposite Vimeiro Hill for most of the battle. This vantage point was very inferior to Wellesley's position for the views it affords yet, considering how much effect Junot's decisions had upon events, it is possibly the most intriguing location. Though the potential for cutting the allies off from the sea must have been enticing, the steepness of the Valongo Ridge on Junot's left is apparent from here and one can see why he decided against mounting an assault there. However, Vimeiro Hill enjoys a higher elevation and the eastern ridge dominates this point totally, denying an observer the ability to detect movement on those heights from here. Therefore it is less easy to imagine how Junot felt justified in sending a large portion of his army east in such a wide flanking manoeuvre. The long slope running down from this point is also evident and its exposed nature clearly reveals how vulnerable large French formations would have been to allied artillery (even at long range) as they marched down towards Vimeiro Hill. Even 200 years after the battle, the topography around Vimeiro reveals a great deal about how events unfolded in 1808.

Porto Novo

If you have time after Vimeiro, finding the small village of Porto Novo is relatively easy by driving through the village and turning left along the river. The short journey to Porto Novo is perhaps more revealing than the destination itself as the river and the high slopes enclosing it present a serious obstacle to forces either retreating or advancing from the Valongo Ridge. Even today, the road to Vimeiro is narrow and, as a supply route, it would have been an easy task to cut it off by forces approaching from some directions. When you reach Porto Novo, you will see that the beaches made a good landing point, although they are not as expansive as those to the north where Wellesley landed at Mondego Bay. There are some small monuments depicting events in 1808, using the tile-work so beloved by the Portuguese.

Notes

1. Solitaire, Elman, *Canto Patriotico*, Portugal, Lisboa na Imressão Regia, 1812, p. 4. Note that in the original old form of Portuguese, the verses of this song are written in rhyming couplets. This effect is virtually impossible to translate into English without altering the writer's original meaning, hence this translation is literal.

Chapter 1: House of Bragança

1. *Annual Register 1807*, p. 761. This was the Fourth Coalition drawn up on 6 October 1806, which included the countries of Britain, Russia and Prussia in an alliance against France.
2. Ibid., p. 761. This refers to the British policy of attacking French colonies, or those of their allies, in South America. Two attempts were made against Buenos Aires in 1806 and 1807, the second ending in near farce when the reverses suffered by General Whitelocke's army forced Britain to abandon the venture.
3. Ibid., p. 761.
4. Chandler, David G, *The Campaigns of Napoleon*, London, Weidenfeld and Nicolson, 1967, pp. 589–590.
5. *The Times*, 15 January 1808, p. 3.
6. *Annual Register* 1808, p. 739. This edict was signed by Brahl on behalf of the Royal Prussian Court of Navigation and Trade at Memel, 2 September 1807.
7. *Annual Register* 1808, pp. 299–300.
8. Jones, Ben R, *Napoleon, Man and Myth*, London, Hodder & Stoughton, 1977, p. 64.
9. Talleyrand-Périgord, Charles, *Mémoires du Prince De Talleyrand*, vol. 1, Paris, Les Editions Henri Javal, 1953, p. 183.
10. Ibid., p. 185.
11. Oman, Charles, *A History of the Peninsular War*, vol. 1, Oxford, The Clarendon Press, 1902, p. 2.
12. Chandler, *The Campaigns of Napoleon*, p. 597.
13. Esdaile, Charles, *The Peninsular War*, London, Penguin Books, 2003, pp. 5–6.

14. Thompson, J M, *Letters of Napoleon*, Oxford, Basil Blackwell, 1934, p. 204. This letter was written on 12 October 1807.
15. Oman, vol. 1, p. 8. Talleyrand claimed that Napoleon ordered Romana to take 20,000 men to defend Denmark remarking: 'It is clear that Napoleon was not taking any chances,' by this action. See Talleyrand, vol. 1, p. 186.
16. Oman, vol. 1, pp. 9–10.
17. See Chandler, p. 597 and Oman, vol. 1, p. 7.
18. Wilcken, Patrick, *Empire Adrift: The Portuguese Court in Rio de Janeiro 1808–1821*, London, Bloomsbury Publishing Plc, 2004, p. 9.
19. Foy, Maximilien, *Junot's Invasion of Portugal (1807–1808)*, p. 12.
20. *The Times*, 18 November 1807, p. 2. In fact Holland was one of the least enthusiastic participants in the Continental System. Although King Louis Bonaparte sat on the Dutch throne, he was reluctant to enforce his brother's embargo as it was not in his subjects' best interests. His failure to comply led to quarrels with Napoleon and his eventual abdication in 1810.
21. Esdaile, pp. 3–4.
22. *The Times*, Tuesday 13 October 1807, p. 2. Viscount Strangford found fame as a Portuguese language expert after his translation of the poet Camões's verse into English. Though the accuracy of his interpretation was criticized by some it won enough praise for him to be seen as an authority on Portuguese affairs and certainly assisted his appointment to such an important position at the age of only 22. See Wilcken, pp. 7–8.
23. *The Times*, Tuesday 13 October 1807, p. 2.
24. Wilcken, p. 17. Strangford also suggested sending the fleet to Madeira as a half measure, which would at least ensure that it was out of French reach.

Chapter 2: The Tempest
1. Abrantes, Duchess d', Laure Junot, *Mémoires de Madame la duchesse d'Abrantes: ou Souvenirs sur Napoléon, le Directoire, le Consulat, l'Empire et la Restauration*, vol. 2, Paris, La Haye Vervloet, 1831–1835, p. 161.
2. Dubreton, J Lucas, *Junot dit 'La Tempête'*, Paris, Gallimard, 1937, p. 7.
3. Ibid., p. 10.
4. Haythornthwaite, Philip J, *Wellington's Military Machine*, Tunbridge Wells, Ravelin Limited, 1989, p. 50. Shrapnel's new form of shell had been used briefly in 1804 but its first serious use in battle would be at Vimeiro 1808. Initially Wellington distrusted them, believing that cutting the fuse accurately enough to ensure it exploded at the right time was too difficult to be entirely reliable.
5. Griffith, Paddy (ed.), *A History of the Peninsular War, vol 9*, London, Greenhill Books, 1999, p. 256.

6. MacKay, Charles Hugh, *The Tempest: The Life and Career of Jean-Andoche Junot, 1771–1813*, Florida, The Florida State University College of Arts and Sciences, 1995, p. 10.
7. MacKay, p. 11. Thiébault referred to his army nickname as being 'the Hurricane'. See Butler, Arthur John (ed.), *The Memoirs of Baron Thiébault*, vol. 2, London, Smith, Elder & Co., 1896, p. 193.
8. Thiébault, vol. 2, p. 191.
9. Ibid., p. 192.
10. MacKay, p. 15. See also Thiébault, vol. 2, p. 192 – 'Polite of these English,' he said, laughing, 'to send me some sand just when I wanted it.' Sand was used to dry the ink and prevent smudging when writing at this time.
11. Thiébault, vol. 2, p. 192. Junot was referring to his contempt for the political commissars by this statement, many fighting men believing that they wielded undue military influence at the time. Indeed, even senior officers were executed for unavoidable failures or 'political unreliability' by men who possessed little military knowledge.
12. MacKay, p. 18. Junot was one of many soldiers utterly captivated by the magnetic personality of Buonaparte. Jean Baptiste de Santeuil 1630–1697 was a French priest, poet and hymn composer whose verses referred to the idea that, in order to know God, one had to become as one with him. However, it is possible that his brother Claude de Santeuil originated this concept, which both Voltaire and Racine also identified with.
13. Ibid., p. 21.
14. Thiébault, vol. 2, p. 192.
15. MacKay, p. 27.
16. Ibid., p. 30.
17. Ibid., pp. 31–32.
18. Ibid., pp. 44–45.
19. Ibid., p. 51.
20. Brindle, Rosemary (ed.), *Memoirs of Napoleon's Egyptian Expedition 1798–1801*, London, Greenhill Books, 2001, p. 71. Moiret was stationed at Damiette at this time and General Dupuy, forewarned of trouble, was attacked just as he was arranging countermeasures against the rebels.
21. Dubreton, p. 34.
22. Ibid., p. 34.
23. Abrantes, vol. 2, pp. 202–203.
24. Cohen, Louis, *Napoleonic Anecdotes*, London, Robert Holden and Co. Ltd., 1925, p. 107. Nevertheless, Bonaparte gave Junot 100,000 francs as a wedding gift and sent Laure 40,000 francs to buy a wedding dress – see MacKay, pp. 74–75.
25. MacKay, pp. 77–78.

26. Ibid., p. 88.
27. Abrantes, vol. 7, p. 234.
28. MacKay, p. 92.
29. Ibid., p. 93. The corpse was stored in Madam Junot's room due to lack of space, although this practice must have been unusual even in rural Spain.
30. Wilcken, p. 15.
31. Dubreton, p. 86.
32. MacKay, p. 96.
33. Chrisawn, Margaret, 'A military bull in a diplomatic China shop: General Jean Lanne's mission to Lisbon 1802–1804', http://www.napoleon-series. org/ins/scholarship98/c_lannes.html, pp. 1–12.
34. MacKay, p. 99.
35. Ibid., p. 107.
36. Ibid., pp. 112–113.
37. Thiébault, vol. 2, p. 193. Napoleon was so angry over Junot's behaviour that he allegedly roared at him: 'Have you lost your mind?'
38. Thiébault, vol. 2, p. 193.
39. Abrantes, vol. 10, pp. 162–166. See also Dubreton, pp. 102–103 and MacKay, pp. 116–117.
40. Abrantes, vol. 10, p. 220.
41. Thiébault, vol. 2, p. 193. Indeed many of Napoleon's high-ranking officers recognized no superior other than the Emperor, whose deliberate favouritism divided them, reducing the chances of one of them supplanting him. Ney and Bessières were good examples of officers who felt answerable only to Napoleon, a fact that caused friction when they were placed under Marshal Massena's command during the Third Invasion of Portugal – see Buttery, David, *Wellington Against Massena*, Barnsley, Pen & Sword, 2007, p. 64, p. 132, p. 143 et al.
42. Foy, Maximilien, *Junot's Invasion of Portugal (1807–1808)*, Tyne and Wear, Worley Publications, 2000 (originally 1829), p. 6. In addition to his renown as a soldier, Junot's recent association with Portugal was well known.
43. Thiébault, vol. 2, pp. 193–194. Thiébault later wrote that: 'Napoleon knew that Junot had not the qualities required for the part assigned to him; and a punishment, because the command, given in anger and accepted with deep vexation, was at the same time one of those pieces of favouritism which, by exciting the jealousy of rivals, form the misfortune of those who are the objects of them and the delight of their enemies.' – Ibid, p. 191.
44. MacKay, p. 36.
45. Oman, vol. 1, p. 8.

Chapter 3: Junot's March on Lisbon

1. Johnston, R M (ed.), *The Corsican*, Boston and New York, Houghton Mifflin Company, 1910, p. 281. Champagny had been Minister of the Interior but became Foreign Minister when Talleyrand resigned in 1807.
2. Foy, pp. 16–17.
3. Ibid., pp. 16–17.
4. Ibid., p. 19.
5. Thiébault, vol. 2, p. 196.
6. Remarking with hindsight, Thiébault wrote: 'What a contrast was there between their present disposition and the deadly hatred for us which before a year was out animated that same population!' Thiébault, vol. 2, p. 196.
7. Johnston, *The Corsican*, p. 281.
8. Foy, p. 21.
9. Ibid., p. 22. Foy recorded how many maps failed to name rivers or indicate roads and tracks.
10. Ibid., p. 19. However, it should be borne in mind that the bulk of Napoleon's campaigning had taken place on the fertile plains of Europe, where plentiful supplies and good roads were the norm. Though he encountered supply difficulties in Egypt 1799 and Poland 1807, this pre-dated his own invasions of Spain and Russia where the French military strategy of 'living off the land' proved unsustainable for long periods.
11. Foy, p. 23.
12. Ibid., pp. 23–26.
13. Ibid., p. 27. This was a derogatory slight on Great Britain's seaborne might.
14. Junot, Jean-Andoche, *Diário da I Invasão Francesa*, p. 95. Junot's letter of 19 November 1807 from Alcántara.
15. Junot, Jean-Andoche, p. 97. Letter dated 19 November 1807.
16. Foy, p. 32.
17. Thiébault, vol. 2, p. 196.
18. Foy, pp. 30–31.
19. Thiébault, vol. 2, p. 197.
20. Boletim do Arquivo Histórico Militar, Vol. 8, 1938 – *Notícias enviadas em 1807, de Lisboa, em cartas escritas por um official português*, pp. 284–289. This letter was written from Principal Sousa on 11 November 1807 to Dr Salinas Colado supõe tartar-se de Filipe.
21. Haythornthwaite, Philip, *The Peninsular War – The Complete Companion to the Iberian Campaigns 1807–14*, London, Brassey's, 2004, p. 169. These districts were the northern provinces of Minho and Tras os Montes, the central regions of Beira and Estremadura and the southern regions of Algarva and Alemtejo.

22. Fortescue, John, *A History of The British Army, vol 6, 1807–1809*, London, Macmillan and Co., 1921, p. 101.

23. Junot, Jean-Andoche, p. 98. Letter written at Abrantes, 25 November 1807.

24. Thiébault, vol. 2, p. 197.

25. Ibid., pp. 197–198.

26. Foy, p. 34.

27. *The Times*, 20 January 1808, p. 2. In a direct quotation from the French newspaper *Le Moniteur* (published 5 December 1807) this article continued that Britain had thus been deprived of her last remaining ally (discounting Sweden and Sicily) and had thereby lost the use of important ports like Lisbon and Porto. Gibraltar would now be the only safe naval staging point on the voyage from Britain into the Mediterranean. It also alleged that Britain was now totally isolated from the Continent and was alienating powers like America with her draconian policy of boarding and searching neutral vessels as part of the trade war.

28. Maxwell, Kenneth, *Conflicts & Conspiracies: Brazil and Portugal, 1750–1808*, London, Routledge, 2004, pp. 233–234. Dom Rodrigo de Sousa Coutinho had been Secretary of State for the Overseas Dominions and was appointed President of the Royal Treasury in 1800.

29. *Annual Register* 1807, pp. 775–776. The proclamation ended: 'Palace of the Ajuda, 27 November 1807 – THE PRINCE.'

30. *Annual Register* 1807, p. 776.

31. Wilcken, p. 22.

32. Ibid., p. 25. The Royal Fleet comprised twelve warships and over thirty smaller craft – see Fortescue, vol. 6, p. 102.

33. *The Times*, 6 January 1808, p. 2. The article went on to state that many of the townspeople were so agitated that they approached the Viceroy demanding: 'to rise *en masse* against the invading French. Their rage was boundless but the Viceroy deemed it proper to repress, instead of encouraging their patriotic ardour.' – Ibid., p. 2.

34. Foy, p. 47. It should be borne in mind that Foy did not personally witness this spectacle, being with Junot's army at the time.

35. Wilcken, p. 24.

36. Thompson, p. 206.

37. Ibid., p. 205. In this dispatch dated 12 November, Napoleon continued that all suitable ships should be kept fully armed, crewed and provisioned: 'so that I may have 7 or 8 battleships ready to sail anywhere.' Ibid., p. 205.

38. Foy, p. 52.

39. Ibid., p. 53. However, Moore had been obliged to wait and rendezvous with Fraser's force sailing from Egypt before embarking from Messina on

25 October. Due to bad weather, the fleet had only reached Gibraltar by 1 December. It is therefore unlikely that the British could have landed enough troops in time to interfere. See Fortescue, vol. 6, p. 103.

40. Thiébault, vol. 2, p. 199. The French newspapers reported that Junot: 'was very favourably received by the inhabitants. Such was the confidence of the French, that the shops were not shut, nor was business interrupted for an instant.' See *The Times* 29 December 1807, p. 2 (translated from the French newspapers, 15 December).

41. Thiébault, vol. 2, p. 199.

42. Ibid., p. 199.

43. Foy, p. 55.

Chapter 4: Brought Before Maneta

1. Oman, vol. 1, p. 37.

2. Ibid., p. 52 (Oman was quoting Escoiquiz here). Oman considered the deposition of the Spanish monarchy to be one of Napoleon's most heinous acts. Contemporary British sources agreed, the *Annual Register* dramatically proclaiming that France had seized Spain's king: 'with the basest treachery, unprecedented in the annals of civilized nations, made him their prisoner, treated him in a manner most disrespectful, and forced him to the deeds of horror, which all Europe has witnessed with astonishment, and every Spaniard with indignation ...' – See the *Annual Register*, 1808, p. 334.

3. *The Times*, 6 January 1808, p. 3. *The Times* was reporting the words of the *Gazette de France* newspaper here, dated 16 December 1807.

4. Foy, p. 82. Junot believed, as did many of his countrymen, that the Regent's flight and supposed desertion of his people effectively endorsed French rule. Some members of Napoleon's Marshalate did eventually become kings, such as Murat and Bernadotte, so the prospect of Junot becoming King of Portugal was a realistic possibility.

5. Ibid., p. 66.

6. Thompson, p. 206. Although this quotation strongly implies that Napoleon held the Portuguese army in contempt, it also reveals that he acknowledged them as a potential threat.

7. Many of these soldiers deserted on the march to France and some even enlisted with the Spanish. However, Foy estimated that over 3,000 men arrived in France and Napoleon used them to form a Portuguese Legion (*Légion Portugaise*) within the French army. Although they were used in detachments and never acted as a complete brigade, these unhappy exiles gave good service, two battalions winning renown at the battle of Wagram 1809 against the Austrians. Napoleon hesitated to use them in the Peninsula

for obvious reasons and the majority of them perished during Napoleon's invasion of Russia 1812.

8. *The Times*, 6 January 1808, p. 3. Here *The Times* was quoting from the French newspaper *Le Moniteur*.

9. Boletim do Arquivo Histórico Militar, vol. 8, 1938 – *Notícias enviadas em 1807, de Lisboa*, pp. 284–289.

10. Foy, p. 78. The Russian fleet comprised one 80-gun battleship, eight frigates and several smaller vessels. They possessed crews totalling around 6,000 sailors and marines with about 100 men from each ship regularly quartered ashore.

11. Ibid., p. 63. To this day, the Rossio is the popular name for the *Praça Dom Pedro IV*, one of Lisbon's most important squares.

12. D'Alorna was later made an Inspector General over the Portuguese regular troops – see Junot, Jean-Andoche, *Diário da I Invasão Francesa*, p. 123 – letter of 27 December 1807. After spending some time in France, he returned to Portugal with Marshal Massena during the Third French Invasion of his nation.

13. Foy, p. 64.

14. Ibid., pp. 65–66. Foy wrote: 'The opportunity was a favourable one to substitute feelings of terror, instead of the impression which had at first been made on the inhabitants of Lisbon by the pitiable state of the French army.' – Ibid., p. 64. Cesar also recorded that riots took place in Lisbon's Commercial Square and that several Frenchmen were murdered afterwards in the night – see Cesar, Victoriano J, *Invasões Francesas em Portugal, 1a parte, Invasão franco-espanhola de 1807, Roliça e Vimeiro*, Lisboa (Portugal), typ. da Cooperativa Militar, 1904, p. 48.

15. Junot, Jean-Andoche, *Diário da I Invasão Francesa*, pp. 115–116 – from a letter written on 16 December 1807.

16. *The Times*, 18 February 1808, p. 3. Translated from Portuguese newspapers on 4 December 1807. Cesar also records that large gatherings of Portuguese citizens were forbidden – see Cesar, pp. 48–49.

17. *The Times*, 19 February 1808, p. 4. Translated from the Portuguese newspapers of 5 December 1807.

18. Thompson, p. 207.

19. Napoleon wrote: 'Your chief of staff is an unscrupulous man: he took a lot of money at Fulde. Insist upon his observing a strict rule and make it known that if there is any thieving, I shall punish it.' – see Thompson, p. 207.

20. *The Times*, 19 February 1808, p. 4. This was translated from the Portuguese newspapers, Francisco Mello making the official proclamation.

21. Foy, pp. 82–83.

22. Ibid., p. 73.

23. Ibid., p. 74.

24. Esdaile, p. 38.

25. Ibid., pp. 39–40. Estimates of the number of people killed in the *Dos de Mayo* vary but Murat recorded that 145 French soldiers and 300 Spaniards lost their lives. Yet the true number of Spaniards killed can only be guessed. Rudorff claims that it was unlikely to have exceeded 1,500. See Rudorff, Raymond, *War to the Death*, London, W&J Mackay Ltd., 1974, pp. 38–39.

26. *The Times*, 8 April 1808, p. 3. The editor chose to keep the writer's identity secret, perhaps fearing that publication might provoke the French authorities to take measures against him. It was printed as: 'an extract from a letter sent from Oporto to a house of the first respectability in the City (London).' The editor would not have gone to press without knowing the true source of such information and therefore must have deliberately published it as an anonymous source.

27. *The Times*, 3 May 1808, p. 4. This article also revealed the French Government's concern that large numbers of qualified professionals were fleeing overseas that Portugal could ill afford to lose. Consequentially stern measures were adopted to deter unauthorized emigration, including confiscation of property and potential death sentences.

28. *The Times*, 8 April 1808, p. 3.

29. Fortescue, vol. 6, p. 187.

30. Foy, p. 101.

31. *Annual Register* 1808, p. 325.

32. Ibid., p. 326. He signed this proclamation the Bishop, Governor and President.

33. Foy, p. 90.

34. Ibid., p. 103.

35. Jomini, Antoine-Henri, Baron de, *The Art of War*, New York, Dover Publication Inc., 2007, p. 29. Marshal Suchet's policies in Aragon and Valencia (Spain) during the Peninsular War and General Hoche's strategy in the Vendée region of France were used by Jomini as models of this approach.

36. Chartrand, René, *Vimeiro 1808*, Oxford, Osprey Publishing Ltd., 2001, p. 24.

37. Ibid., pp. 24–25.

38. Foy, p. 92. Foy claims that this attack took place at Mesao Frio before the rearguard left the banks of the Douro but Chartrand claims that it took place later during the battle – see Chartrand, p. 26. Indeed, Foy either ignored or was unaware of the main conflict that took place at Teixeira.

39. Cesar, p. 67 – Cesar wrote that the worst possible atrocities were committed, including the slaughter of women and children.
40. Foy, p. 98.
41. Chartrand, p. 28. However, Napier disputes tales of atrocities at Guarda, claiming they were exaggerated. Loison had only 3,000 men and to kill as many as 1,200 in an action that lasted little over thirty minutes by a force that lacked artillery was unlikely, he claimed. He believed that confusion arose due to the number of townsfolk who fled into the hills when the town fell – see Napier, vol. 1, p. 102. Nonetheless, Chartrand asserts that Loison did have artillery and, if innocents were slain in the aftermath of the fighting, this figure is certainly possible. Portuguese historian Valente comments that harsh methods employed against civilians could either crush resistance or exacerbate the problem. In the case of the 1808 Revolt, further rebellion was provoked by atrocities and, as soon as the French punitive columns marched on, resistance sprang up again. See Valente, Vasco Pulido, *Ir Pro Maneta*, Lisboa, Portugal, Alethia Editores, 2007, p. 69.
42. Napier, Major General Sir W F P, *History of the War in the Peninsula*, vol. 1, London, Frederick Warne and Co., 1851, p. 102.
43. Foy, p. 129.
44. Cesar, pp. 82–83.
45. Foy, p. 130.
46. Oman puts the figure closer to 2,000 but in fact the true figure will probably never be known. See Chartrand, p. 29.
47. Valente, p. 73. Valente also refers to Thiébault, Baron, *Relation de l'expedition du Portugal, faite en 1807 et 1808, par le 1.er Corps d'Observation de la Gironde, devenu Armee de Portugal*, Paris, 1817, pp. 172–173.
48. Valente revealed that this phrase rapidly became a part of the Portuguese language; see Valente, p. 68. Foy claims that Loison had actually lost an arm rather than just a hand in combat and also refers to his reputation for ferocity, though he considered it exaggerated. See Foy, p. 122.
49. Foy, p. 99.
50. Ibid., p. 108. Tales of how the Spanish city of Zaragoza withstood two major sieges also proved an inspiration for those who resisted the French. Though strategically unimportant, the people of the city defied attempts to storm it between 15 June and 17 August 1808. The city only fell on 20 February 1809, after the French were forced to fight from house to house within the city and destroy large sections of Zaragoza before its defenders finally submitted.
51. Thiébault, vol. 2, pp. 200–201. Thiébault's scheme is curiously similar to Wellington's later plan to defend Lisbon, though admittedly on a lesser

scale. Rather than fortify the Setúbal Peninsula, Wellington constructed the Lines of Torres Vedras roughly 25 miles north of Lisbon, cutting off the entire Lisbon Peninsula to protect the capital. Building began in 1809 and was only fully completed by 1812. Marshal Massena's advance on the capital was stopped in its tracks by these fortifications in 1810.
52. Napier, vol. 1, p. 101.

Chapter 5: The Lion Awakes

1. Glover, Michael, *Britannia Sickens*, London, Leo Cooper Limited, 1970, pp. 26–28.
2. *Cobbett's Parliamentary Debates*, vol. 10, 21 Jan–8 April 1808, London, T.C. Hansard, 1808, p. 35. A motion had been added to the protests over Copenhagen that was supported by a number of influential members including Lord Lauderdale, Lord Grey, Lord Norfolk, Lord Suffolk, W. Frederick and Vassal Holland.
3. *Cobbett's Parliamentary Debates*, vol. 11, 11 April–4 July 1808, p. 1138.
4. Ibid., p. 1139.
5. Ibid., pp. 1139–1145.
6. Oman, vol. 1, pp. 221–222.
7. Keegan, John, *The Mask of Command*, London, Penguin Books, 1988, pp. 114–115. It should be noted that cattle such as bullocks, or oxen, were used to pull carts and carry baggage in India and later in the Peninsula.
8. Glover, p. 36. Famous for his love of concise speech and orders, Wellesley may have preferred the oft-quoted shorter version of this endorsement: 'I never met any military officer with whom it was so satisfactory to converse. He states every difficulty before he undertakes any service, but none after he has undertaken it.' See Stanhope, Earl, *Life of the Right Honourable William Pitt*, vol. 4, London, John Murray, 1867, p. 375.
9. Fortescue, vol. 6, p. 190.
10. *Wellington's Supplementary Dispatches*, vol. 6, p. 87.
11. Warre, Lieutenant General Sir William, *Letters from the Peninsula 1808–1812*, London, John Murray, 1909, p. 6. Letter dated 8 June 1808.
12. *Wellington's Dispatches*, vol. 4, p. 16 – Castlereagh to Wellesley, 30 June 1808.
13. Fortescue, vol. 6, p. 194.
14. Pool, Bernard (ed.), *The Croker Papers 1808–1857*, London, B.T. Batsford Ltd., 1967, p. 11.
15. Glover, p. 49. However, Fortescue claims that the fleet sailed the day afterwards on 13 July 1808 – see Fortescue, p. 191.
16. *Wellington's Dispatches*, vol. 4, p. 19. Castlereagh to Wellesley, 30 June 1808.

17. Oman, vol. 1, pp. 227–228. 13,700 French under Bessières had defeated 22,000 Spaniards at this battle, inflicting around 2,000 casualties upon them. Though the Spaniards had fought hard, 1,000 newly-recruited men deserted and ten Spanish guns were lost. The French suffered around 400 casualties. Also see Glover, pp. 53–54.

18. Glover, p. 52. Wellesley formed the impression that: 'There is no such thing as a French party in the country, and I believe there is no man who dares avow that he wishes well to the French cause.' – See *Wellington's Supplementary Dispatches*, vol. 13, p. 292.

19. Glover, p. 55.

20. *Wellington's Dispatches*, vol. 4, p. 47.

21. NAM: 5903-127, The Letters of Captain William Granville Eliot, Royal Artillery.

22. Warre, pp. 21–22. Letter from Camp at Lavos, near Figueira, 8 August 1808.

23. Wardell, John (ed.), *With 'The Thirty-Second' in the Pensinsular and other Campaigns*, Dublin, Hodges, Figgis & Co. Ltd., 1904, p. 96.

24. Ibid., p. 97.

25. *Wellington's Dispatches*, vol. 4, p. 55 – Wellesley to Castlereagh, 1 August 1808.

26. *Wellington's Supplementary Dispatches*, vol. 6, p. 95. Wellesley also wrote that he expected to be joined by Spencer and his troops within two days. He had heard from Spencer, who believed there were 20,000 French troops in Portugal, a figure Wellesley discredited – ibid., p. 95.

Chapter 6: 'One of our most important affairs'

1. Warre, p. 22. Letter from the camp at Lavos.

2. NAM: 1964-04-76 and 6594-1808-14, Anonymous, *Journal of a Soldier of the 71st or Glasgow Regiment, Highland Light Infantry from 1806–1815*, Edinburgh, Balfour & Clarke, 1819. In recent years research has been carried out concerning the identity of this anonymous soldier of the 71st, identified in the original manuscript only as 'Thomas'. The best project so far has been conducted by Stuart Reid who discovered that John Howell of Edinburgh probably compiled the book using the recollections of two men. The vast majority of the narrative is attributable to one Joseph Sinclair of the 71st, including the bulk of the Peninsular War material, and the final chapters are probably from the reminiscences of James Todd of the same regiment. See Reid, Stuart, 'The Mysterious Highlander', *Military Illustrated*, 245 (October 2008), pp. 16–23.

3. *Wellington's Supplementary Dispatches*, vol. 6, p. 97. Two letters from Wellesley to Lord Burghersh from Lavos 3 and 5 August 1808.

4. Ibid., p. 98. Written to Lord Burghersh under his command on 5 August.

5. *The Times*, 5 September 1808, p. 3. Nevertheless, Carvalho lists nine other men of rank who accompanied him in this enterprise, including non-commissioned officers.

6. Ibid., p. 3.

7. Ibid., p. 3. Note that De Novion was anxious to capture and publicly punish some of the deserters, no doubt hoping to discourage others from joining the revolt. He also cautioned Gambus that the cavalry were armed with sabres, pistols and six cartridges per man. De Novion was a French émigré who had spent some years in Lisbon. He dated this order Lisbon 1 August 1808.

8. *The Times*, 5 September 1808, p. 3.

9. Ibid., p. 3. Pereira's account was translated directly from Portuguese and dated Coimbra 8 August 1808. The spelling of Baron *Deviomenil* is in accordance with this account but the author has not been able to find any confirmation of this officer's name and command.

10. Ibid., p. 3.

11. Ibid., p. 3. Pereira rode his men to Thomar and stayed there overnight but French forces failed to materialize and they left the following day.

12. *Wellington's Supplementary Dispatches*, vol. 6, pp. 102–104. Writing to Admiral Sir Charles Cotton from Lavos, 8 August 1808.

13. Foy, p. 148.

14. Ibid., p. 149.

15. Oman calculated that Delaborde probably fielded 5,779 men at the subsequent Battle of Roliça but conceded that through sickness and other factors he might have had as few as 4,350. See Oman, vol. I, p. 235. French accounts place the figure much lower and Oman criticizes Thiébault's figure of 1,900 as a gross underestimate, see Thiébault, vol. 2, p. 204.

16. *Wellington's Supplementary Dispatches*, vol. 6, p. 106. General Order concerning carts, 8 August 1808 from camp near Lavos.

17. Ibid., pp. 104–105. To the Lord Bishop of Oporto, camp near Lavos, 8 August 1808.

18. Weller, Jac, *Wellington in the Peninsula 1808–1814*, Whitstable, Purnell Book Services Ltd., 1973, pp. 32–33.

19. Ross-Lewin, Harry, Major, *With 'The Thirty-Second' In the Peninsular and other Campaigns*, Dublin, Hodges, Figgis & Co. Ltd., 1904, p. 98. In fairness, the junta had provided supplies for 'allied' usage.

20. Oman, vol. 1, p. 233.

21. Leslie, Colonel K H, *Military Journal of Colonel Leslie whilst serving with the 29th Regt in the Peninsula, and the 60th Rifles in Canada, etc, 1807–1832*,

Aberdeen, Aberdeen University Press, 1887, p. 38. In reference to Hill's subsequent remark, Leslie wrote: 'The poor fellows had little or no uniform, but were merely in white jackets, and large broad-brimmed hats turned up at one side, some having feathers and others none, so that they cut rather a grotesque appearance.' Ibid., p. 40.

22. Oman, vol. 1, pp. 235–236.
23. Curling, Henry (ed.), *Recollections of Rifleman Harris*, London, Peter Davies Ltd., 1929, p. 27. The position the riflemen took up was to counter a feared cavalry attack. Wellesley later commented that this 'little affair of advanced posts' had been 'foolishly brought on by the over-eagerness of the riflemen in the pursuit of an enemy's piquet'. However, though critical of their impetuous action, he felt the troops had fought well – see *Wellington's Supplementary Dispatches*, vol. 6, p. 115.
24. *Wellington's Supplementary Dispatches*, vol. 6, p. 115. Wellesley to the Duke of Richmond, from Caldas, 16 August 1808.
25. Ross-Lewin, p. 100.
26. Oman, vol. 1, p. 237.
27. Ross-Lewin, p. 101.
28. Leslie, p. 41. Ross-Lewin stated that his battalion also suffered un-necessary losses at this stage in the battle, blaming the slowness of the flanking forces getting into position – see Ross-Lewin, p. 100.
29. Everard, Major H, *History of Thomas Farrington's Regiment subsequently designated the 29th (Worcestershire) Foot 1694 to 1891*, Worcester, Littlebury & Co., The Worcester Press, 1891, p. 278. This incident was witnessed by Dr Guthrie (regimental surgeon) who was positioned just behind the colour party. A regiment would carry two colours (or standards) bearing the regiment's own flag and that bestowed upon them by the sovereign.
30. Everard, p. 279. See also Wills, p. 74 and Landmann, *Recollections of my Military Life*, vol. 2, London, Hurst and Blackett, 1854, pp. 137–138.
31. Fortescue, vol. 6, p. 210.
32. Leslie, p. 42. Leslie conceded that the 29th was only supposed to occupy Columbeira and make a demonstration against the French position but there were no orders about making a general advance. He surmised that Lake probably misunderstood his instructions – see ibid., pp. 44–45. However, Willis cites evidence that Lake's actions in India imply considerable recklessness, such as the incident when he attacked a vastly superior force at Laswaree 1803 in a good defensive position, without even waiting for the artillery to deploy. See Willis, Clive, 'Colonel George Lake and the Battle of Roliça', *Portuguese Studies*, vol. 12 (1996), pp. 68–77.
33. Leslie, p. 42.

34. Letter of Major Gregory Way, 29th Foot, written on board the *Vasco da Gama*, a Portuguese gunship on the Tagus, 26 August 1808.
35. Ibid. Following his capture, Way was marched with other prisoners to Lisbon and imprisoned aboard a ship on the Tejo. Fortescue claims that four officers and thirty men of the 29th were taken prisoner in this fight, see Fortescue, vol. 6, p. 212.
36. Maxwell, W H, *The Victories of the British Armies*, vol. I, London, Richard Bentley, 1839, pp. 106–107.
37. Harris, p. 22. Harris was comparing the losses of his battalion to those suffered by the 29th. By 'too near' Harris referred to the fact that the 95th could not utilize the superior range of the Baker Rifle to advantage as, by the time they saw the French skirmishers deployed on the reverse slope, they were well within musket range. At one point he was forced to use a comrade's body for protection due to lack of cover.
38. Ibid., pp. 25–26. Riflemen carried a 'sword bayonet' that clipped on to the side of the Baker rifle rather than the usual socket bayonet carried by line infantry.
39. Everard, p. 283.
40. Warre, p. 24. The preceding casualty figures are taken from Smith, Digby, *The Greenhill Napoleonic Wars Data Book*, London, Greenhill Books, 1998, p. 266.
41. Oman, vol. 1, p. 239.
42. Ibid., p. 240. Fortescue also wrote that: '... he had fought a most gallant though perhaps unduly rash rearguard-action ...' See Fortescue, vol. 6, p. 213.
43. Hadaway, Stuart, 'Roliça: A Most Important Affair', http://www. napoleon-series.org/, pp. 1–9. Fortescue also commented that Roliça's: '... chief historic interest lies in the curious fact that he, who showed such surpassing skill in hiding his troops in a defensive position, should in his first action against the French have to deal with an enemy concealed with a dexterity that he himself might have envied.' See Fortescue, vol. 6, p. 214.
44. Hadaway, pp. 1–9. In Weller's opinion, Sir Arthur showed great confidence in fighting at Roliça with the potential threat of Loison attacking his left flank, commenting: 'Many commanders in Wellesley's position would not have advanced at all.' See Weller, p. 39. Fortescue also comments that Wellesley's caution was largely due to his fear that Loison might make an appearance – see Fortescue, vol. 6, pp. 213–214.
45. Thiébault, vol. 2, p. 204.
46. Stanhope, Henry, Earl of, *Conversations with the Duke of Wellington 1831–1851*, London, Prion, 1998, p. 29.

Chapter 7: The Lion and the Eagle

1. Fortescue, vol. 6, p. 214.
2. *Wellington's Supplementary Dispatches*, vol. 6, p. 121. General Order, Vimeiro, 20 August 1808.
3. Fortescue, vol. 6, pp. 215–216. Oman believed that the allies fielded 16,778 British troops along with 2,000–2,100 Portuguese under Trant – see Oman, vol. 1, p. 251. Smith puts the combined Anglo-Portuguese forces at 18,669 – see Smith, Digby, *The Greenhill Napoleonic Wars Data Book*, p. 267.
4. Foy, pp. 158–159. On 11 August Junot dispatched General Kellerman to relieve the garrison at Setúbal, who were threatened by insurgents from the south after Loison crossed the Tejo. Kellerman partially destroyed Setúbal's defences and returned to the capital with the garrison – see Fortescue, vol. 6, pp. 216–217.
5. Oman, vol. 1, pp. 243–244. Oman believed that Russian marines and sailors would have sufficed to defend Lisbon but Siniavin obstinately denied Junot any real assistance, declining even to lend guards for the prison hulks moored in the Tejo that contained many Spanish prisoners of war – ibid., p. 244.
6. Foy, pp. 159–160. The visible presence of veteran battalions aboard transports, which Wellesley had lent to the Royal Navy, added substance to this rumour. Junot's panicked reaction also demonstrated his reluctance to leave Lisbon.
7. Ibid., p. 160.
8. Ibid., pp. 160–161.
9. Chartrand, p. 92. According to Oman, the 3rd Regiment of Volunteer Cavalry comprised French expatriate merchants from Lisbon – see also Foy, p. 174. He also commented that Junot's army was already disordered by his haphazard deployment of units in garrisons around Portugal, which had not left a single brigade intact. Junot compounded this by forming his reserve from the grenadier companies from all eighteen of his line regiments – see Oman, vol. 1, pp. 244–245.
10. Oman, vol. 1, p. 252. Junot allowed his men to pause and eat at Villa Facaia, roughly 4 miles from the allied position. Having marched through the night, it was good sense to allow the men some respite but it also denied Junot the advantage of surprise.
11. Fortescue, vol. 6, p. 222.
12. Foy claims that the cavalry: '... which had approached nearest ... merely reported that the English were all concentrated around Vimeiro and that three lines of fires had distinctly been seen during the night.' See Foy, p. 167. See also Thiébault, vol. 2, p. 205.

13. Thiébault, vol. 2, p. 206. Fortescue argued that the French believed there was a British presence at Lourinha, which may explain Brenier's movement. Junot may have believed that the two positions were too far apart to offer mutual support and that Brenier's troops could easily deal with anything they encountered – see Fortescue, vol. 6, p. 224. Such a scenario might also explain why Junot mounted a frontal assault before Brenier was established on the eastern ridge.
14. Foy, p. 168.
15. Chartrand puts the strength of Thomières' brigade at 1,945 men from the 1st and 2nd Battalions of the 86th Ligne along with 246 men from the 4th Swiss infantry in two companies. He estimates Charlot's brigade as 1,034 men from the 3rd Battalion of the 32nd Ligne and 963 men from the 3rd Battalion of the 82nd Ligne – see Chartrand, p. 92. Note that the full strength of the brigades may not have been deployed, hence the approximation of 1,500–2,000 men in each attack column.
16. Keegan, p. 115.
17. Weller believed that the fire-fight began at a distance of about 100 yards and the British in line could use every one of their 900 muskets. In reply the French could only use about 200 of their 1,200 muskets while still in column formation. General Thomières tried to deploy into line but, at such close range and under heavy fire, this proved impossible. See Weller, p. 47. For further analysis of this struggle, see Griffith, p. 238.
18. Foy, p. 172.
19. Hulot, J L, *Souvenirs du Baron Hulot*, Paris, *Spectateur Militaire*, 1886, pp. 234–235.
20. Harris, p. 39. Harris continued that repeated firing demonstrated the disadvantage of black powder weapons. The gunpowder of the day produced large amounts of smoke, which rapidly obscured a rifleman's vision unless a breeze struck up to blow it away. This resulted in men firing almost blind and, consequently, a rifle's advantage over a musket was drastically reduced. In contrast, infantry firing massed volleys with muskets would soon be masked by the smoke of their own discharge and hitting their targets was a matter of educated guesswork on the part of officers and sergeants, who estimated ranges and listened for the sounds of impact to judge whether they were effective or not.
21. Ibid., p. 39.
22. Leslie, p. 49.
23. Ibid., pp. 49–50.
24. Harris, p. 53.

25. Landsheit, Norbert & Gleig G R (ed.), *The Hussar*, England, Leonaur Ltd., 2008, p. 137 and later p. 139 for the 20th's outraged reaction to their alleged timidity. Fortescue distrusts Landsheit's claims about the Portuguese as there are some unsubstantiated claims in his account – see Fortescue, vol. 6, p. 229. Foy also mentions that the Portuguese charged but fails to record them falling back en masse at any stage before they were counter-charged – see Foy, p. 172.

26. Landsheit, p. 137.

27. Ibid., p. 138.

28. Maxwell, p. 115 – for a primary account of this incident see Landsheit, pp. 137–138.

29. Foy, p. 172. Foy records that the 4th and 5th Dragoons were led by Majors Leclerc and Theron. Oman claimed that the 20th Light Dragoons suffered twenty killed, twenty-four wounded and lost eleven men as prisoners in this incident, adding that it was a wonder that any of them regained their own lines without being cut off – see Oman, vol. 1, p. 257.

30. NAM: 1964-04-76 and 6594-1808-14, Anonymous, *Journal of a Soldier of the 71st.*

31. Ibid.

32. Hathaway, Eileen (ed.), *A Dorset Soldier*, Staplehurst, Spellmount Ltd., 1993, p. 34. In fact the British had captured only three guns, all of those that Solignac had with him – see Weller, p. 52. It is possible that Lawrence confused this figure with the total number of guns captured from various parts of the battlefield after hostilities had ceased.

33. Leslie, p. 50.

34. Ibid., p. 51.

35. Ibid., p. 51, also see Fortescue, vol. 6, p. 231.

36. Anonymous, *The Whole Proceedings upon the conduct of Sir Hew Dalrymple, late commander-in-chief of His Majesty's forces in Portugal, relative to the Convention of Cintra*, London, Sherwood, Neely & Jones, 1809, p. 96. This is a quotation from the evidence of Colonel Torrens presented to the Board of Enquiry later that year.

37. Fortescue, vol. 6, pp. 232–233.

38. Ibid., pp. 232–233. Maxwell commented that: 'Sir Harry appeared to have formed a stubborn resolution of remaining quiet that no argument or remonstrance could disturb ...' – see Maxwell, p. 110.

39. Glover, p. 124 – here Glover is using a quotation from Moyle Sherer's memoirs. Another version of what Sir Arthur said was: 'Now we can go and shoot red-legged partridges,' – see ibid., p. 184. Regardless of the wording of his retort, this apparent insubordination did not sit well with the Board of Enquiry, which later examined these events.

Chapter 8: A Tainted Victory

1. Hulot, pp. 234–235.
2. Ibid., p. 235. By 'pieces', Hulot was of course referring to his guns. Other French officers also expected an immediate general advance by the allies at this time – see Foy, pp. 174–175.
3. Thiébault, vol. 2, p. 209. In regard to Thiébault's bias, Junot's surly fits of temper almost drove him to resign on several occasions, despite their friendship – see ibid., p. 200. However, the British later claimed to have captured an *Ordre de Bataille* on the battlefield belonging to Junot that placed the number of the French army at 14,000, which implies that a hurried departure took place – see *Wellington's Supplementary Dispatches*, vol. 6, p. 206.
4. Oman, vol. 1, p. 260. These troops naturally formed a rearguard to cover the retreat along with Margaron's cavalry. Foy claimed that the reinforcements other than the battalion of the 66th consisted of picked companies from the Hanoverian Legion and the Legion of the South – see Foy, p. 175.
5. Thiébault, vol. 2, p. 209 – see also Foy, p. 174.
6. Ross–Lewin, p. 110.
7. Warre, p. 35. Ross–Lewin also refers to this incident but claimed that the Piper's name was George Clerk – see Ross–Lewin, p. 111. For the incident regarding Brenier's watch referred to immediately afterwards, see Warre, p. 35.
8. Warre, p. 30, writing from Lisbon, 17 September 1808. For Warre's damning comments immediately after the battle see ibid., p. 28 and for the soldier of the 71st's comments see NAM: 1964-04-76 and 6594-1808-14, Anonymous, *Journal of a Soldier of the 71st*.
9. *The Times*, Tuesday 6 September 1808, p. 2. This passage was quoted from an unnamed Portuguese newspaper published in Coimbra on 23 August.
10. For the French and British figures see Smith, pp. 266–267. For the Portuguese losses and Paes de Sa's recollection, see Chartrand, p. 81.
11. *Wellington's Supplementary Dispatches*, vol. 6, p. 122. To the Duke of Richmond from the camp at Vimeiro, 22 August 1808.
12. Thiébault, vol. 2, pp. 207–208.
13. Ibid., pp. 205–206. Thiébault thought the French should have made a demonstration against the allied front from the south and attacked directly along the eastern ridge. Had this strategy been adopted, he believed the troops on the isolated Vimeiro Hill would have been cut off and the British forced back into the sea. Such a course would have seen the allies receive far less benefit from the steep ground they occupied, assuming that the French could have achieved this.

14. Ibid., p. 208.
15. Ibid., p. 208.
16. Napier, vol. 1, p. 127. He continued that, by maintaining garrisons in various parts of the country, Junot denied himself the use of 50 per cent of the forces available in Portugal. See Oman, vol. 1, pp. 243–244 for his views on the French garrisons.
17. Fortescue, vol. 6, p. 233.
18. Weller, pp. 55–56.
19. See Griffith, p. 259 for a more detailed analysis of line versus column tactics.
20. Fortescue, vol. 6, p. 195.
21. Glover, pp. 22–23.
22. Ibid., pp. 127–128.
23. Ibid., p. 129.
24. Foy, p. 176.
25. Hulot, p. 236.
26. Glover, pp. 137–138.
27. Ibid., p. 138.
28. Ibid., p. 138.

Chapter 9: An Infamous Act

1. *Wellington's Supplementary Dispatches*, vol. 6, p. 122. Wellesley to Viscount Castlereagh from the camp at Ramahal, 23 August 1808.
2. Ibid., p. 123.
3. Foy, pp. 179–180.
4. Napier, vol. 1, pp. 147–148. Kellerman tried to argue that the *Vasco da Gama* (a Portuguese ship of the line) along with several frigates left by the Regent had been refitted at their expense and should be deemed French. However, Murray rejected this demand and the French failed to press the matter – see Glover, p. 147.
5. Glover, pp. 147–148, quoting Moore's *Diary*, vol. 2, pp. 257–258.
6. *Wellington's Supplementary Dispatches*, vol. 6, p. 125 – Castlereagh to Wellesley from Downing Street, 4 September 1808.
7. Glover, p. 147.
8. Foy, p. 182.
9. Glover, pp. 150–151.
10. Napier, vol. 1, p. 152.
11. Cesar, p. 146.
12. *Annual Register* 1808, p. 266.
13. Ludovici, Anthony (ed.), *On the Road with Wellington*, London, William Heinemann Ltd., p. 41. Warre also commented on 29 September that:

'The indignation expressed in all the English Papers at the Capitulation ... is scarce equal to what has been felt by every individual of the Army, whose glory and the gratitude of their countrymen (their best reward) has been so completely frittered away.' He also remarked that the worst clause in the Convention was the stipulation that French soldiers with fighting experience in Iberia would be free to return to the region – see Warre, p. 36.

14. Foy, p. 185.
15. NAM: 1964-04-76 and 6594-1808-14, Anonymous, *Journal of a Soldier of the 71st*.
16. *Wellington's Supplementary Dispatches*, vol. 6, p. 130. Letter from Major General Beresford to Arthur Wellesley.
17. Scattolin, Roberto A, 'General Junot and the Holy Bible of Belém,' http://www.napoleon-series.org/, pp. 1–3. The Prior of the Heironymite Order was exiled for three years for letting Junot take the bible and several attempts were made to restore it to its rightful owners over the following years. Napoleon was approached but felt disinclined to pursue the matter as the then widowed duchess had fallen upon hard times and in any case was beset with numerous other difficulties during the years 1813–1815. Eventually the Marquis de Palmella, Portuguese Ambassador in Paris and Count de Funchal, his counterpart in Rome, prevailed upon Louis XVIII to instruct the duchess to return it for the sum of 80,000 francs. Today it resides in the Mosteiro dos Jerónimos at Belém.
18. *The Times*, 1 November 1808, p. 3. *The Times* received these reports in letters from Lisbon and Porto.
19. Foy, p. 186.
20. Ibid., p. 187.
21. *Wellington's Supplementary Dispatches*, vol. 6, pp. 134–135. Dalrymple to Wellesley, 9 September 1808.
22. *Wellington's Dispatches*, vol. 4, p. 156. Wellesley to Moore, 17 September 1808.
23. *Annual Register* 1808, p. 223.
24. Wordsworth, William, *Wordsworth's Tract on the Convention of Cintra*, London, Humphrey Milford, 1915, p. VIII – A V Dicey wrote the introduction to this edition of Wordsworth's work in 1915.
25. *Wellington's Supplementary Dispatches*, vol. 6, p. 151. Wellesley to the Duke of Richmond, London, 10 October 1808.
26. Ross-Lewin, p. 123.
27. *The Times*, 29 September 1808, p. 3. The *Morning Chronicle* commented: 'Do Sir Arthur Wellesley's friends mean to give out that he was reduced to the level of one of Maillardet's machines, that he was nothing more than

the pen in Sir Hew Dalrymple's hand, and that he had not even the power to annex to his signature, "by order of the commander?" ' See Glover, p. 169 – quoting the *Morning Chronicle* of 19 September 1808.

28. The deputation presented their petition on Wednesday 12 October 1808, listing many grievances and ending with the request: 'we therefore humbly pray your Majesty, in justice to the outraged feelings of a brave, injured, and indignant people ... to remove from its character so foul a stain in the eyes of Europe, that your Majesty will be graciously pleased, immediately to institute such an enquiry into this dishonourable and unprecedented action as will lead to the discovery and punishment of those, by whose misconduct and incapacity the cause of the country and its allies have been so shamefully sacrificed.' – Anonymous, *The Whole Proceedings upon the conduct of Sir Hew Dalrymple, late commander-in-chief of His Majesty's forces in Portugal, relative to the Convention of Cintra*, London, Sherwood, Neely & Jones, 1809, p. 16.

29. Glover, pp. 178–179. The members of the Board were Generals Sir David Dundas, Earl Moira, Peter Craig and Lieutenant Generals Lord Heathfield, Earl Pembroke, Sir George Nugent and Oliver Nicolls.

30. Stockdale, John Joseph, *The Interesting Proceedings on the Enquiry into the Armistice and Convention of Cintra, and into the conduct of officers concerned*, London, 1809, pp. 35–36. This is taken from Sir Hew Dalrymple's evidence, who also stated that the discussion between Wellesley, Burrard and himself continued from 2:30 pm until 9:00 pm that evening.

31. Glover, pp. 186–187.

32. Stockdale, p. 81.

33. *The Times*, 23 November 1808, p. 2.

34. *Wellington's Supplementary Dispatches*, vol. 6, p. 155. Wellesley to George Burrard Esq. from London, 14 October 1808. Sir Arthur's generosity in this matter, written as it was during the time the board was sitting, was appreciated by the Burrards who sent an equally gracious reply.

35. *Wellington's Supplementary Dispatches*, vol. 6, p. 161. Wellesley to Earl Temple, 19 October 1808. Fortescue wrote that fate had been unkind to Burrard since, had he come ashore the previous evening, he would have commanded the army and probably won the victory himself. 'Never was there a more unfortunate man,' he concluded – see Fortescue, vol. 6, p. 216.

36. Glover, pp. 189–190.

37. *Annual Register* 1808, pp. 280–281.

38. Ibid., p. 282. In fact Dalrymple wrote his dispatch on 3 September but Wellesley and others had written to England regarding these matters some days beforehand.

39. *Wellington's Supplementary Dispatches*, vol. 6, p. 186. Wellesley to the Duke of Richmond, 23 November 1808.
40. *Cobbett's Parliamentary Debates*, vol. 12, comprising the period between the 19th January and the 7th March 1809, London, T C Hansard et al., 1809, p. 150.
41. Wordsworth, William, *Wordsworth's Tract on the Convention of Cintra*, pp. 187–188.
42. Byron, Lord George, *The Complete Poetical Works of Lord Byron*, vol. 1, London, George Routledge and Sons, 1886, p. 264 – for both quotations.

Chapter 10: Europe in Flames

1. Thiébault, vol. 2, p. 238.
2. Ibid., p. 238.
3. Thiébault, vol. 2, p. 209.
4. Johnson, R M (ed.), *The Corsican*, Boston and New York, Houghton Mifflin Company, 1910, p. 299. Napoleon to Junot, 19 October 1808.
5. Napier, vol. 1, p. 173 – using a quotation from Napoleon's Correspondence.
6. Johnson, p. 299. Napoleon to Junot, 19 October 1808.
7. Napier, vol. 1, p. 172.
8. *Annual Register* 1808, p. 276.
9. Willis, Clive, 'Colonel George Lake and the Battle of Roliça', *Portuguese Studies*, Volume 12 (1996), pp. 68–77. Here Willis refers to Brandão, Raul, *El-Rei Junot*, Lisbon, Imprensa Nacional-Casa da Moeda, 1982, p. 243.
10. *Abrantes Mémoires*, vol. 12, pp. 99–102.
11. Buttery, David, *Wellington Against Massena*, Barnsley, South Yorkshire, Pen & Sword Military, 2007: p. 109 for Coimbra, p. 111 for the Lines of Torres Vedras and p. 169 for the Battle of Fuentes de Oñoro.
12. Caulaincourt, Armand de, *At Napoleon's Side in Russia*, New York, Enigma Books, 2008, p. 69.
13. MacKay, p. 431.
14. Caulaincourt, p. 69. Rapp pleaded with Napoleon to give Junot another chance, citing his many wounds and campaigns, saying: 'Do not forget in a moment of disfavour his twenty years of faithful service.' – see MacKay, p. 433 quoting Saint-Hilaire.
15. MacKay, p. 444.
16. *Abrantes Mémoires*, vol. 15, pp. 165–166.
17. MacKay, p. 446.
18. Ibid., p. 449.
19. Dubreton, p. 253.
20. Ibid., pp. 253–254.
21. Thompson, p. 333. Napoleon to General Savary, Dresden, 7 August 1813.

22. MacKay, pp. 453–454.
23. Ibid., p. 456.
24. Guedalla, Philip, *The Duke*, London, Hodder and Stoughton, 1933, p. 165.
25. *Wellington's Dispatches*, vol. 7, p. 427. Wellesley to Beresford, 4 April 1811.

Bibliography

Archives Consulted
The British Library
The National Army Museum
The National Newspaper Archive (Colindale)
The University of Leicester

Contemporary Sources
Museu Militar – Lisbon, Portugal
Boletim do Arquivo Histórico Militar, Vol. 8, 1938 – *Notícias enviadas em 1807, de Lisboa, em cartas escritas por um official português*, pp. 284–289. (Two letters written by Principal Sousa.)
I am also indebted to the Museu Militar for the use of several books that appear in the Secondary Source section of this bibliography.

National Army Museum – London, England
NAM: 1964-04-76 and 6594-1808-14, Anonymous, *Journal of a Soldier of the 71st or Glasgow Regiment, Highland Light Infantry from 1806–1815*, Edinburgh, Balfour & Clarke, 1819.
NAM: 5903-127, The Letters of Captain William Granville Eliot, Royal Artillery.

Worcester Regiment Museum
Letter of Major Gregory Way, 29th Foot, written on board the *Vasco da Gama*, a Portuguese gunship on the Tagus, 26 August, 1808.
I am also indebted to this archive for the use of several contemporary and secondary book and journal sources relating to the 29th Regiment, which appear in the relevant sections of this bibliography.

Newspapers and Periodicals
The Annual Register
Cobbett's Parliamentary Debates
The Gentleman's Magazine
The Times

Primary Sources

Books

Abrantes, Duchess d', Laure Junot, *Mémoires de Madame la duchesse d'Abrantes: ou Souvenirs sur Napoléon, le Directoire, le Consulat, l'Empire et la Restauration*, in 18 vols (Paris, La Haye Vervloet, 1831–1835)

—— Laure Junot, *Mémoires: souvenirs historiques sur Napoléon, la Revolution, le Directoire, le Consulat, l'Empire et la Restauration*, in 10 vols (Paris, Garnier, 1900–1923)

Anonymous, *The Whole Proceedings upon the conduct of Sir Hew Dalrymple, late commander-in-chief of His Majesty's forces in Portugal, relative to the Convention of Cintra* (London, Sherwood, Neely & Jones, 1809)

Brindle, Rosemary (ed.), *Memoirs of Napoleon's Egyptian Expedition 1798–1801* (being the recollections of Captain Joseph-Marie Moret), (London, Greenhill Books, 2001)

Butler, Arthur John (ed.), *The Memoirs of Baron Thiébault*, in 2 vols (London, Smith, Elder & Co., 1896)

Byron, George, *The Complete Poetical Works of Lord Byron*, in 3 volumes (London, George Routledge and Sons, 1886)

Caulaincourt, Armand de, *At Napoleon's Side in Russia: The Classic Eyewitness Account* (New York, Enigma Books, 2008)

Clausewitz, Carl von, *On War* (Oxford, Oxford University Press, 2007, originally 1976). Translated by Michael Howard and Peter Paret.

Curling, Henry (ed.), *Recollections of Rifleman Harris* (London, Peter Davis Ltd., 1929)

Foy, General Maximilien, *Junot's Invasion of Portugal 1807–1808* (Tyne and Wear, Worley Publications, 2000 (originally published 1829))

Hathaway, Eileen (ed.), *A Dorset Soldier: the Autobiography of Sergeant William Lawrence 1790–1869* (Staplehurst, Spellmount Ltd., 1993 (originally published 1886))

Hibbert, Christopher (ed.), *A Soldier of the Seventy-first* (Moreton-in-Marsh, Gloucestershire, The Windrush Press, 1996 (originally 1970))

Hulot, J L, *Souvenirs du Baron Hulot, général d'artilleries, 1773–1843* (Paris, Spectateur Militaire, 1886)

Jomini, Antoine-Henri, Baron de, *The Art of War* (New York, Dover Publication Inc., 2007 (originally published 1862))

Junot, Jean-Andoche, *Diário da I Invasão Francesa* (Lisboa, Portugal, Livros Horizonte, 2008)

Junot, Laure, *Memoirs of Madame Junot Duchess of Abrantes*, 4 vols (London, Richard Bentley & Son, 1893)

_____ *Memoirs of Madame Junot*, 6 vols (Paris and Boston, The Napoleon Society, 1895)

_____ *Mémoires de Madame la duchesse d'Abrantes: ou Souvenirs sur Napoléon, le Directoire, le Consulat, l'Empire et la Restauration*, in 18 vols (Paris, La Haye Vervloet, 1831–1835)

_____ *Mémoires de Madame la duchesse d'Abrantes: ou Souvenirs historiques sur Napoléon, la Revolution, le Directoire, le Consulat, l'Empire et la Restauration*, in 10 vols (Paris, Garnier Frères, 1893)

Landmann, George, *Recollections of my Military Life*, in 2 vols (London, Hurst and Blackett, 1854)

Landsheit, Norbert & Gleig G R (ed.), *The Hussar: A German Cavalryman in British Service throughout the Napoleonic Wars* (England, Leonaur Ltd., 2008 (originally 1837))

Leslie, Colonel K H, *Military Journal of Colonel K.H. Leslie whilst serving with the 29th Regt in the Peninsula, and the 60th Rifles in Canada, etc, 1807–1832* (Aberdeen, Aberdeen University Press, 1887)

Ludovici, Anthony (ed.), *On the Road with Wellington* (London, William Heinemann Ltd., 1924)

Napier, Major General Sir W F P, *History of the War in the Peninsula and in the South of France, vol 1* (London, Frederick Warne and Co., 1851)

Pool, Bernard (ed.), *The Croker Papers 1808–1857* (London, B.T. Batsford Ltd., 1967)

Ross-Lewin, Harry, Major, *With 'The Thirty-Second' In the Peninsular and other Campaigns* (Dublin, Hodges, Figgis & Co. Ltd., 1904)

Solitaire, Elman, *Canto Patriotico, em que se Redordao os Gloriosos Tiunfos do Illustrissimo e Excellentissimo Sehnor Conde Wellington e do Vimeiro Marquez de Torres-Vedras, Marechal General dos Exercitos Cominados em Portugal, etc, etc, etc* (Portugal, Lisboa na Imressão Regia, 1812)

Stanhope, Henry, Earl of, *Conversations with the Duke of Wellington 1831–1851* (London, Prion, 1998 (numerous other editions and publishers – originally 1888))

Stockdale, John Joseph, *The Interesting Proceedings on the Enquiry into the Armistice and Convention of Cintra, and into the conduct of officers concerned* (London, 1809)

Talleyrand-Périgord, Charles, *Mémoires du Prince De Talleyrand, in 7 volumes* (Paris, Les Editions Henri Javal, 1953)

Thompson, J M, *Letters of Napoleon* (Oxford, Basil Blackwell, 1934)

Wardell, John (ed.), *With 'The Thirty-Second' in the Peninsular and other Campaigns* (Dublin, Hodges, Figgis & Co. Ltd., 1904)

Warre, William, Lieutenant General Sir, *Letters from the Peninsula 1808–1812* (London, John Murray, 1909)

Wellesley, Arthur, *A narrative of the campaign which proceeded the Convention of Cintra to which is annexed the report for the Board of Enquiry – copied from The Proceedings of the Enquiry by John Joseph Stockdale* (London, Stockdale Junior, 1809)

Wellington, Arthur Field Marshal, Duke of, *The Despatches of Field Marshal the Duke of Wellington during his various Campaigns*, in 13 vols (London, John Murray, 1834–1838 (compiled by Lieutenant Colonel Gurwood))

Wellington, Second Duke of (ed.), *Supplementary Despatches, Correspondence, and Memoranda of Field Marshal the Duke of Wellington*, in 15 vols (London, John Murray, 1858–1872)

Wordsworth, William, *Wordsworth's Tract on the Convention of Cintra* (London, Humphrey Milford, 1915 – previously published in 1809)

Wybourn, Emily (ed.) – also Petrides, A (ed.) and Downs, Jonathan (ed.) in 2000, *Sea Soldier: An Officer of Marines with Duncan, Nelson, Collingwood and Cockburn, The Letters and Journals of Major T. Marmaduke Wybourn RM, 1797–1813* (Tunbridge Wells, Parapress Limited, 2000)

Secondary Sources

Books

Bell, Douglas, *Wellington's Officers* (London, Collins Clear-Type Press, 1938)

Birmingham, David, *A Concise History of Portugal* (Cambridge, Cambridge University Press, 2007)

Buttery, David, *Wellington Against Massena: The Third Invasion of Portugal 1810–1811* (Barnsley, South Yorkshire, Pen & Sword Military, 2007)

Cesar, Victoriano J, *Invasãos Francesas em Portugal, 1a parte, Invasão franco-espanhola de 1807, Roliça e Vimeiro* (Lisboa, Portugal, typ. da Cooperativa Militar, 1904)

Chandler, David G, *The Campaigns of Napoleon* (London, Weidenfeld and Nicolson, 1967)

____ *Dictionary of the Napoleonic Wars* (Ware, Hertfordshire, Wordsworth Editions Limited, 1999 (originally 1979))

Chartrand, René, *Vimeiro 1808* (Oxford, Osprey Publishing Ltd., 2001)

____ *The Portuguese Army of the Napoleonic Wars, in 3 volumes* (Oxford, Osprey Publishing Ltd., 2000)

Cohen, Louis, *Napoleonic Anecdotes* (London, Robert Holden and Co. Ltd., 1925)

Dickinson, Patric (ed.), *Byron: Selected Poems* (London, The Grey Walls Press Limited, 1949)

Dubreton, Lucas, J, *Junot dit 'La Tempéte'* (Paris, Gallimard, 1937 (4th edition))

Esdaile, Charles, *The Peninsular War* (London, Penguin Books, 2003)

Everard, Major H, *History of Thomas Farrington's Regiment subsequently designated the 29th (Worcestershire) Foot 1694 to 1891* (Worcester, Littlebury & Co., The Worcester Press, 1891)

Fortescue, John, *A History of The British Army, in 13 volumes* (London, Macmillan and Co., 1921)

—— *Wellington* (London, Williams and Norgate Ltd., 1925)

Glover, A S B, *Byron: Poems* (London, Penguin Books Ltd., 1987 (originally 1954))

Glover, Michael, *Britannia Sickens: Sir Arthur Wellesley and the Convention of Cintra* (London, Leo Cooper Ltd., 1970)

Grant, Charles, *Wellington's First Campaign in Portugal* (Leigh-on-Sea, Essex, Partizan Press, 2007)

Griffith, Paddy (ed.), *A History of the Peninsular War: Modern Studies of the War in Spain and Portugal, 1808–1814, vol 9* (London, Greenhill Books, 1999)

Guedalla, Philip, *The Duke* (London, Hodder and Stoughton Ltd., 1933 (originally 1931))

Haythornthwaite, Philip, *The Peninsular War – The Complete Companion to the Iberian Campaigns 1807–14* (London, Brassey's, 2004)

Haythornthwaite, Philip J, *Wellington's Military Machine* (Tunbridge Wells, Ravelin Limited, 1989)

Hibbert, Christopher, *Wellington: A Personal History* (London, HarperCollins Publishers, 1997)

Hutchinson, Major General H D, *The Operations in the Peninsula, 1808–1809: A Lecture Delivered at Aldershot on June 5th, 1905* (London, Hugh Rees Ltd., 1905)

Johnston, R M (ed.), *The Corsican* (Boston and New York, Houghton Mifflin Company, 1910)

Jones, Ben R, *Napoleon, Man and Myth* (London, Hodder & Stoughton, 1977)

Keegan, John, *The Mask of Command* (London, Penguin Books, 1988)

Kennedy, Paul, *The Rise and Fall of British Naval Mastery* (London, Penguin Books, 2001 (originally 1976))

MacKay, Charles Hugh, *The Tempest: The Life and Career of Jean Andoche Junot, 1771–1813* (Doctor of Philosophy Dissertation, Florida, The Florida State University College of Arts and Sciences, 1995)

Maxwell, Kenneth, *Conflicts & Conspiracies: Brazil and Portugal, 1750–1808* (London, Routledge, 2004)

Maxwell, W H, *The Victories of the British Armies* in 2 vols (London, Richard Bentley Publisher in Ordinary to Her Majesty, 1839)

Oman, Charles, *A History of the Peninsular War* in 7 vols, 1807–1809 (Oxford, The Clarendon Press, 1902)

Pope, Stephen, *Dictionary of the Napoleonic Wars* (London, Cassell, 1999)

Rathbone, Julian, *Wellington's War* (London, Book Club Associates, 1984)

Robertson, Ian C, *Wellington at War in the Peninsula 1808–1814* (Barnsley, South Yorkshire, Pen & Sword Books Ltd., 2000)

Rudorff, Raymond, *War to the Death: The Sieges of Saragossa 1808–1809* (London, W&J Mackay Ltd., 1974)

Smith, Digby, *The Greenhill Napoleonic Wars Data Book: Actions and Losses in Personnel, Colours, Standards and Artillery, 1792–1815* (London, Greenhill Books, 1998)

Stanhope, Earl of, *Life of the Right Honourable William Pitt, in four volumes* (London, John Murray, 1867)

Valente, Vasco Pulido, *Ir Pro Maneta: A Revolta contra os Franceses (1808)* (Lisboa, Portugal, Alethia Editores, 2007)

Weller, Jac, *Wellington in the Peninsula 1808–1814* (Whitstable, Kent, Purnell Book Services Ltd., 1973 (originally 1962))

Wilbur, Richard, *Byron* (New York (USA), Dell Publishing Co. Inc., 1965 (originally published 1962))

Wilcken, Patrick, *Empire Adrift: The Portuguese Court in Rio de Janeiro 1808–1821* (London, Bloomsbury Publishing Plc, 2004)

Journals and Magazines

Reid, Stuart, 'The Mysterious Highlander', *Military Illustrated* 245 (October 2008), pp. 16–23.

Willis, Clive, 'Colonel George Lake and the Battle of Roliça', *Portuguese Studies*, volume 12 (1996), pp. 68–77.

Electronic Sources

Chrisawn, Margaret, 'A military bull in a diplomatic China shop: General Jean Lanne's mission to Lisbon 1802–1804', http://www.napoleon-series.org/, pp. 1–12.

Hadaway, Stuart, 'Roliça: A Most Important Affair', http://www.napoleon-series.org/, pp. 1–9.

Scattolin, Roberto A, 'General Junot and the Holy Bible of Belém', http://www.napoleon-series.org/, pp. 1–3.

Index